World Hunger Series

Hunger and Markets

WFP

World Food Programme

earthscan

Map A – Underweight among children under 5 years old

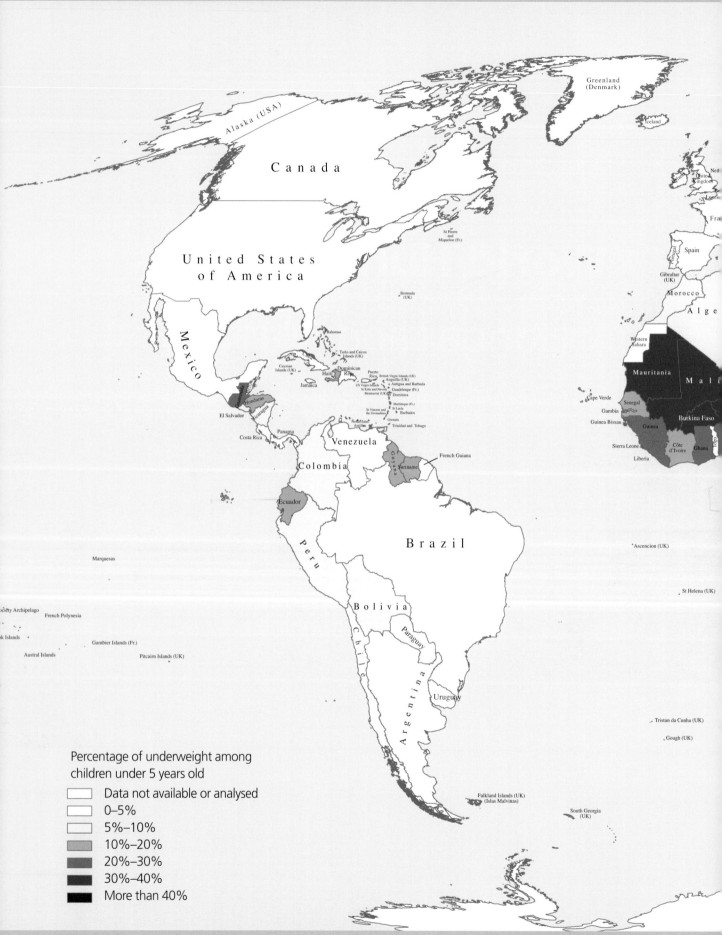

Percentage of underweight among children under 5 years old

- Data not available or analysed
- 0–5%
- 5%–10%
- 10%–20%
- 20%–30%
- 30%–40%
- More than 40%

The boundaries and names shown and the designations used on this map do not imply official endorsement or acceptance by the United Nations.

Data source: Resource Compendium, Table 1
Map produced by the WFP Food Security Analysis Service (OMXF), February 2009

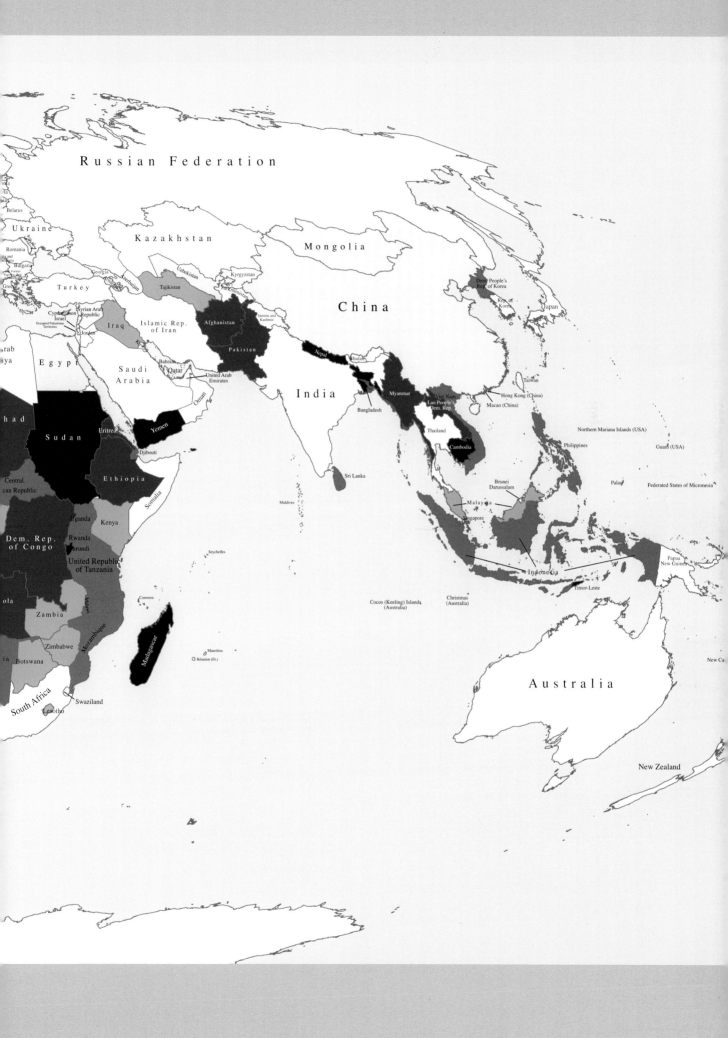

There are countless economists and market specialists in the world, and numerous people specializing in food security issues. However, only a limited number of people work on the links between markets and food security. WFP has been very fortunate that many of these people have been involved in its analysis of these links and in the preparation of this report. Without them, this report would not have seen the light of day.

This edition of the *World Hunger Series* on *Hunger and Markets* was produced under the general supervision of Stanlake Samkange, former Director of the Policy, Planning and Strategy Division, and David Stevenson, current Director. Henk-Jan Brinkman was the lead author and team leader, very capably assisted by Ceren Gürkan. Together with Ludovic Subran, they drafted major parts of the report. Ugo Gentilini, Ulrich Hess, Vivien Knips and Issa Sanogo provided additional inputs. All are WFP staff. Jan Lundius and Jane Shaw provided editorial assistance. A number of interns and volunteers provided excellent support: Mathias André, Emilio Batzella, Alessandra Gaia, Adam Goldenberg, Farzad Kapadia, Gilles Koumou, Marc Lundwall, Adeline Renat, Mariateresa Silvi and Stefania Spoto. Their contributions and hard work are much appreciated.

Background papers were prepared by Erin Lentz for Chapter 9, Phumzile Mdladla for Intermezzo 6.1 and Johan Swinnen for Chapter 5. Figure 4.1 has been adapted from earlier work by Steven Haggblade, David Tschirley and colleagues at Michigan State University on the COMESA Regional Food Security Strategy for Pillar Three of the Comprehensive African Agricultural Development Programme (CAADP). Lia van Wesenbeeck and Max Merbis prepared Figure 1.2.

Jenny Aker helpfully provided the data for Figure 2.3. Paul Dorosh kindly updated Figure 6.4. These inputs were very valuable and WFP is thankful for them.

The drafting process benefited from a consultation in Rome in February 2008. Contributions from participants, particularly Stephen Devereux, Cynthia Donovan, Paul Dorosh, Gary Eilerts, Kisan Gunjal and Lili Mohiddin, are gratefully acknowledged.

Several experts provided very useful comments on drafts: Shukri Ahmed, Gustavo Anriquez, Aziz Arya, Liliana Balbi, Chris Barrett, Stephen Devereux, Marie Claude Dop, Ali Gürkan, Lawrence Haddad, Steven Haggblade, David Hallam, John Hoddinott, Henri Josserand, David Kahan, Marco Knowles, Erin Lentz, Justin Yifu Lin, Kostas Stamoulis, Francoise Trine and Patrick Webb. WFP is very appreciative of their generosity in sharing their expertise.

WFP colleagues provided helpful comments or inputs: Thomas Beuter, Sabine Bongi, Nick Crawford, Agnes Dhur, Adama Faye, Alberto Gabriele, Deborah Hines, Suan Khaffaf, George Mu'Ammar, Steven Were Omamo, Robert Opp, Simon Renk, George-André Simon, Joanna Syroka, Gaurab Tewari, Andrew Thorne-Lyman, Tina van den Briel and Sonali Wickrema.

Production of the report was supported by Cristina Ascone of the Communications and Public Policy Strategy Division and Paolo Grillo of the Translation and Documents Unit.

The majority of the draft was produced between mid-2007 and mid-2008. The analysis in Chapter 3 and some figures were updated at the end of 2008.

Hunger is on the march throughout the world, fuelled by record high food prices. During 2007 and 2008, 115 million people were added to the ranks of the urgently hungry. Today, almost 1 billion people struggle to find their next meal, and a child dies every six seconds from hunger-related causes.

Ensuring affordable and adequate access to nutrition for all people, especially the next generation, is therefore one of the most pressing challenges of our time. In their elusiveness, well-functioning food markets have long been a bane to policy-makers searching for answers to this challenge. But their potential for spurring the structural transformation, innovation and broad-based growth that lead to deep and rapid hunger reduction means that well-functioning food markets are also a boon.

This third edition of the *World Hunger Series* examines the complex relationship between markets and hunger. The report could not be more relevant or timely. In recent years, we have witnessed how high food prices have adverse impacts on the nutritional status of vulnerable populations, particularly children under the age of 2. Now we are facing another market failure of unprecedented proportions. The current financial crisis is a global one, destroying livelihoods and adding to the negative impacts of high food prices, which had already eroded the coping capacities of millions around the world. Global and national food systems are in disarray, unable to respond adequately.

Policy-makers and practitioners are therefore currently preoccupied by the risks posed by food markets. This is appropriate. But this report reaffirms a major lesson from history: as we accommodate these risks, we must not ignore or undermine the potential of markets for helping to put food on tables in widely ranging contexts, including during humanitarian crises.

This edition of the *World Hunger Series* comes at an important moment in the history of WFP. A new Strategic Plan has positioned the agency as a frontline actor and innovator in the fight against hunger. A central dynamic framed in the plan is WFP's transition from a food aid to a food assistance agency. This shift is partly rooted in trends in global and national food markets, and hinges on the design and implementation of an expanded toolbox of programming interventions to address the food needs of vulnerable people. Many of the most exciting elements of that expanded toolbox – such as Purchase for Progress, vouchers, cash transfers and insurance instruments – require a deeper and more nuanced understanding of opportunities and threats posed by the current functioning of food markets.

At WFP, we firmly believe that the innovative use of market-based instruments can help us meet the needs of the hungry poor more effectively. We also recognize the perils associated with these opportunities. But we believe that, working closely with partners, we can identify and implement market-based hunger solutions in which the potential benefits outweigh the prospective dangers.

Through this report, we invite you to join us in this challenging but exciting venture.

Josette Sheeran
Executive Director
World Food Programme

Figures

Tables

Maps

Well-functioning food markets are central to ending hunger. Not only must enough food be produced to meet consumption needs, but this food must also be accessible. Food markets link food production and consumption sectors. But they can do much more. When food markets are functioning well, they can create jobs and stimulate economic growth by spurring diversification of food systems based on comparative advantage. This can lead to more equal distributions of income and purchasing power, and thus increased nutritional well-being and enhanced food security.

This issue of the *World Hunger Series* considers this potential, highlights the major opportunities and risks facing households seeking to realize it, and outlines strategic priorities for policies and investment.

Markets and hunger – a complex relationship

Sustainable hunger reduction hinges on helping growing numbers of the hungry poor to participate in the process of economic growth. Where food markets play a role, they must perform two inherently opposing functions: they must help keep food affordable, especially for the poor; but they must also promote efficiency in resource allocation, especially through the signals they send to food producers, who favour high prices. To contribute to hunger reduction, food markets must therefore help raise incomes for farmers and returns to food traders, processors, transporters, wholesalers and retailers sufficient to induce these groups to perform services that keep nutritious food affordable to consumers. Experience suggests that this is an extremely complex challenge.

This food price dilemma is well recognized. Strategies are required that provide significant price incentives to create rural purchasing power that, in turn, stimulates the rural growth needed to support broader economic growth. History shows that when implemented in the context of large-scale investments in rural infrastructure, human capital and agricultural research, such strategies can spur rapid income growth.

However, the relationship between hunger and income is not consistently strong. In many of the countries where market development has led to substantially increased incomes, malnutrition has not declined correspondingly, and targeted nutrition interventions have been needed. Paradoxically, the households with least access to market-sourced food are precisely those that must rely on markets to fill their basic food needs. Food markets tend to fail most often and most severely for those who need them the most – the hungry poor.

Markets can benefit the hungry poor

The proportion of a household's budget devoted to food declines as the family's income increases, as does the share of food expenditure on staples. Markets can confer benefits on the hungry poor through these two powerful and related channels: first by lowering the costs of basic staples, and thus also the costs of meeting fundamental calorie requirements; and second by making available an expanded range of the non-staple food items that supply key nutrient needs, which reduced expenditures on basic staples allow households to afford.

There is considerable evidence that because poor households spend large shares of their incomes on food and because staples loom large in their food expenditures, lower prices of staple foods significantly increase purchasing power and real incomes. Higher real incomes allow greater purchases of non-staples, leading to substantial short- and long-term nutritional benefits. Conversely, high prices for staple foods lead to reduced consumption of nutritious foods, with long-term negative effects on health, education and productivity.

Markets can also benefit the world's poorest farmers. In much of the developing world, no more than 40 percent of the total output of any food item produced is marketed, and fewer than one-third of farmers sell food. Most of the smallholder farmers who produce the bulk of the world's food are themselves net food buyers. More efficient markets would benefit both net sellers and net buyers of food. Net sellers would face lower barriers to market entry and have greater incentives to produce and sell surpluses. Net buyers would face lower food prices and thus greater access to food supplies. Experience from Asia's green revolution suggests that with sufficient support and correct incentives, net food buyers can become net sellers, raising their own incomes, driving down food costs in urban areas, and thereby pulling not only themselves but also millions of urban consumers out of the ranks of the hungry poor.

Markets can also increase hunger risks

However, markets may not yield these benefits, especially where basic marketing infrastructure is lacking. Most food producers, traders and consumers face a plethora of trade-impeding constraints, which keep many of them in a hunger–poverty trap. Their access to credit is severely limited. The costs of obtaining market information, searching for buyers or sellers, and enforcing contracts are high. Food trade is risky, personalized and cash-based, with limited long-term investment by private traders in transport or storage. Limited and inadequate storage capacity leads to high post-harvest losses. With poor access to formal financing mechanisms, traders exchange small volumes within limited geographical areas, rendering prices highly volatile. Other important constraints include a general lack of grades and standards, and thus low levels of market transparency, and frail legal environments governing property rights and contract enforcement.

Added to these long-standing problems are challenges raised by recent developments in global food markets. Food prices have risen sharply over the last few years, sparking protests and riots in several countries. The impacts on poor producers are less clear, not least because many poor producers are net food buyers. Higher food prices should improve production incentives, but only when food markets efficiently transmit these prices and reliably absorb new surpluses. Increased farm input costs, especially for fertilizers, have contributed significantly to rising food costs and have led to fears of lower harvests and increased food insecurity in the future.

Market-related opportunities to cut hunger must be seized

Recent experience of food market liberalization has uncovered several deeply rooted limitations on market-based solutions to hunger, including major capital and infrastructural constraints, high transaction costs, weak coordination between buyers and sellers, inadequate trade financing, highly skewed distributions of market power, high risk, and – as a result – several non-competitive elements. Opportunities for developing market-based solutions to hunger depend on overcoming these constraints.

Most opportunities are likely to centre on reducing transaction costs, unleashing new sources of demand for food, increasing value addition in food marketing chains, and creating enabling environments for efficient food marketing, with an emphasis on risk-mitigating instruments. With such support, traders and other actors in food markets would be more likely to invest in low-cost, low-margin food marketing practices that provide reliable and rewarding outlets for the expanded volumes of food commodities that would be produced and sold by farmers pursuing high-input, high-output, high-income food production methods. Such developments would lead to lower food costs to consumers, especially in rapidly expanding urban areas.

Ready-to-eat foods developed through technological advances in agroprocessing are providing new scope for market-based hunger reduction. When properly prepared, packaged and stored, these foods can be efficient sources of key nutrients, especially micronutrients, while reducing health risks associated with food handling and preparation under poor hygienic conditions. Burgeoning populations of poor people in urban areas with limited water and sanitation services imply increasing benefits from delivering such foods through market outlets.

Increased privatization, integration and globalization of food systems define and reflect the growing importance of supermarkets. These dynamics suggest new opportunities for farmers who are able to diversify from staples towards higher-value products. There is a risk that high quality and quantity requirements will exclude small-scale farmers, but they can also improve the positive nutrition impacts of ready-to-eat foods, to which access is often easiest through supermarkets.

Strategic priorities for hunger-reducing market development

Left to themselves, food markets may not promote hunger reduction.

Policy-makers in countries with significant hunger challenges must find opportunities for developing food markets in ways that help overcome the fundamental trade-off between the food needs and welfare of poor people in rural and urban areas and the incentives for food production.

The Asian green revolution induced sharp reductions in rural and urban poverty and hunger, partly through significant government intervention in markets. Policy-makers increasingly agree that there is little historical precedent for complete reliance on free market forces to drive agricultural and broader economic development, and to cut hunger. Thus, while policy-makers recognize and applaud the private sector for its dynamism and resilience, many resist calls for full public sector withdrawal from food marketing. Motives for continued resistance are likely to remain strong under the new high food price regime in global markets and the evolving global financial crisis.

This edition of the *World Hunger Series* is intended to help create a better understanding of the complexity of hunger and markets. It is divided into four parts: **Part I** (Chapters 1 to 3) sets the stage by presenting the basic concepts related to hunger and the importance of markets; **Part II** (Chapters 4 to 8) provides a broad analysis of key aspects of the relationship between hunger and markets, including livelihoods and food security at the household level, market access for the poor, determinants of food availability, risks faced by the hungry poor in relation to markets and the impact of emergencies on market performance; **Part III** (Chapters 9 and 10) identifies policy options and actions that various stakeholders may adopt for the benefit of the hungry poor; and **Part IV** is a compendium of data on the state of

hunger, malnutrition, food availability and access and other aspects of the effort to fight hunger.

To use markets as instruments in the fight against hunger, the report suggests that governments, international actors, the private sector and other stakeholders all have roles to play in ten market-based priority actions:

1   *Incorporate food market dynamics into hunger alleviation initiatives:* Knowledge of markets is crucial for understanding the drivers of hunger and vulnerability and for designing responses.

2   *Support food markets with targeted investments in institutions and infrastructure:* Governments should support markets with appropriate infrastructure and institutions, including strong legal and regulatory frameworks, a robust system for setting and enforcing quality standards, and policies that support fair competition among market entrants.

3   *Improve access to complementary markets, such as financial markets:* Access to secure financial services is critical in efforts to reduce hunger and poverty. Increased education opportunities, employment information and work programmes can also support access to labour markets.

4   *Use the power of markets to transform market dependency into opportunities:* The potential for generating income through food markets can be harnessed for the hungry poor by assisting their access to agricultural inputs, value chain innovations and public–private partnerships.

5   *Reduce market-based risks and vulnerabilities and safeguard markets:* The risk of market failure or inefficiency can be reduced by improving the monitoring of food prices and trade flows, promoting market resilience, establishing disaster risk management frameworks and facilitating markets during relief and recovery operations.

6   *Invest in social protection measures that reduce risk and vulnerabilities and complement markets:* Programmes to protect the most vulnerable populations are critical. Insurance,

vouchers and cash transfers and other market-based social protection measures should accompany growth strategies and market policies.

7 ***Invest more in nutrition and differently in agriculture:*** Smallholder agriculture needs the support of investments, including in appropriate crop research, rural infrastructure and storage systems, which improve the hungry poor's access to markets. These measures should be complemented by cost-effective investments in nutrition, such as the development of affordable nutritious food products that combat micronutrient deficiencies.

8 ***Ensure that trade supports food security:*** Trade and food security policies need to be made more consistent through continued discussions on international and regional platforms. Reducing export restrictions and ensuring exemption of humanitarian food are important parts of this effort.

9 ***Engage international and domestic actors in the fight against hunger:*** Official development assistance (ODA) and international and domestic public–private partnerships involving governments, the private sector and civil society are important in supporting emergency interventions, market innovations and the post-crisis recovery of markets.

10 ***Create and leverage knowledge on markets and hunger:*** There is need for additional research into key questions, including the nutritional impact of high food prices and the global financial crisis, ways of minimizing the negative effects of speculation in food markets and the potential for a global grain reserve.

Part I Setting the Stage

High food prices illustrate how important markets are for the hungry poor.

Part I presents major concepts related to hunger and markets, and illustrates the importance of markets by discussing the recent episode of high food prices. **Chapter 1** defines food insecurity, hunger and malnutrition, introduces the hunger–poverty trap, presents aggregate data on hunger and highlights the link between hunger and markets. **Chapter 2** discusses what markets are, how they work and why they fail, and illustrates some key changes regarding food markets and the evolving policy approaches towards markets. **Chapter 3** presents recent trends in food prices and their causes and impacts on countries and households.

1 Hunger

"There are many different ways of seeing hunger. The dictionary meaning of the term, e.g. 'discomfort or painful sensation caused by want of food', takes us in a particular and extremely narrow direction."

Amartya Sen, 1993

Severe hunger is life-defining. It wrecks people's health, reduces their productivity, diminishes their learning capacity, overcomes their sense of hope and upsets their overall well-being. Lack of food stunts growth, saps energy and hinders foetal development. Hungry people's constant struggle to secure food consumes valuable time and energy, reducing their possibilities of receiving education and finding alternative sources of income.

Worldwide, there were 848 million undernourished people in 2003–2005 (FAO, 2008c). The undernourished population in developing countries increased from 824 million in 1990–1992 to 832 million in 2003–2005. Although this was a relatively small increase, the long-term trend is worrying, as high food prices increased the number by 75 million in 2007 and 40 million in 2008, when it reached 963 million (FAO, 2008c). This jeopardizes the prospect of reaching the Millennium Development Goal (MDG) of halving the proportion of hungry people worldwide by 2015.

No statistic can embody the sheer terror of hunger. For hundreds of millions of people, hunger is a fact of life that imperils their health, reduces their productivity and diminishes their educational attainment.

Food insecurity and hunger

Hunger is an outcome of food insecurity, which in turn is often caused by poverty. Understanding hunger and its causes depends on identifying the necessary conditions for food security. The 1996 World Food Summit defined food security as: "Food security exists when all people, at all times, have physical and economic access to sufficient, safe and nutritious food to meet their dietary needs and preferences for an active and healthy life." It involves four aspects: availability, access, utilization and stability (see the box on page 18).

Identification of the factors necessary for food security has fostered a new, more heterogeneous conception of hunger. A seminal work by Amartya Sen (1981) proposed that famines, hunger and malnutrition are related less to declines in food availability than to people's access to food. Sen demonstrated that during famines in Bengal (1943), Ethiopia (1973) and Bangladesh (1974) food availability did not decline significantly – and sometimes it even increased. These famines were caused by such factors as falling wages, rising food prices, loss of employment and declining livestock prices, all of which relate to the food access dimension – and to markets. Lack of food availability is neither a sufficient nor a necessary condition for famines or hunger.

Sen's analysis is relevant in today's environment of high food prices. Although food is available, many households cannot afford the same quantity and quality as before, because incomes have not kept up with prices.

Markets play a role in many of the dimensions of hunger and food insecurity.

1 Hunger

What is hunger?

Most people understand the concept of being hungry, but specialists working on hunger issues have developed a range of technical terms and concepts to help describe and address the problem more effectively. Unfortunately, there is disagreement about what these terms mean and how they relate to each other. This box provides a short glossary of terms and concepts used in this report. These are not the only "correct" usages, but they provide a relatively clear and consistent overview of the issues.

Hunger: A condition in which people lack the required nutrients – both macro (energy and protein) and micro (vitamins and minerals) – for fully productive, active and healthy lives. Hunger can be short-term/acute or longer-term/chronic, and has a range of mild to severe effects. It can result from insufficient nutrient intake or from people's bodies failing to absorb the required nutrients – hidden hunger. Two billion people suffer from vitamin and mineral shortages. It can also result from poor food and childcare practices.

Malnutrition: A physical condition in which people experience either nutrition deficiencies (undernutrition) or an excess of certain nutrients (overnutrition).

Undernutrition: The physical manifestation of hunger that results from serious deficiencies in one or several macro- and micronutrients. These deficiencies impair body processes, such as growth, pregnancy, lactation, physical work, cognitive function, and disease resistance and recovery. It can be measured as weight for age (underweight), height for age (stunting) and height for weight (wasting).

Undernourishment: The condition of people whose dietary energy consumption is continuously below the minimum required for fully productive, active and healthy lives. It is determined using a proxy indicator that estimates whether the food available in a country is sufficient to meet the population's energy requirements, but not its protein, vitamin and mineral needs. Unlike undernutrition, undernourishment is not measured as an actual outcome.

Food security: A condition that exists when all people at all times are free from hunger. It has four parts, which provide insights into the causes of hunger:

- availability: the supply of food in an area;
- access: a household's ability to obtain that food;
- utilization: a person's ability to select, take in and absorb the nutrients in food;
- stability.

Food insecurity, or the absence of food security, implies either hunger resulting from problems with availability, access and use, or vulnerability to hunger in the future.

How is hunger related to undernutrition and food insecurity?
Hunger, undernutrition and food insecurity are nested concepts. Undernutrition is a subset, a physical manifestation of hunger, which in turn is a subset of food insecurity (see the diagram below). This publication discusses hunger as a specific manifestation of food insecurity.

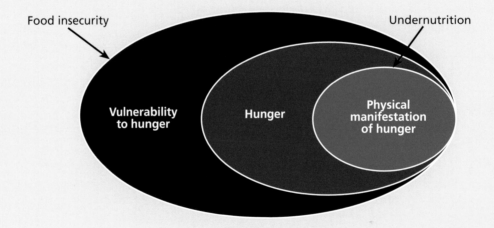

The hungry poor

Hunger is the bottom-line of poverty, and food is central to poor people's concerns (Narayan et al., 2000). Poverty and hunger are not easy to disentangle. Not all poor people are hungry, and malnutrition, such as micronutrient deficiencies, also occurs among the non-poor. However, all hungry people are considered poor. Hunger is an intergenerational phenomenon passed from mother to child. An undernourished mother generally passes the condition on to her child as low birth weight, which has an impact on the child's future health and well-being. This process is known as the "hunger trap".

Hunger traps are linked to poverty conditions. Poverty and hunger are interlinked and mutually reinforcing; hunger is not only a cause of poverty, but also its consequence (Figure 1.1). Development economists recognized this phenomenon half a century ago: "[A] poor man may not have enough to eat; being underfed, his health may be weak; being physically weak, his working capacity is low, which means that he is poor, which in turn means he will not have enough to eat; and so on" (Nurkse, 1953). Hunger and poverty drive each other in a vicious cycle, generating a hunger–poverty trap. The impact of hunger on health, education and productivity is long-term, which reinforces the hunger–poverty trap (Behrman, Alderman and Hoddinott, 2004; Victora et al., 2008). The damage done by malnutrition before the age of 24 months is irreversible, making escape

from the hunger–poverty trap difficult. This not only hampers individuals, but also imposes a crushing economic burden on the developing world. Economists estimate that the cost of child hunger and undernutrition can amount to as much as 11 percent of a country's gross domestic product (GDP) (CEPAL and WFP, 2007).

Several factors can contribute to a hunger–poverty trap (Collier, 2007; United Nations, 2000), including shocks related to diseases or weather, lack of assets and institutions, risks, small-scale and physical isolation, all of which affect access to markets and transaction costs.

Lack of access to markets, assets, technology, infrastructure, health facilities and schools breeds hunger. So does women's exclusion from land, education, decision-making and mobility – a situation that is reinforced by laws and/or cultural norms in many places. Higher malnutrition tends to be concentrated in remote, resource-poor rural areas. This indicates that visible and invisible barriers to access to productive assets, or "asset poverty", are important drivers of high hunger and poverty levels (Ahmed et al., 2007; Webb, 1998; Carter and Barrett, 2005). An uneven initial distribution of assets is important in generating and perpetuating poverty and hunger traps. The initial distribution of assets and the asset base of households matter because households use their assets to increase their wealth and well-being (Williamson, 2003b). The access of groups that are

Figure 1.1 – The hunger–poverty trap: a vicious cycle of poverty and hunger

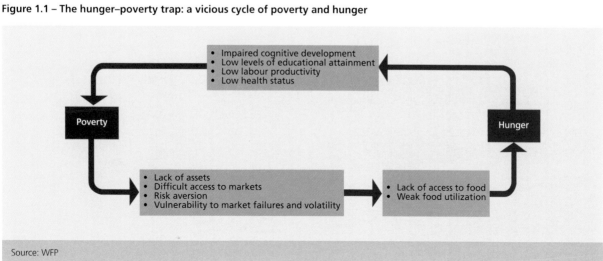

Source: WFP

19

marginalized or discriminated against, including indigenous peoples and ethnic minorities, might be compromised.

"Poor and hungry people often face social and political exclusion, unable to demand their rights. They have little access to education, health services, and safe drinking-water" (United Nations Millennium Project Task Force on Hunger, 2005). They suffer an extreme lack of economic, political or social freedom and choice. These deprivations are deep-rooted and prevent poor people from lifting themselves out of the trap. It is difficult to discuss hunger without discussing poverty. Hence, the focus on the *hungry poor* throughout this publication.

Hunger may be expected where widespread asset deprivation, of land, education and financial and social capital, and underinvestment in technology, infrastructure and institutions prevent poor households from increasing their incomes. The hungry poor are stuck in a poverty trap of low productivity, high transaction costs and poor access to markets.

Where are the hungry poor?

Global numbers on hunger hide regional variations. Asia and Africa contain more than 90 percent of the world's hungry, with China and India accounting for 42 percent and sub-Saharan Africa for a quarter (FAO, 2008c). Although undernourishment has declined in South Asia, this region still has the highest overall prevalence of underweight children in the world, at 42 percent of all those under 5. Sub-Saharan Africa ranks a distant second with 28 percent (UNICEF, 2008).

Aggregate numbers do not provide a comprehensive understanding of what poverty and hunger mean, who the hungry poor are and where they live. It is a bitter irony that 75 percent of the world's hungry poor live in rural areas, where most people are engaged in agricultural activities. Although they produce food, these people are vulnerable to risks associated with economic, weather-related and other shocks, and are unable to grow or buy enough food to meet their families' requirements. According to the United Nations Millennium Project Task Force on Hunger (2005): "estimates indicate that the majority of hungry people live in rural areas. The task force believes that

Figure 1.2a – Underweight prevalence and high transportation costs (>US$1.5 per MTkm) in sub-Saharan Africa

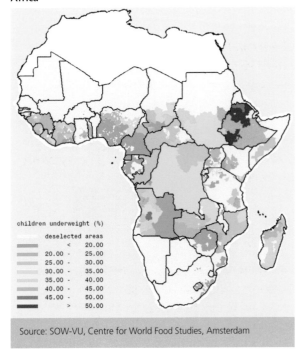

Source: SOW-VU, Centre for World Food Studies, Amsterdam

Figure 1.2b – Underweight prevalence and low transportation costs (<US$1.5 per MTkm) in sub-Saharan Africa

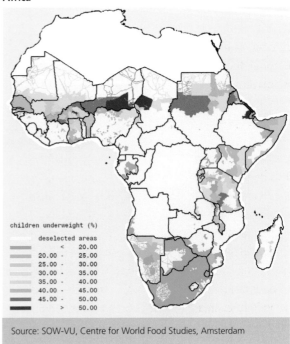

Source: SOW-VU, Centre for World Food Studies, Amsterdam

about half of the hungry are smallholder farming households unable either to grow or to buy enough food to meet the family's requirements... We estimate that roughly two-tenths of the hungry are landless rural people. A smaller group, perhaps one-tenth of the hungry, are pastoralists, fisher folk, and people who depend on forests for their livelihoods... The remaining share of the hungry, around two-tenths, live in urban areas".

Rural poverty is often greatest in areas furthest away from roads, markets, schools and health services. For example, a survey in the United Republic of Tanzania found a significant correlation between child nutrition status and access to major roads (Alderman, Hoddinott and Kinsey, 2006). The maps in Figure 1.2 show the associations between child undernutrition and transportation costs, which are a proxy for access to markets and other basic services. Areas where transportation costs are high – more than US$1.5 per metric ton kilometre (MTkm) – generally have a high prevalence of underweight children (Figure 1.2a). Where roads and infrastructure are present and well-connected, as in Southern Africa, the prevalence of underweight children is low (Figure 1.2b). These associations suggest the existence of geographical poverty traps.

Underweight rates in rural areas of developing countries are on average twice those of urban areas (UNICEF, 2007). This is linked to lower access to health services, safe water and sanitation in rural areas. In Burundi, for example, skilled health personnel attend 83 percent of births in urban areas, but only 16 percent in rural areas (Sahn and Stifel, 2003). Dietary quality is also much lower in rural than in urban areas (Ahmed et al., 2007).

This does not mean that there are no hungry poor in urban areas. In fact, poverty is tending to become increasingly urbanized because of high levels of migration by poor people from rural areas (Ravallion, Chen and Sangraula, 2007). However, poverty remains highly concentrated in rural areas. A higher proportion of poor people live in rural areas, and of the people living in rural areas, a higher proportion are poor. Poverty is more extensive and deeper in rural areas.

Urban populations can face food access challenges because they depend on markets and often tackle difficult trade-offs among competing demands on their income, such as housing, health or transport, which may be more expensive in urban areas (Ravallion, Chen and Sangraula, 2007). The urban poor are particularly vulnerable to high food prices. The 1997/1998 financial crisis in Indonesia, for example, showed that micronutrient deficiencies can grow rapidly in urban areas when staple food prices increase (Block et al., 2004). Across the world, high food prices have helped provoke demonstrations and riots in urban areas, where political mobilization is much easier. Only careful monitoring can tell whether the impact of high food prices on nutrition is worse in urban than in rural areas.

There is evidence that poor people pay higher prices than rich people (Muller, 2002). The reasons are not clear, but could be related to market failures, including market power, poor market integration and lack of credit in remote areas, forcing poor households to buy goods in small quantities and during the lean season at higher prices.

To address global hunger efficiently, its local manifestations must be taken into account. The heterogeneous character of the hungry poor demands consideration of their specific natural, political, cultural, religious and socio-economic environments.

Hunger and poverty are deeper and more extensive in rural areas. Whether or not high food prices and the global financial crisis will change this pattern needs to be monitored carefully. Maintaining a focus on the hungry poor and the specific obstacles they face is a key to breaking the cycle of hunger and poverty across the developing world.

Markets and hunger

Amartya Sen's *Poverty and Famines: An Essay on Entitlement and Deprivation* (1981) emphasized the role of markets in the emergence of famines. He called attention to economic relationships, arguing that endowment bundles provide access to food, through either own production or the market. These bundles, which he divided into assets, such as investments and storage, and claims, such as patronage and kinship ties, provide individuals with access to food.

In periods of scarcity, entitlements are threatened by increasing staple grain prices, or diminishing values of assets as the market becomes swamped by crisis sales. Wages may be insufficient to meet the costs of staple crops. Restricted access to food leads to a decline in nutrition status, which could culminate in starvation.

As Sen acknowledges, his model has limitations, for example, because of the roles of diseases, extra-legal entitlement transfers and ambiguous entitlements resulting from "fuzzy" property rights (Devereux, 2007b). Sen's model has been criticized for retaining conventional "Western" models and viewing famine-stricken populations as passive victims of external shocks. It has been suggested that the perceptions of people in famine-stricken communities should be acknowledged and that famines and chronic hunger must be conceived as a collective experience, threatening not only the lives of affected people, but also their livelihoods (Rangaswami, 1985). Nevertheless, Sen's analysis puts market functioning at the centre of debates concerning severe hunger and starvation.

Markets are critical in the fight against hunger because they determine food availability and access. They play an important role in averting or mitigating hunger by adjusting to shocks and reducing risks. Markets provide employment and trading opportunities and are centres for exchanging vital information for the decision-making processes that determine survival. During periods of production failure, communities become increasingly dependent on markets, as households seek to exchange assets, such as livestock, for grain. Even households that engage in subsistence agriculture depend on markets, at least to buy necessities and diversify their diets beyond the food crops they produce themselves.

The structure and dynamics of food markets and the threats and opportunities they generate are key to the lives of millions. High food prices emphasize this importance. Markets' capacity to help or hurt hungry people depends on market institutions, infrastructure, policies and other interventions that protect the hungry poor from the vagaries of markets. An understanding of markets as a whole is therefore critical for understanding the basis of hunger and vulnerability and designing appropriate responses.

The hungry poor – even those who seem scarcely connected to the rest of the world – depend on markets for their overall well-being, livelihoods, food and nutrition. This report identifies the dynamics and processes through which markets affect the prevalence and nature of hunger, either positively or negatively.

Poverty and hunger are intimately connected with access to food. As markets enable the exchange of services and goods, they are essential for achieving food security. To fight hunger, knowledge is needed about how markets function, why they fail and how they relate to their institutional context. The following chapter deals with the nature, role and functioning of markets.

"No single solution to [the] … food policy dilemma is likely to emerge for all societies, but the underlying importance of markets as a key to all the solutions is being recognized."

C. Peter Timmer, Falcon and Pearson, 1983

"[W]ithout development of supporting institutions, the free market remains nothing but a flea market[:] … no placement of order, no invoicing or payment by check, no credit, and no warranty."

Marcel Fafchamps, 2004

Every society, ancient or contemporary, determines what to produce, who will produce it, how it will be produced and who will receive it. Social customs and bureaucrats figure in the equation, but increasingly these issues are decided by markets.

A market is a social structure that facilitates change of ownership of services and goods. It has been described as establishing "rules of the game" by enabling services, firms and products to be evaluated and priced. Markets can therefore be characterized as "institutions which provide the incentive structure of an economy" (North, 1991).

Markets aggregate demand and supply across actors distributed in space and time, delivering goods and services from sellers to buyers. The way in which goods are distributed and the effectiveness of markets in aggregating demand depend on market functioning, or performance. This, in turn, depends on the structure of the market and the conduct or behaviour of market agents and actors. For policies and institutions to be effective, markets must function well, and for markets to function well, they need supportive institutions and policies.

Omnipresence of markets

Markets range from local marketplaces for fruits and vegetables to international export markets. Most of the world's population depends on these markets for food security. Many people rely on markets for employment, to earn sufficient income to buy food from markets; farmers rely on them to sell their produce.

Market participation does not guarantee positive outcomes. Individuals who are able to use the market to augment their income may enter a "virtuous cycle". Those with low or non-existent assets are not able to benefit from the market (Perry et al., 2006); their returns do not provide sufficient income to invest in the technology, education and health that lead to greater productivity and higher-return activities. There may be obstacles at the national level, when a country does not earn enough money to invest in technology and infrastructure (Dorward et al., 2003). A lack of marketable surplus and high costs to participate in markets contribute to a "market trap", with deficient market mechanisms confining individuals and nations to low levels of development.

The hungry poor depend on markets, not just for directly acquiring their food, but also for obtaining incomes that allow them to buy food.

What are markets and how do they work?

The core distributive role of markets was characterized by Adam Smith as an "invisible hand". Although a free market seems chaotic and uncontrolled, the transactions among agents are guided by self-interest, and yield beneficial results. If one party would not gain from trading with another, an exchange will not take place. When there is a free market and a conducive institutional framework, the self-interested actions of independent economic agents tend to promote the general well-being and prosperity of society.

There is a wide variety of markets, including primary, producer, retail, output and input, and factor markets. What all markets have in common is that they constitute institutional arrangements that facilitate the exchange of goods and services. Exchanges take place in a marketplace – a public sphere where goods are bought and sold. Markets do not necessarily occupy a tangible location; "cyberspace" also provides marketplaces (McMillan, 2002). Concretely or abstractly – as in market economy, free market or market mechanisms – a market always involves buyers and sellers. The exchange process is regulated by supply and demand, which are reflected in prices that vary according to the relative scarcity of goods or services.

Markets are institutions that attempt to facilitate exchange among individuals in spite of the many problems and obstacles that exist, particularly in the developing world.

Market functioning and market failure

Markets allocate resources, including food. They set prices, and coordinate buyers and sellers. In theory, markets perform these functions perfectly, yielding optimal outcomes. However, the conditions for free markets are demanding:

- There must be many buyers and sellers, no one of which is large enough to influence the price.

- New buyers and sellers must be able to enter the market at no significant cost.

Figure 2.1 – The support structure of markets

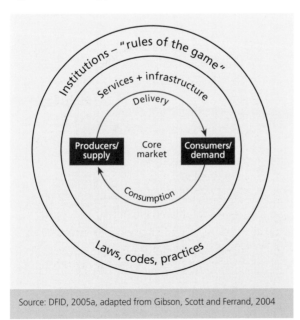

Source: DFID, 2005a, adapted from Gibson, Scott and Ferrand, 2004

- All buyers and sellers must know everything and have the same cost-free information.

- All products must be identical.

In most cases, none of these conditions are fulfilled, so markets do not generate optimal outcomes. Information tends to be costly, and sellers usually know more than buyers. Trade and processing are generally dominated by a few actors. Products are very heterogeneous – less so in agriculture, but even there. There are transaction costs and barriers to trade everywhere, particularly in the developing world. To overcome marketing problems and coordinate the exchange of goods and services, certain mechanisms have to be in place. It is only in an imaginary, perfect world that markets can be completely left to their own devices.

Markets require legislation, regulation, oversight and enforcement. To benefit as many as possible, markets also need an institutional framework that provides adequate and efficient incentives (Figure 2.1). Important mechanisms for reducing market frictions are:

- protection of property rights;

- contract enforcement;

- a system of standards, for example on weights and quality; and

- accurate information flows.

These mechanisms stimulate the strengthening and expansion of existing markets (North, 1995). They are especially important when markets expand and local exchanges – based on social networks, trust and personal ties – are transformed into impersonal exchange and long-distance trade, when third-party enforcement of rules, generally by government, becomes necessary (North, 1990; Fafchamps, 2004).

Trust is important for markets, especially when formal institutions are less developed. When there is no official grading system, buyers rely on trust to ensure that the quality of perishable goods is satisfactory. They also rely on trust to ensure that they are getting the right quantity for the price charged when no scales are present. When costs increase, sellers often try to

Market failures

Economists identify four causes behind market failures:

- **Market power**: A single large buyer or seller, sometimes in collusion with others, can influence the price. This can result from economies of scale, which provide incentives to operate on a large scale.
- **Externalities**: These exist when the costs and benefits of a particular good or service are not fully observed in the prices prevailing on the market. Examples are the costs of pollution or the benefits of bee-keeping.
- **Public good**: This is a good that can be used by anyone to whom it is available, as long as such use does not preclude others. Examples are sea-defence walls and lighthouses. Roads and market information are less perfect examples. Public goods or services are likely to be in short supply, for example because of the "free-rider problem" where people benefit from resources without paying for them, so suppliers have insufficient incentives to supply goods in socially optimum quantities.
- **Imperfect information**: Markets do not work well when information is inadequate, wrong or uncertain, or when some actors know more than others. Information is a costly public good, and knowledge creates market power. When more information is available, actors gain power and can bargain for better deals.

The term "market failure" can refer to:

Market imperfections: Economists disagree about many things, but they all accept the law of supply and demand, i.e. that prices increase when demand is larger than supply, and vice versa. Sometimes, however, prices and quantities do not adjust, owing to lack of information, market power, social conventions, etc. Such circumstances are particularly frequent in agriculture, partly because supply responses take time – at least until the next harvest.

Segmented or fragmented markets: Transaction and transportation costs are often high in developing countries. This means that markets can be segmented and not fully integrated. Market integration implies that price differences across different markets are based on the costs of moving goods from one market to another. If these costs are large, as is common in developing countries with poor infrastructure, the prices in one area can be unconnected with those in another. This can result in a food-surplus area being close to one with a food deficit. Sellers sometimes use product differentiation to segment markets deliberately in order to extract additional profits when richer buyers are willing to pay higher prices.

Missing markets: Markets could also be non-existent because of high transaction costs or a lack of demand. A prominent example is the lack of financial services in many rural areas.

Markets failing to coordinate: Coordination failures can result from externalities and public goods. Public goods are often produced in quantities that are too small to generate significant benefits, mainly because there are insufficient incentives to produce them. A typical example is when low demand for fertilizers or tractors keeps production low and prices high, thereby hampering agricultural development; another is when information about bad payers is not shared.

Markets yielding incorrect results: Public goods and externalities mean that prices do not entirely reflect the benefits derived from them. Two extreme examples are research and pollution. Research results are public goods – unless they are patented, as is becoming increasingly common – and yield positive externalities. For example, a drought-resistant seed may yield huge benefits, but the price of the seed is not likely to, and probably should not, reflect those benefits. Pollution is a negative externality, and prices of polluting activities are often too low to yield a desirable outcome.

Markets yielding undesirable results: Even when markets yield efficient outcomes, they respond to demand and not to need, so these outcomes are not necessarily equitable or socially optimal. Thus, if drought-affected farmers lose their crops, and therefore also their income, markets are unlikely to move food into the affected area. If people do not have enough money to buy nutritious food, markets will not supply them. Markets do not ensure proper nutrition for everybody. They can contribute to under- or overnutrition because of imperfect information – parents do not always know what food or care practices are best – or externalities leading to higher productivity, better health and reduced spread of contagious diseases.

Markets in equilibrium when demand does not equal supply: Examples of this are cases where the demand for a product, service or job is larger than what the supplier is willing to sell or provide. This happens in the labour market, resulting in unemployment, or in financial markets, where banks refuse to lend as much as a borrower wants because they might not get paid back. Another example is when wages are so low that workers cannot buy enough food for healthy and productive lives. Higher wages would lead to higher productivity, but markets are unlikely to produce such an optimal outcome.

keep prices nominally constant by adjusting the quantities sold (Hoffman and Bernhard, 2007).

Markets need institutions and legal systems to facilitate exchange.

Information on milk quality

"The quality of milk [in Karachi, Pakistan, in the mid-1970s] varied from seller to seller, and information about quality was asymmetric: the sellers knew more than the buyers. The consumer knew that a common practice of sellers was to add water to milk, but the consumer could not easily judge whether and how much a particular vendor had watered his milk down on a given day… [T]he market contained no institutions to certify that the milk had such-and-such an amount of butterfat. There were no grades, no brand names and no minimum levels of quality. There was only one market price of milk… In the absence of better information about quality, Karachi's milk market functioned poorly, leading to suboptimal levels of milk production and consumption"

Source: Klitgaard, 1991

Market performance requires the complementarity and coordination of policies, institutions and individual market actors, otherwise markets may fail. Market failures are common in developing countries because of poorly developed market institutions, weak or non-existent market information, extensive market power, and the absence of several markets, particularly financial markets. There may also be high risks, widespread uncertainties and poor infrastructure, which make participation and transactions costly and thus contribute to market segmentation and power (Kydd and Dorward, 2004).

Unregulated formation of market forces has produced uneven development (Brett, 2001). Poor rural areas have suffered from slow market development, especially compared with urban centres with high population density, or high-potential rural areas with greater levels of agricultural production and surpluses (IFAD, 2003b). Isolated and deprived rural areas, where most of the hungry poor live, generally lack efficient markets and are more likely to suffer from market failures.

Market failures are particularly common in developing countries, and the hungry poor are the most affected. Effective market performance requires the coordination of various policies, institutions and individual market actors.

Market functioning versus market failure

The law of demand and supply dictates that prices increase when demand is larger than supply, and vice versa. A higher maize price, for example, stimulates farmers to produce more maize and makes consumers buy less. This should bring supply closer to demand and reduce the maize price. Economists refer to this as the allocative and distributional roles of markets; for example, maize growers allocate more land, labour and inputs to maize production, while their crop is increasingly bought and distributed through markets. This means that prices drive market actors' decisions. As a result, analysis and close tracking of market prices can provide much valuable information, especially regarding market functioning and market failure.

Marketing and market functioning

Evaluation of the market functioning can be based on the process through which food leaves producers and makes its way to consumers in retail food markets. This process is the marketing chain. Assessment of the marketing chain identifies its structure and the behaviour of various actors along the chain.

The marketing chain transforms products over space and time through storage, transportation and processing. The various costs and prices along the marketing chain can provide insights into the functioning or non-functioning of markets. Prices along the chain reflect transaction costs. The differences in prices between each stage of the marketing chain – from farmer to trader or processor, and from wholesale/retail trader to consumer – can reveal how competitive a market is and whether or not traders' marketing costs are reasonable (Baulch, 2001), as well as indicating where markets may be weak, failing or functioning well.

Agriculture markets are typically concentrated at one point of the marketing chain. In remote locations, there may be very few traders, and farmers have little

Figure 2.2 – Marketing margins for raw cashew nuts, April 2007

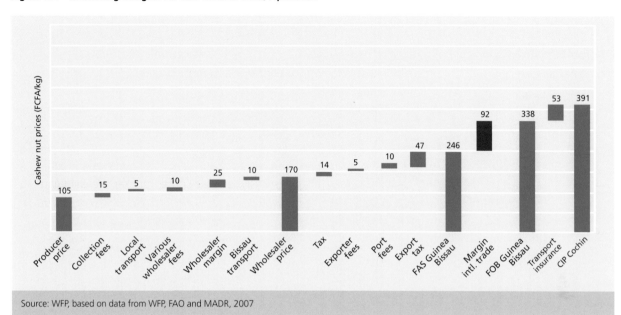

Source: WFP, based on data from WFP, FAO and MADR, 2007

choice. The more traders competing to buy farmers' output, the better the information available to farmers about prevailing prices and the easier it is for them to switch from one buyer to another (Timmer, Falcon and Pearson, 1983).

The spread, or difference, between prices at two points of the marketing chain – for example between the retail price at an urban market and the wholesale price – may indicate if gross marketing margins are large. This could mean that traders are making excessive profits. In Guinea Bissau, for example, inefficiencies and failures in raw cashew nut markets led to declined food security in 2007.

Figure 2.2 indicates a large difference between the free alongside ship (FAS) price, which is what the seller pays to move goods from the depot to the port of shipment, and the free on board (FOB) price received by the buyer at the border. This difference was larger than the costs of transportation, insurance and port fees, implying that either the exporter or the importer received profits beyond typical costs. Only three companies exported raw cashew nuts from Guinea Bissau to India, while 60 percent of the population was engaged in cashew nut production. The market at one end of the chain was therefore very concentrated, pointing to oligopolistic market power (WFP, FAO and MADR, 2007).

The marketing chain provides an insight into price formation. Although non-competitive price formation affects market performance and efficiency, it may not stop market functioning altogether: food or other goods may still move from producer to consumer.

Another dimension of market functioning is spatial integration. If the price differentials between one market and another are larger than the transaction costs, traders have incentives to move food from surplus regions, where prices are low, to deficit regions, where prices are higher. This process is referred to as arbitrage. If markets are integrated and arbitrage takes place, prices should follow similar patterns (Figure 2.3). If traders are not responding to such price differentials, there are significant barriers to trade and markets no longer function in their distributive and allocative roles.

This situation occurs in East and Southern Africa, where trade from surplus to deficit regions is hindered by natural market boundaries, based on agro-ecological zones, policies and trade procedures. There are no quotas, bans or taxes on cross-border rice and wheat trade between South Africa and Mozambique, but a 17 percent value added tax (VAT) is applied to the movement of maize, unless it is imported for meal. Policies therefore favour the trade of rice, wheat and maize for meal over maize grain. In practice, despite

Figure 2.3 – Real millet prices in regions of Niger and Nigeria, 1995–2005

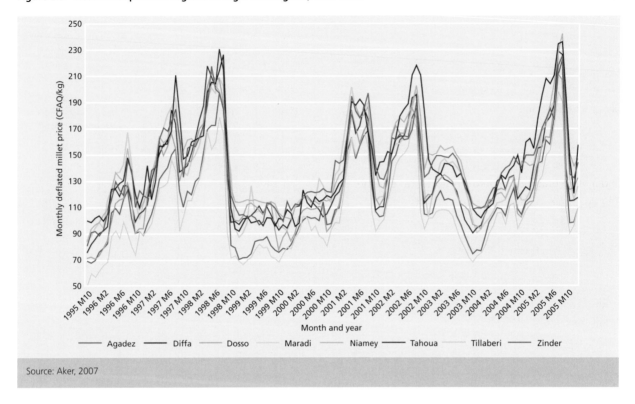

Source: Aker, 2007

several prolonged periods when they would have been profitable for traders, there have been no grain imports into Mozambique because of the scale and complexity of import procedures in the South African marketing chain (Govereh et al., 2008).

Prices provide the key to understanding market behaviour. Costs and price differences along the marketing chain, from farmer to trader and from wholesale/retail trader to consumer, need to be studied carefully because they indicate where markets may be weak, failing or functioning well.

Changing market structures

The role of public actors and markets

Until the 1980s, development economists generally believed that prevalent market imperfections in developing countries could be overcome by a coordinated, state-led investment push. Through the creation of marketing boards, government-controlled cooperatives and parastatal processing units, many African and Asian governments became heavily involved in agricultural marketing and food processing.

Governments had an interest in keeping food prices low to enhance support for themselves. Government institutions turned into monopoly buyers of agricultural products, especially basic food and important export crops.

In the 1980s, this paradigm lost ground, mainly because of constraints imposed by slower growth and an unfolding debt crisis. In its place, a market paradigm known as the "Washington consensus" emerged, whose fundamental tenets were stabilization, liberalization and privatization.

The theoretical case for markets having a larger role is mainly based on the argument that markets' allocative function improves if prices are free to move and are determined by markets, rather than governments. There are limitations, however. For example, the gains from liberalizing markets can only be realized once, and are small or non-existent if controls on markets are not all removed or if other market failures persist (Brinkman, 1996).

When markets function, macroeconomic policies, such as exchange rates, and trade, fiscal or monetary policies, may change the incentives and constraints for market actors such as farmers, processors and traders (Barrett, 2005b). Conversely, macro-level policies can either facilitate or dampen market formation. In certain cases, this can benefit food security and hunger reduction; in others, it works against a population's general well-being.

By the 1990s, generally disappointing results, financial crises and rising inequalities triggered a reassessment, and a more pragmatic approach started to emerge. This approach included roles for markets and governments and emphasized the importance of institutions (Williamson, 2003b). More room was left for "humility, policy diversity, selective and modest reforms, and experimentation" (Rodrik, 2006). Concepts such as externalities, asymmetric information, economies of scale, poverty traps, strategic complementarities among sectors, and coordination failures were again used to explain development experiences and guide policies. Development practice and theory began to converge (United Nations, 2000).

Sub-Saharan Africa: Finding the balance between liberalization and domestic policies

Many colonial governments taxed agriculture – largely through marketing boards – as an easy way to generate revenues. In Africa, the structure and nature of intervention in agricultural sectors varied from region to region: in East and Southern Africa, government intervention was concentrated in grain markets; in West Africa, marketing boards operated primarily in the export crop sector (Kherallah et al., 2002).

After independence, African governments emphasized industrialization, as opposed to agriculture, as a means of achieving growth and development. They continued to extract agricultural revenue to support industry and provide social services.

As well as collecting tax revenue, marketing boards ensured price stability and provided farmers with cheap inputs and a guaranteed outlet for crops. As there was only one buyer, contract enforcement was straightforward.

An advantage of such systems of vertical coordination was that they served all farmers equally, and the marketing boards bore all transportation (pan-territorial pricing) and storage costs (pan-seasonal pricing). Unfortunately, however, most of them did this inefficiently – farmers received low prices and had few production incentives. When international prices declined, losses became unsustainable. Intervention had been "clumsy and heavy-handed, [and] has provided means and opportunities for rent-seeking and capture" (Lundberg, 2005). From the 1980s, structural adjustment loans extended by the World Bank and bilateral donors obliged governments to scale down marketing agencies and provide an enabling environment for traders.

Agricultural liberalization appears to have had some positive impacts on the supply chains for cash crops (Kydd and Dorward, 2004), but input, output and financial markets for staple food crop production have not been successfully developed. Problems include loan default by farmers; low producer prices offered by traders at harvest, when farmers are desperate for cash, and in remote areas, where farmers have no other sales outlets; sale of adulterated inputs; and the use of inaccurate/loaded weights and measures. Central to these issues are depressed investment, thin markets and weak institutions (Kydd and Dorward, 2004).

Government intervention is still prevalent in African food commodity markets. One reason is the political sensitivity of issues concerning a country's national food supply: under total liberalization, consumers and smallholders could be vulnerable to speculators, particularly when prominent traders come from minority ethnic groups. Governments are wary of becoming over-dependent on international grain trading firms owing to the vulnerabilities such dependence entails (Dorward, Kydd and Poulton, 1998).

In East and Southern African countries such as Kenya, Malawi, Zambia and Zimbabwe, governments continue to pursue price stabilization and food security objectives through marketing boards. Their operations are now more modest, but boards continue to be major actors in the maize market. Maize export bans have been asserted several times, generally without notice, and with devastating effects on the private sector. In Kenya, maize import tariffs are regularly waived without notice, resulting in market distortions and shortages as traders postpone imports in anticipation of tariff removal.

Food market liberalization is controversial. Some argue that implementation has been erratic and not far-reaching enough. Others maintain that the reforms were wrong-headed, as demonstrated by the limited private sector response. A balance between these two views would lead to judicious and gradual reforms that support market development (Chapter 9).

The role of private actors and markets

Markets are dynamic and continuously changing. A recent example is the growing importance of large retail chains, often referred to as the "supermarket revolution" (Reardon and Berdegué, 2002; Reardon et al., 2003; Weatherspoon and Reardon, 2003; Reardon and Swinnen, 2004). Worldwide food distribution is increasingly organized around large super- and hypermarket chains, driven by four interrelated trends: privatization, liberalization, integration and globalization.

Supermarkets first emerged in developed countries. Since the 1990s they have spread rapidly in developing countries, starting in Latin America's larger and richer nations, and expanding to East and Southeast Asia, smaller and poorer countries in Latin America, Southern and then East Africa, and most recently South Asia. Supermarkets now account for 50–60 percent of food retailing in Latin America and East Asia (Figure 2.4). It is expected that supermarkets will continue to proliferate across Latin America, Asia and Africa (Traill, 2006). Supermarkets cater increasingly to poor segments of the population, which may have negative implications for these people's access to nutritious food. Supermarkets offer new market opportunities for farmers, but smallholders generally have limited possibilities to meet the quantity, quality and timeliness requirements (Chapter 5).

Although recent debates have centred on the role of markets rather than states in spurring development, there must be coordination and complementarity between markets and government action for markets to work properly. Markets cannot operate in a vacuum. Finding the right balance between markets and interventions is a challenge for any government.

Understanding how markets help or hinder the fight against hunger and poverty is only one step towards lasting solutions to the hunger–poverty trap. Markets have a great variety of direct or indirect impacts on the prevalence of hunger and poverty. High food prices have large, global implications for countries and households, particularly those vulnerable to food insecurity. The risks have further increased because of the global financial crisis. The following chapter disentangles some of the possible reasons for and consequences of this distressing development.

Figure 2.4 – Supermarkets' share in food retailing in selected developing countries

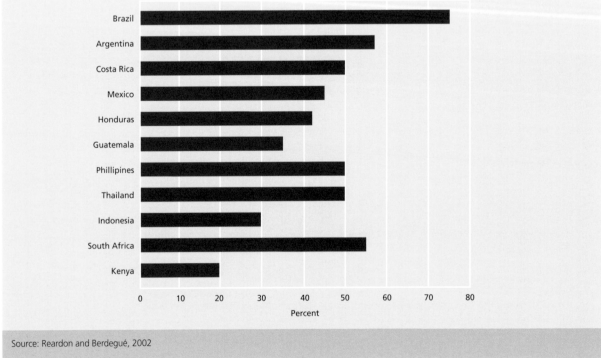

Source: Reardon and Berdegué, 2002

Intermezzo 2.1: The Chinese model – beating hunger with reforms

One of the largest famines of the twentieth century occurred in China. Since then, however, the country has experienced a remarkable reduction in poverty and hunger. Reforms in the agriculture sector were central to this success.

Before the reforms, the agricultural sector was characterized by the commune system, which prohibited people from cultivating on private plots. This substantially reduced the incentives for small farmers to work productively (Fang and Yang, 2006).

In 1978, individual farm households received the right to use collectively owned land under long-term leases. This reform, known as the "household responsibility system" (HRS), also granted farmers access to markets where they could sell their surplus crops, after meeting the collectives' production quotas. Over the years, production quotas were reduced, and mandatory production plans were abolished in 1985. These reforms were supplemented by increased procurement prices, provision of hybrid seeds and investments in irrigation, agricultural research and extension, and rural infrastructure (United Nations, 2000; Fang and Yang, 2006).

During the early years of the reform period, 1978–1985, grain production increased by 30 percent, while the land area cultivated decreased by 6 percent (Lohmar, 2006). This success was a result of flexibility at the local and regional levels, which allowed the specifics of each region to be taken into account when local leaders divided land among small farmers (FAO, 2006b). The leaders also ensured that crop yields would satisfy urban needs, by allocating a part of each crop for delivery to cities (Lohmar, 2006).

Between 1978 and 1998, the number of poor citizens in rural China fell from 260 to 42 million. More than half of that decrease occurred in the first six years (Lohmar, 2003). Food availability per capita rose from 1,717 kcal in the 1960s, to 2,328 kcal in 1981 and 3,000 kcal in the late 1990s. China proved able to respond to emergencies during the reform period, such as during the government's massive and timely response to the 1990s floods (FAO, 2006b).

The Chinese model – reasons for success

- Government action – *policy-makers identified solutions and implemented them.*
- Incentives for farmers – *a market space was created.*
- Market reforms – *reforms were implemented gradually to smooth the transition.*

"Progress in reducing hunger is now being eroded by the worldwide increase in food prices."

United Nations, 2008b

The world has experienced increased food prices in recent years, with a dramatic peak in 2008. Prices are likely to remain relatively high in the next few years. The impact of high food prices on hunger has long-term consequences, and has jeopardized the fight against hunger and the prospects for achieving the Millennium Development Goals (MDGs).

Trends and causes: demand is outpacing supply

Food prices have increased since 2001, and rose particularly steeply in 2007 and 2008, declining sharply in the second half of 2008 (Figure 3.1). The causes can be categorized as demand and supply factors (Table 3.1). Demand for food has been increasing as a result of rising incomes in rapidly growing economies, particularly Asia. Higher incomes usually mean less cereal consumption and more meat production, which requires intensive use of cereals.

The production of food crops for conversion into biofuels has expanded rapidly in recent years, particularly in developed countries. This is largely because of high energy prices and policy measures to reduce the dependence on fossil fuels, such as through mandatory mixing and use requirements, subsidies and tariffs. Most experts agree that biofuels have a significant impact in boosting demand and prices. Although biofuels account for only about 1.5 percent of global liquid fuel supply, they accounted for nearly half the increase in consumption of major food crops in 2006/2007 (IMF, 2008d). Globally, 126 million MT of grains will be used to produce ethanol in 2008/2009, accounting for about 6 percent of global production and about a third of US maize production (IGC, 2008b).

Biofuels have pushed up the prices not only of the crops used for energy, such as maize and vegetable oil, but also of other foods, because of production or consumption substitutions or through cost-push effects. When the prize of maize increases, farmers are encouraged to grow more maize and use less land for other crops. Moreover, consumers might prefer other cereals, increasing the demand for and prices of these

Figure 3.1 – Food prices have increased to different degrees and remain volatile (1998–2000 = 100)

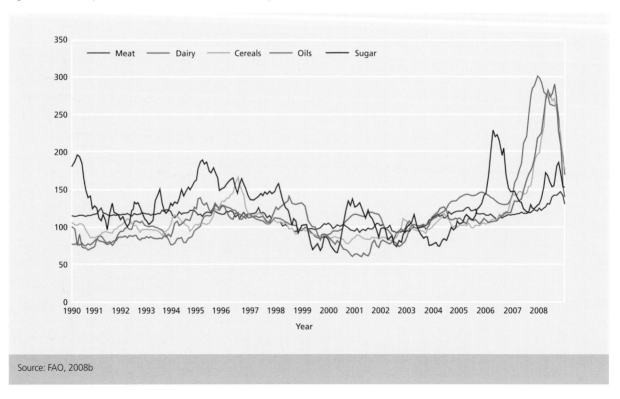

Source: FAO, 2008b

Table 3.1 – Factors causing high food prices

Demand factors	Supply factors
• Higher incomes and changing demand	• Low stocks
• Population growth	• Weather-related shocks
• Biofuels	• Low investments in agriculture and low productivity growth
• Low US$ exchange rate	• Export restrictions
• Institutional investment (speculation)	• Energy prices: fertilizer, mechanization, transport
	• Low US$ exchange rate

crops. Approximately 60 percent of global maize production is currently used for animal feed, pushing up the prices of meat and dairy products. Several institutions estimate that biofuels account for about 20–30 percent of the price increases, but some put this figure as high as 70 percent or as low as 3 percent (von Braun, 2007; IMF, 2008d; OECD-FAO, 2008; World Bank, 2008c and 2009).

Demand has probably also been increased by the large amount of money flowing into commodity markets from institutional investors. There is, however, no consensus on the extent to which these investments – or speculation – have pushed food prices up. Investors have been looking for portfolio diversification, as stock markets show low correlation with commodity markets, and higher returns, driven by low interest rates and financial turmoil. Investments by institutional investors add a new, and sometimes puzzling, dynamic to the market (Intermezzo 3.2).

The fact that most food commodities are denominated in US dollars (US$) affects prices through demand and supply. The lower dollar exchange rate makes commodities relatively cheap for countries whose currencies are appreciating against the dollar, stimulating demand. However, these same countries also receive less domestic currency for their food exports, which pressurizes farmers to raise prices to cover costs.

On the supply side, global cereal production declined by 3.6 percent in 2005 and 6.9 percent in 2006, largely because of weather-related shocks (FAO, 2008c). These declines were small, but as demand had outpaced supply for a few years, cereal stocks were low and could not fully absorb the supply shocks. Currently, cereal stocks are at their lowest levels for 30 years (Figure 6.3), which has contributed to price volatility.

Supply has not kept pace with demand, partly because investments in agriculture have been low and the growth rate of yields has fallen. Yields of maize, rice and wheat generally grew by more than 2 percent a year between 1960 and 1985 – reaching 5 percent for wheat. Around 2000, the annual growth rate for rice and wheat yields was less than 1 percent. Subsequently, this rate has been increasing, but the rate for maize has fallen to less than 1 percent (World Bank, 2007c).

Policy measures have exacerbated the supply situation. In mid-2008, about 40 countries had agricultural export restrictions, including major exporters such as Argentina, Kazakhstan and Viet Nam (World Bank, 2008a). The rice export ban imposed by India on 9 October 2007 had a significant impact on the rice price (Figure 3.2). Countries introduced export restrictions to increase the availability of domestic supplies. In the short run, such measures can be helpful domestically, but have significant negative effects on neighbouring and other importing countries. In the long run, they are not effective because they are a disincentive to production and trade. They can be ineffective in the short run as well, if borders are porous or traders increase their margins (and prices) because of the restrictions. In the second half of 2008, several countries eased export restrictions, helping to lower prices.

Higher energy prices are the final factor behind high food prices. Energy prices have influenced food prices for a long time, because some fertilizers and pesticides are based on hydrocarbons and the production of food is very energy-intensive in many countries (see IMF, 2008c). Food also needs to be transported. In recent years, the output prices of food have been connected to energy prices rather than input prices. This phenomenon is largely a result of biofuels' emergence as an alternative to fossil fuels when prices are high (Schmidhuber, 2006; World Bank, 2009).

33

Figure 3.2 – Thai rice prices and India's export ban (US$/MT)

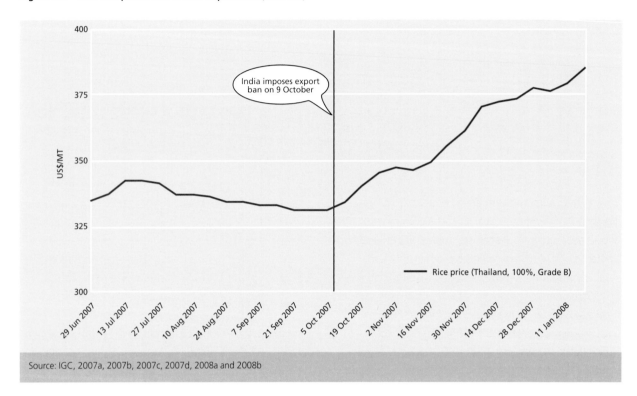

Source: IGC, 2007a, 2007b, 2007c, 2007d, 2008a and 2008b

Analysts generally agree that a combination of these factors, with the possible exception of speculation, has contributed to food price increases. However, there is disagreement about the relative weight to ascribe to each factor, particularly for specific commodities and time periods.

Food prices are likely to remain high and volatile

Food prices peaked in mid-2008, and declined in the second half of that year. Several factors behind the fall, such as slower demand growth, lower energy prices and a stronger US dollar, can be attributed to the global financial crisis that erupted in September 2008. Other factors, such as the easing of weather-related supply constraints and export restrictions, also played a role.

However, a number of structural factors, including low stocks, low productivity growth, climate change, relatively high energy prices and demand for biofuels, are still in place. Growth in developing countries is also expected to remain or be relatively strong in the medium to long term, even if income growth is slowing in the short term.

Structural changes could herald a new era. The recent increases come after a prolonged decline in the prices of many agricultural commodities, reaching historic lows in the late 1990s. Cereal prices declined because productivity benefited from the green revolution, while demand grew more slowly as a result of slowing population growth, persistent poverty in some countries, and the reaching of medium to high cereal consumption levels in other countries, such as China (FAO, 2002).

Forecasting is difficult, particularly for the medium and long term, and economists have been wrong in the past. Fears about rising food prices have often turned out to be exaggerated or just wrong (Intermezzo 3.1). Most forecasting is done by mechanically extrapolating into the future, and structural changes in underlying dynamics or the model are often not foreseen.

"The only function of economic forecasting is to make astrology look respectable."

John Kenneth Galbraith

Commodity prices are inherently volatile, particularly those for agricultural commodities, because of low supply and demand responses to price changes.

Demand and supply curves are steep, and small changes in supply can have large effects on prices, especially when stocks are low. Figure 3.3 illustrates this. A drought would move the supply curve to the left, while the demand curve stays put. A small decrease in production, from Q_0 to Q_1, yields a much larger increase in prices, from P_0 to P_1. A similarly large price increase can be deduced if the demand curve shifts to the right because of higher incomes or biofuels.

Many factors affect future patterns of demand and supply, and most of them are considerably uncertain (Table 3.2). Temporary factors, such as a slowing of the world economy, will wane, but changing demand patterns, climate change and higher energy and fertilizer prices are more structural. Higher prices should lead to higher production – and lower prices. However, this requires investments in agriculture, including in research and development to improve yields, and in expanding the cultivated area, where land is available, while protecting the rights of current users and promoting sustainable use of natural resources. The global financial crisis, effects of climate change on agricultural production, institutional investors and the demand for biofuels are creating considerable uncertainty about the normal market mechanism.

Most institutions predicted that prices would peak in 2008 or 2009, and then decline gradually (Figure 3.4).

Figure 3.3 – Demand and supply curves for food commodities

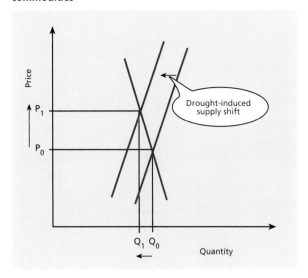

This has largely materialized, although the drop has been more sudden and steeper. In November 2008, the FAO Cereal Price Index was still 70 percent above the 2005 level and double that of 2000. Average food prices for the next ten years will be significantly higher than for the previous ten years. Whatever the time frame of food price rises, they have an immediate and long-term negative effect on population groups and countries vulnerable to food insecurity.

Medium- and long-term forecasting is difficult; temporary factors such as a slowdown in the

Table 3.2 – Factors influencing future food prices

	Demand	Supply
Short-term	• Slowing of the world economy	• Low stocks • Export restrictions • Weather-related shocks • Biofuel competition for land • Area expansion, where appropriate • Higher energy (input) prices
Long-term	• Increasing and changing demand from emerging markets • Population size increasing, but more slowly • Demand for biofuels • Institutional investments	• More investment in agriculture? • (Bio)technology to raise yields? • Climate change will increase frequency and intensity of extreme weather events • Second-generation of biofuels: competition for land declining? • Higher energy (and fertilizer) prices

Figure 3.4 – Averages of the food price forecasts of six institutions (2000 = 100)

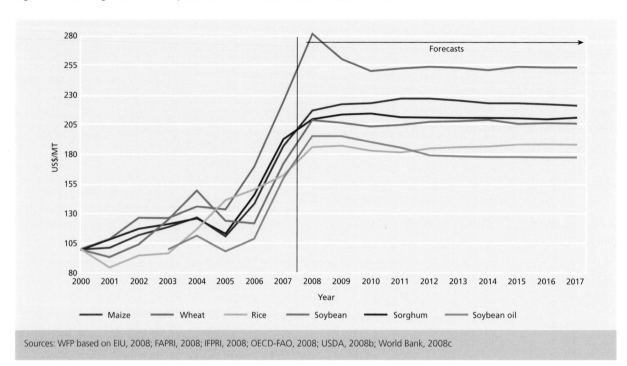

Sources: WFP based on EIU, 2008; FAPRI, 2008; IFPRI, 2008; OECD-FAO, 2008; USDA, 2008b; World Bank, 2008c

world economy will wane, but higher demand, climate change and higher fuel and fertilizer prices are more structural, and are likely to remain.

Impact on countries

The transmission of international to domestic food prices is imperfect and depends on several factors

The risk that a country is negatively affected by high food prices depends on the country's vulnerability and the extent of the food price increase (Chapter 7 for terminology). Higher international prices do not necessarily mean higher domestic prices. Transmission of international prices to domestic prices depends on several factors. First, there are structural factors that cannot be changed in the short term:

- *Food imports* as a share of domestic food supplies: Countries importing less food are less exposed.

- *Transportation costs*: Areas with expensive transport routes, such as remote, landlocked or mountainous regions, usually face higher prices that are less correlated to international prices.

- *Competitiveness of markets*: More competitive markets are likely to pass through price changes more directly.

- *Cost structure*: Foods with higher processing, transport and retail costs are better insulated.

Second are the policy measures that governments take to reduce the transmission from international to domestic prices:

- *Trade barriers* – import tariffs, import quotas, export restrictions: Higher import barriers generally mean higher domestic prices that are less correlated to international prices. Export restrictions can increase domestic food availability and lower prices in the short term.

- Domestic food *taxes and subsidies*: Lower taxes and higher subsidies reduce the pass-through.

- Other government *interventions*: For example, releasing food reserves can reduce the transmission.

Almost three-quarters of 80 developing countries surveyed in March 2008 had taken policy measures to reduce the transmission and mitigate the impact on consumers (World Bank, 2009).

Exchange rates are another major factor affecting the transmission of international to domestic prices. Appreciating exchange rates make imports less expensive, reducing the pass-through. This has benefited the CFA zone in West Africa, for example; the CFA franc is tied to the euro. The extent to which governments can influence the exchange rate depends on the exchange regime. If the regime is floating or intermediate (between fixed and freely floating), governments have instruments that influence the rate.

A recent study in seven Asian countries found that world prices in US dollars increased by an average of 52 percent between the end of 2003 and the end of 2007, while domestic prices increased by only 17 percent in local currencies (Dawe, 2008). Another study estimated that between 1995 and 2008 about 15 percent of the change in international food prices was passed-through to domestic prices (IMF, 2008c). Domestic demand and supply conditions are more important when the pass-through is limited, which was, for example, the case in Burundi and Uganda (Sanogo, 2009).

Incomplete pass-through also occurs when prices decline. For example, at the end of 2008, there was evidence that the steep decline in international food prices had not translated into similar declines in domestic prices. The reasons could include:

- delayed price transmission because of transportation time;

- sticky prices and the ratchet effect, when prices adjust more easily upwards than downwards;

- the effects of reduced fuel subsidies on food prices (IMF, 2008b); and

- second-round price effects – higher prices leading to higher wages and back to higher prices (IMF, 2008c).

Food-importing countries suffer

High world food prices have made food-importing developing countries more vulnerable. Imports are an important safety valve for many developing countries facing domestic production shortfalls. Such imports have a dampening effect on prices (Chapter 6). High

international prices and export restrictions have hampered this safety value.

The international environment has also highlighted the "tragedy of the commons" (Timmer, 1986). When one country suffers a production shortfall because of a shock, it is often fairly easy to import the difference. However, when many countries face the same situation, they are likely to face higher prices, and imports might not be available, because there are far more importers than exporters (Chapter 6). Until recently, the probability that many countries would need to import more food than normal was rather low. This probability is growing, however, as climate change increases the frequency and intensity of weather-related production shortfalls.

High food prices can have several macroeconomic effects. Regarding the balance of payments, net-exporting countries have benefited from higher food prices, experiencing higher terms of trade. Net-importing countries have faced lower terms of trade and larger food import bills. This is especially worrying for developing countries, the majority – 55 percent – of which are net food importers. Almost all countries in Africa are net importers of cereals.

Since the end of 2004, higher food prices have led to terms-of-trade losses amounting to 0.5 percent of GDP in low-income countries, rising to an average of 1 percent of GDP in 29 countries and nearly 5 percent in the most affected country, Eritrea (World Bank, 2008c). For 33 net food-importing countries, the adverse balance-of-payment impact amounted to 0.9 percent of 2007 GDP for the period January 2007 to July 2008 (IMF, 2008b).

From 2006 to 2008, the total costs of food imports rose from US$86 billion to US$117 billion in low-income food-deficit countries (LIFDCs), and from US$13 billion to US$24 billion in least developed countries (LDCs) (FAO, 2008a). In 2008, the annual food import bill of LIFDCs and LDCs was four times that of 2000.

In addition, petroleum prices have also risen sharply over recent years, and many net food-importing

Figure 3.5 – Weight of food in the consumer price index, and per capita income

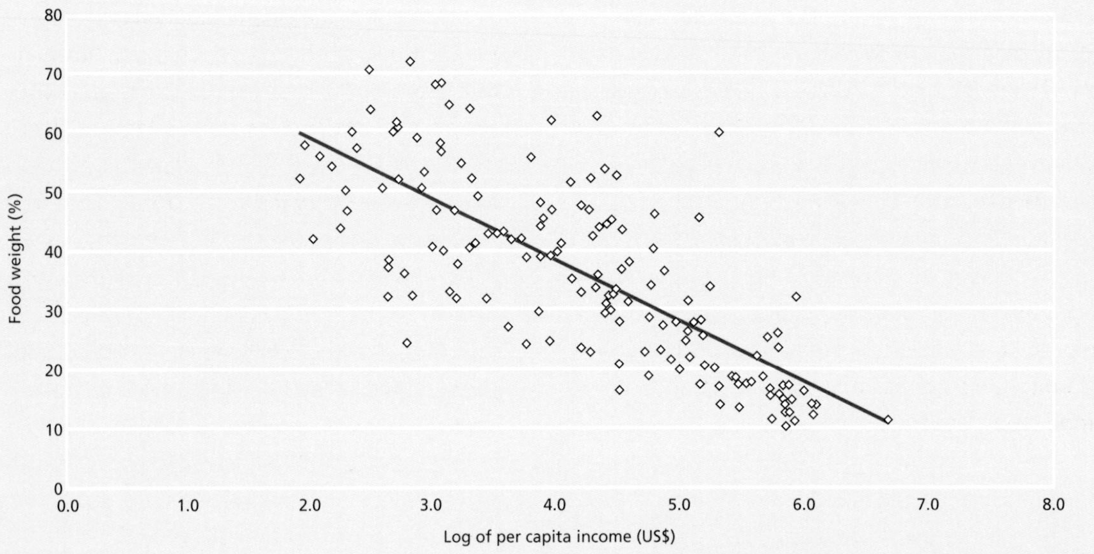

Note: Equation: Food weight = 79.8 − 10.4 × per capita income; with $R^2 = 0.5835$ and t-ratio = −14.59.
Source: IMF, 2008d

countries are also net oil-importers, so face two price shocks. For nearly all food-importing countries, the oil price shock is greater than the food price shock in terms of impact on the balance of payments (IMF, 2008a). International financial institutions have increased financial support to cover these balance-of-payment difficulties. After mid-2008, both food and fuel prices dropped, benefiting importers.

Higher food prices have pushed up inflation rates across the world. Developing countries are particularly vulnerable, because food typically accounts for a large share of the consumer price index (Figure 3.5). Inflation in developing economies accelerated from 5.4 percent in 2006 to 9.4 percent in 2008 (IMF, 2008c). In the 12 months to June 2008, food price inflation was about 17 percent in 35 low-income countries, more than double the rate in 2006 (IMF, 2008b).

Higher food prices have also contributed to fiscal imbalances. Several governments have lowered

taxes and tariffs on food to mitigate the impact, but some have benefited from higher export taxes. Government expenditures on safety net programmes, food-based and other, have also increased, because numbers of beneficiaries, costs per beneficiary, or both have risen. About half the countries surveyed by IMF reported a net increase in the fiscal cost of policy responses; the median annualized increase for 2007/2008 was 0.7 percent of GDP, but exceeded 2 percent of GDP in many countries (IMF, 2008b; World Bank, 2009). Many have emphasized the need for targeted approaches – rather than, for example, general subsidies – to reduce costs and increase effectiveness and efficiency. For example, direct compensation of the poor for higher food prices between January 2005 and December 2007 would amount to only US$2.4 billion (World Bank, 2009).

High food prices have had a significant negative impact in many developing countries.

Impact on households

Higher food prices pushed 115 million people into hunger in 2007 and 2008 (FAO, 2008c), and between 130 and 155 million into poverty between late 2005 and early 2008 (World Bank, 2009). Higher food prices make food access more difficult for households. The most vulnerable population groups are those who buy more food than they sell (net buyers), spend a large share of their income on food and have few coping strategies at their disposal. These groups include the urban poor, rural landless, pastoralists and many small-scale farmers and agropastoralists, because they grow non-food crops, depend on limited livestock sales or buy more food than they sell. Pastoralists are often particularly vulnerable, because they face falling livestock prices at the same time as high food prices. This can cause steep, and often rapid, drops in the terms of trade between cereals and livestock.

According to Engel's law, the share of food in total household expenditures declines when income increases (see Figure 3.5). A rich family that spends about 10 percent of its income on food can manage a 25 or 50 percent increase in food prices. Poor families in developing countries spend between 50 and 80 percent of their incomes on food, a similar price increase poses severe hardship. Poor households usually have few coping mechanisms at their disposal and risk being hardest hit (FAO, 2008c). In many countries, the middle class might also be at risk. For a middle-class family spending a total of US$6 to US$10 a day, food still accounts for 35–65 percent of expenditures (Banerjee and Duflo, 2008). In most developing countries, more than 80 percent of the population lives on less than US$10 per day; in some, such as Côte d'Ivoire, India, Indonesia, Pakistan and the United Republic of Tanzania, this proportion is more than 98 percent.

For vulnerable households, higher prices have an immediate impact on the quantity and quality of food consumed. They switch to cheaper foods, and reduce the number and size of meals and the expenditures on non-staple foods. Non-staple foods are often the main sources of fat, minerals and vitamins, which are essential for growth and maintenance of a healthy and productive life. These strategies have significant consequences, especially for the most vulnerable groups: the sick, the elderly, children and pregnant women. Households also reduce expenditures on other basic needs, such as education and health, or sell productive assets, with negative effects on their current and future livelihoods. These consequences are long-term – even life-long.

WFP assessments found widespread evidence of reductions in the quality and quantity of food consumed and some evidence of increased school drop-out rates or sale of economic assets, for example in Liberia, Lesotho, Nepal, Pakistan, Tajikistan and Yemen (Sanogo, 2009).

In Bangladesh, for example, households facing rising rice prices try to maintain rice consumption and reduce non-rice expenditures. This has a strong effect on nutrition status because of the high micronutrient content of non-rice foods, such as fruit, vegetables, eggs and fish. Non-rice food expenditures are strongly correlated to the percentage of underweight children (r = –0.91) (Torlesse, Kiess and Bloem, 2003; see Figure 3.6). A similar pattern was found in Indonesia during the financial crisis of 1997/1998, resulting in worsening micronutrient status and maternal wasting, but no increase in child underweight was observed. Child nutrition indicators had not recovered to their pre-crisis levels by January 2001 (Block et al., 2004). In Brazzaville, after devaluation of the CFA in 1994, stunting and wasting increased because of the lower quality of complementary foods, associated with higher food prices (Martin-Prével et al., 2000). It should be noted that the impact may vary among contexts, depending on such factors as pre-existing nutrition status and vulnerability to food insecurity, dietary intake patterns, consumption of micronutrient-rich foods and the severity of the crisis.

When households face higher staple food prices, they try to maintain the quantity of calories, but reduce the quality of their diets. This has serious immediate and long-term consequences because of micronutrient deficiencies, the severity of which can increase quite rapidly (WFP and UNICEF, 2008). One-third of the world's population already suffers from micronutrient

Figure 3.6 – Undernutrition and expenditure in rural Bangladesh, 1992–2000

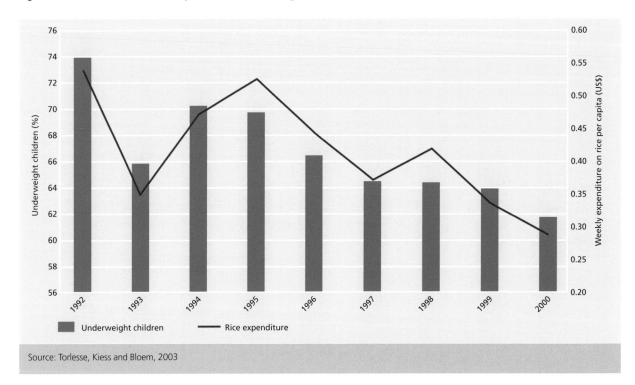

Source: Torlesse, Kiess and Bloem, 2003

deficiencies, resulting in reduced immunity – increasing morbidity and mortality – weakened work productivity, diminished school performance, hampered cognitive development and slower growth.

Even a few months of inadequate nutrition can do irreversible damage, especially for children under 24 months and pregnant women. The longer the high food prices last, the more households exhaust their coping capacities and the greater the impacts on nutrition, education, productivity, health and livelihoods. A recent study highlights the large impact that proper nutrition can have. In Guatemala, men who had benefited from a nutritious drink when they were aged 0 to 24 months in the early 1970s, were – 30 years later – earning wages that were 46 percent higher than those of men who had received a less nutritious drink at the same age (Hoddinott et al., 2008). About 300 million children under 24 months and pregnant women, in 61 countries, were at risk to high food prices during the period 2006–2008.

Because they vary across different settings, the effects of high food prices on livelihoods, food purchasing, food consumption and nutrition status must be carefully monitored. Interventions appropriate to the specific population and subgroups can then be designed for the short, medium and longer terms. Interventions may include:

- transfers of vouchers, for specific nutrient-rich food products, cash or food with adequate micronutrient content;

- when purchasing power is restored, ensuring the availability of nutritious foods or food supplements at affordable prices, such as complementary foods for young children, or micronutrient powders;

- blanket feeding of children 6 to 23 months with a fortified-blended food that contains micronutrients and some milk or whey powder;

- treatment of children with moderate acute malnutrition with ready-to-eat therapeutic foods or (improved) fortified-blended food mixed with sugar and oil; and

- distribution of additional micronutrients, such as micronutrient powders for home fortification, particularly for children aged 6 to 59 months.

High food prices may have severe impacts on household food security, particularly in

The high food prices of recent years have already caused irreversible damage to nutrition, education, assets and coping capacities. The global financial crisis is another shock that might have severe implications for hunger across the globe. The poorest and most vulnerable people in the developing world are likely to experience the greatest hardships – paying the price for a crisis they had no hand in creating.

The crisis, which erupted in the US in September 2008, is "the most dangerous shock in mature financial markets since the 1930s" (IMF, 2008d) and likely to cause the worst recession in the developed world since then. It rapidly spread to developing countries, which are affected by lower export revenues because of lower volumes and prices, fewer tourists, job losses, lower capital flows, lower remittances and budgetary pressures. These could lead to reduced government services and spending on social protection systems. Aid levels might also decline, even if developed countries maintain their GDP-based aid targets.

For vulnerable groups, the channels and impacts of the financial crisis are different from those of high food prices. High food prices have affected households mainly through prices; the impact of the financial crisis will affect mainly incomes and employment. Both reduce access to food. Based on previous crises (Fallon and Lucas, 2002), these are some of the results that might affect households:

- more hunger and malnutrition;
- higher poverty rates;
- lower school enrolment;
- more open unemployment and fewer formal jobs;
- lower real wages; and
- lower remittances.

developing countries where most households spend the majority of their incomes on food. Poor households have few coping mechanisms at their disposal and will be at risk. When confronted with high staple food prices, vulnerable households are likely to reduce first the quality of their diets. Micronutrient deficiencies will increase, with life-long consequences. This requires immediate action.

Response

Supported by the international community, governments have been responding to the crisis by:

- *assessing and analysing* the extent of the food price increase, its causes and impacts;

- *adjusting* existing programmes and targeting;

- *adding* activities (including monitoring) and programmes (in urban areas and to address micronutrient deficiencies); and

- *amending* government policies to address food availability and access problems.

The international community has focused on:

- *advising* governments on policies and programmes;

- *assisting* governments with technical and financial support; and

- *advocating* for funding and collective responses with partners.

High food prices call for urgent and comprehensive actions. Immediate food needs require food and nutrition assistance. Investments in agriculture must be increased to boost the supply of food. Policies need adjustments to improve food security in the short, medium and long terms. And social protection systems should be strengthened. Table 3.3 highlights some good practices for responses; Chapters 9 and 10 provide a fuller discussion of the various policy interventions (see also United Nations, 2008a).

Table 3.3 – Good practices for responding to high food prices

	Intended consequence	Issues to watch
Policies that mitigate the impact of high food prices		
Reduce taxes and tariffs on food	Lower food prices	• Lower fiscal revenues • Might disrupt production and trade incentives
Targeted food subsidies	Lower food prices for targeted vulnerable groups	• Fiscal burden • Careful targeting is essential, but difficult • Might disrupt production and trade incentives
Release food reserves	Increased availability and lower prices	• Creating and maintaining reserves might be costly • Might disrupt production and trade incentives
Emergency food assistance		
Emergency food assistance: vouchers, cash or food, e.g. through work programmes and school feeding	Improved access to food	• Targeting • Needs market assessment • Requires implementation capacity
Nutrition interventions	Better access to nutritious food	• Requires implementation capacity
Investments in agriculture		
Improve access to inputs	Increased production	• Potential fiscal burden • Needs careful planning, coordination and implementation
Provide public goods, e.g. infrastructure, institutions, market information	Improved market functioning	• Needs careful planning, coordination and implementation
Strengthened social protection systems		
Enhance domestic capacity to design, implement and finance social protection systems	Improved food security	• Needs careful planning, coordination and implementation

The extent to which households are affected by high food prices depends partly on their livelihood strategies. These in turn depend on the type of production systems and income-generating activities that households rely on. The following chapter deals with the different strategies households use, and the role of markets in these.

Intermezzo 3.1: The "Dismal Science" all over again – a comparison with the 1970s

"Don't look for this global pressure on our food prices to ease off."

Changing Times, March 1974

"The era of cheap food is over."

The Economist, 19 April 2008

Is the current food crisis unprecedented? It is difficult to compare events across time, but the crisis that occurred in the first half of the 1970s seems similar to the current one.

At that time, the world experienced very rapid increases in the prices of nearly all food commodities. This spike in prices was triggered by drought in several countries, including the Soviet Union. High prices were accompanied by record low stocks – just as they are now – contributing to very high volatility. The world was also facing large increases in oil prices, a depreciating US dollar exchange rate, and export restrictions imposed by major exporters.

During the 1970s, analysts talked about a structural shift in the food markets caused by high population growth in developing countries and increasing incomes. Concerns about population growth and demand outpacing supply go back centuries.

Thomas Malthus wrote in 1798 "that population, when unchecked, increased in a geometrical ratio (1, 2, 4, 8, 16, 32, etc.), and subsistence for man (food) in an arithmetical ratio (1, 2, 3, 4, 5, 6, etc.)." As a result, he gave economics a reputation of being a "dismal science". Despite additional agricultural land in the "new world", expansion of international trade in grains in the nineteenth century, and rapid productivity growth with slowing population growth in the second half of the twentieth century, Malthus has continued to appeal, including in the Club of Rome's *Limits to Growth* report, published in 1972 (Meadows et al., 1972). Increasing population and limited resources, such as land and water, continue to feature strongly in the food crisis debate.

However, the price peaks in the 1970s – and those in the mid-1990s – only temporarily interrupted a long-term decline, and prices reached historic lows in the late 1990s. Despite the similarities, there are also several differences between the 1970s food crisis and the current one.

First, the percentage price change for rice and wheat was larger in the 1970s. Real prices are still lower now than in the 1970s (see the figure below).

Real prices of maize, rice and wheat (adjusted with US inflation rate)

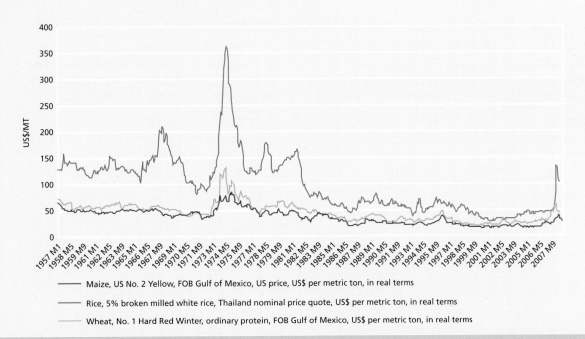

——— Maize, US No. 2 Yellow, FOB Gulf of Mexico, US price, US$ per metric ton, in real terms

——— Rice, 5% broken milled white rice, Thailand nominal price quote, US$ per metric ton, in real terms

——— Wheat, No. 1 Hard Red Winter, ordinary protein, FOB Gulf of Mexico, US$ per metric ton, in real terms

Source: WFP, based on IMF data

What is different? What is the same?

	Features of both crises	Features of the current crisis
Magnitude		• Smaller percentage change and lower prices in real terms
	• Broad-based, affecting nearly all food commodities	
		• Longer-lasting high prices
	• High volatility	• Higher volatility
Supply	• Weather-related supply shocks	• Climate change is "unequivocal"
		• Falling productivity growth
	• High oil prices, through input prices	• High oil prices are demand- not supply-driven, and linked to the food market through output prices because of biofuels
Demand	• Higher demand because of higher incomes	• Higher demand in developing rather than developed countries
	• Population growth	• Population growth rate declining
	• Low stocks	
	• Export restrictions	
	• Depreciating dollar	
	• Speculation	• Institutional investors

Second, the 1970s crisis was shorter. For real prices of maize, rice and wheat, the period from trough to peak was about two years, and that from trough to peak and back to trough, four to five years. In the 2000s, the trough to peak period was about two and a half years for real prices of maize and rice, and three years for wheat, based on the peaks in the first half of 2008.

Third, volatility was lower in the 1970s. The standard deviation for maize, rice and wheat has been 30–60 percent higher in the 2000s than in the 1970s.

Fourth, rising incomes pushed up demand for meat and feedstocks in both crises. Rising incomes in the 1970s were primarily in developed countries, while higher incomes in developing countries play an important role in the current crisis.

Fifth, for a long time, oil prices have influenced food prices through the use of inputs that are heavily influenced by energy prices, such as fertilizer, mechanization and transportation. This influenced both the 1970s and the current crises. The oil crisis in the mid-1970s was temporary and supply-driven by an embargo. The current oil price is fuelled by higher demand, which is more structural, and the emergence of biofuels creates an additional link between food and energy markets (Schmidhuber, 2006).

Sixth, in the 1970s experts were concluding that "climate itself is changing" (*Time*, 1974). Now, climate change is "unequivocal" and contributes to more extreme weather events, such as droughts and floods (Bates et al., 2008).

Seventh, trader speculation is often blamed for high food prices – and it was in both the current and the previous crises. Recently, however, far more speculative capital seems to be going into commodities than in any previous episode (Intermezzo 3.2).

Eighth, yields were increasing rapidly in the 1970s, fuelled by the green revolution, but productivity growth is currently declining.

Intermezzo 3.2: Did speculation push up food prices and create a bubble?

When a phenomenon such as high food prices is difficult to explain and affects many people negatively, "speculators" are often blamed. They were blamed in 1958 when onion prices soared, in the first half of the 1970s and again in 2008. Is there any ground for this?

Hedging and speculation: two sides of the same coin

What the media and politicians label as speculation is a critical market function. Economists define speculation as buying and selling to make profits from price changes. This is in contrast to buying and selling for use, to generate income as an investment, or to add value through transformation or transportation. Speculation in commodities involves buying and selling futures contracts – pieces of paper. Without it, traders would have to buy, sell – and store – the actual commodities.

A futures contract guarantees the price its holder will pay or receive for a good at a certain delivery date. This is very useful for farmers in reducing risk, particularly when there is a time lag between spending on inputs, such as seeds and fertilizer, and receiving revenues from harvested crops sales.

When a farmer decides what to grow, s/he would like to know, or even lock in, the price s/he will receive for the crop. A farmer can do this by hedging in the futures market. The farmer sells a futures contract that commits her/him to deliver, say, 1 MT of wheat six months from now at a certain price. If the actual price in the market is higher at the delivery date, the farmer will lose on the futures contract, but gain by selling the crop at a higher price than expected. If the actual price in the market is lower at the delivery date, the farmer will gain on the futures contract, but lose by selling the crop at a lower price.

For every seller, there is a buyer. What the farmer sells, a speculator buys. A futures contract transfers the price risk from the farmer to the speculator. The commodities underlying futures contracts are seldom delivered. On large futures markets, such as in Chicago or London, there is very active trade in futures contracts, which traders buy and sell before they expire. Most traders offset their contracts before they expire, with each party to the original contract selling/buying an opposite futures contract.

Because the contracts are not related to actual deliveries, the number of futures contracts is unlimited. In a way, futures contracts are bets on the future price of a commodity. The volume of underlying commodities exceeds the volume actually harvested (OECD, 2008).

There are thus two kinds of participants in futures markets. The *hedgers* are the farmers, commercial traders and processors who want to hedge against the price risks they face, and who are heavily involved in actual deliveries of commodities. The *speculators* are the non-commercial traders who seek profits through speculation and are often not involved in delivering commodities. Hedgers and speculators are two sides of the same coin.

Speculation and prices

Do prices quoted in futures contracts have an effect on spot prices? For actual deliveries, the futures price should be equal to the spot price plus the storage and insurance costs of holding the commodities until the contract expires. As that date approaches, the spot and futures prices should converge. Arbitrageurs make sure that this happens. If, for example, the futures price is considered too high, arbitrageurs will sell a futures contract, buy the commodity, store it and deliver it when the contract expires, making a profit by doing so (OECD, 2008).

One anomaly of the commodities markets is that spot and futures prices do not always converge at the time of delivery, for example in the maize, wheat and soybean markets (OECD, 2008). Another anomaly is that the difference between spot and futures prices seems to be widening. These anomalies reduce the usefulness of the futures market in transferring risk, and are difficult to explain. A lack of convergence could be caused by storage problems, but some argue that large amounts of new money from institutional investors are distorting the markets. Further research is needed, but the coincidence of these anomalies with the influx of new money has raised suspicions.

A speculative bubble?

The amount of money that institutional investors put into commodities has increased rapidly in recent years. The number of futures contracts doubled or tripled between the end of 2004 and 2006 (see the figures on page 47). In early 2008, so-called index funds, used by institutional investors to track a representative index of commodities, were holding US$120 billion of agricultural futures contracts, according to one estimate (Young, 2008).

Push and pull factors seem to be at work. Low returns on stocks and bonds, low interest rates and financial turmoil in developed country housing markets have pushed money into commodities. Investors have been attracted because, historically, returns on commodities have compared well with and been negatively correlated to returns on stocks and bonds, providing good portfolio diversification and risk reduction (Garton and Rouwenhorst, 2004).

Some economists believe that speculation can be excessive or destabilizing, giving rise to a speculative bubble. The fundamental characteristics of bubbles are usually the same, and include rising prices, leading to profit opportunities and attracting more investments. More investment pushes up prices, creating positive feedback, and a bubble. The critical characteristic of a bubble is that it cannot be supported by fundamental economic factors, and generates a psychological element, often described as a mania, hysteria or irrationality (Kindleberger, 2000; Shiller, 2000).

A mania can easily become a panic, transforming the bubble into a crash. There are also positive feedback loops. When prices and profits decline, the value of collateral declines as well. Loans become more difficult to obtain, and people withdraw money, exacerbating the price decline. A famous example of this boom–bust scenario is the tulip mania in the Netherlands in the 1630s. Another is the housing bubble, whose bursting in the US triggered the current global financial crisis.

It is difficult to distinguish a bubble from fundamental economic factors. As explained in this chapter, a number of structural demand and supply factors can explain the worldwide rise in food prices of recent years. Many of these factors have been changing rather gradually, however, making it difficult for them to explain a jump in rice prices (of Thai, 5 percent broken) from less than US$400/MT in January 2008 to about US$1,000/MT in May 2008, or an increase in wheat prices (of US hard red winter) from about US$200/MT in May 2007 to more than US$500/MT in February 2008, followed by a fall to about US$250/MT in May 2008.

It is particularly difficult to distinguish a bubble from fundamental factors before it bursts. Uncertainty about the future creates plenty of space for psychology. An important feature of futures markets is that market participants do not know the true value of the contracts or assets they are trading. As a result, they act on average opinion. Traders act according to what everybody else believes. If everybody believes that a particular asset a trader owns is overvalued, s/he will be wise to sell, irrespective of whether s/he agrees or not. This kind of mechanism can easily create herd behaviour – and bubbles and crashes.

New information – true or false, positive or negative – can lead to reactions and overreactions in commodity markets. One expert suggests a link between the emergence of speculative bubbles and the advent of newspapers in the 1600s (Shiller, 2000). He draws attention to information cascades, when one story, perhaps at first judged minor, leads to others. Through these cascades, average opinion changes and bubbles can emerge. Media coverage of the biofuel expansion and rising food prices seems to follow this pattern: a Google search for "biofuel food price" got 3,070,000 hits on 25 July 2008, 85 percent of them dating from the previous year. It is too early to draw conclusions, however, and scholars will have to determine the precise unfolding of events and the factors that contribute to it.

Is there evidence that a speculative bubble has been building? Some facts imply there is. First, large amounts of new money from institutional investors have moved into commodity markets (see the figures on page 47). Second, the share of non-commercial traders has increased in many of these markets (Sanders, Irwin and Merrin, 2008). Third, index traders expect prices to increase for 90–98 percent of the contracts they hold ("long positions"), compared with 20–65 percent of commercial traders who think that prices will decline ("short positions") (Sanders, Irwin and Merrin, 2008), even though the percentage of contracts outstanding ("open interests") attributable to index traders has been relatively stable (Sanders, Irwin and Merrin, 2008). Fourth, there is some evidence that the ratio of volume to open interests influenced futures prices for rice and wheat, and that the ratio of non-commercial positions to short positions influenced futures prices for maize and soybeans (von Braun, Robles and Torero, 2008).

However, other facts imply the opposite. First, commodity prices have also increased for commodities not traded on futures market, such as edible beans and durum wheat, or not commonly included in index funds, such as rice. Second, some

Wheat prices and open positions on Chicago Board of Trade

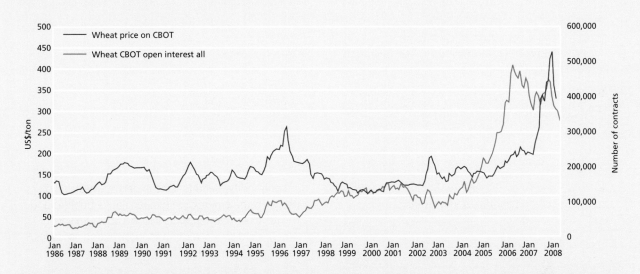

Maize prices and open positions on Chicago Board of Trade

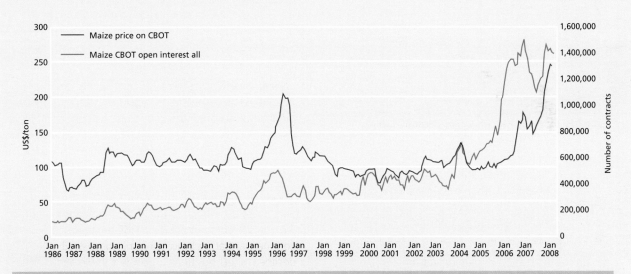

argue that if speculation is increasing, inventories should also increase, but – as far as they are known – inventories are declining (IMF, 2008c). However, others suspect increased holding of stocks, particularly by households, traders and processors, because of the large rewards of increasing prices (Young, 2008; World Bank, 2009). Third, speculation in proportion to hedging did not seem to have increased by much from 1995 to 2008 and was not extraordinarily high, at approximately 14 percent more than what is needed to meet hedging needs in 2006–2008, compared with

12 percent for the period before 2005 (Sanders, Irwin and Merrin, 2008). Fourth, using three different methods, IMF (2008c) found little evidence that futures have driven up prices.

Speculation has also drawn the attention of policy-makers. Futures trading has been suspended in some countries, and several are considering policy measures, such as reducing the quantity that can be traded by one entity, imposing delivery requirements and increasing margins (down payments on futures contracts). The effects of these measures on price levels and volatility are not clear (Sanders and Irwin, 2008). Financial markets need regulation and supervision, but striking a balance between effectiveness and efficiency is difficult. Improving reporting and transparency, including on over-the-counter trade, would also help, by enhancing knowledge about the futures market, enabling new research and determining more precisely the role of speculation.

In conclusion, the evidence regarding speculators pushing up food commodity prices is mixed. These markets have been very volatile, the amounts have been huge, and recent anomalies have been difficult to explain. Money flowing in from institutional investors may be pushing prices up, or down, and even if speculators do play a role, this does not imply that fundamentals are not important. Speculation is more likely to be riding the bandwagon than pulling the train.

Intermezzo 3.3: The cost-of-food-basket approach

When food prices started to increase significantly in 2007, WFP looked at how many people were affected and to what extent. This information is needed to determine whether, where and how much assistance would be required.

In 2007, WFP developed a method for estimating the proportion of households that become vulnerable as a result of food price increases. The tool starts by calculating the cost of a food basket in a baseline period, and estimates the proportion of households that can no longer afford this food basket when food prices rise.

The comprehensive food security and vulnerability analysis that WFP conducts in many countries classifies households into food consumption groups – poor, borderline, acceptable and good – based on a diet diversity and frequency score: the food consumption score.

The underlying rationale of the tool is that households might not be able to afford their previous food basket and are at risk of dropping from one food consumption group to a lower one. This happens if higher food prices push their current real food expenditure above the baseline figures.

The tool assumes the following:

- Dietary diversity is a proxy for the quality of the diet and is highly correlated to adequate caloric and protein intake, quality of protein consumption and household income (Hoddinott and Yohannes, 2002).

- Expenditures are a proxy for income.

- The food basket of the good food consumption group is nutritionally balanced. The quantities of food consumed are derived from the food frequency and diet diversity in a way that they provide the quantities of necessary nutrients. The quantities and calories consumed by other food consumption groups are extrapolated from the food consumption score of the good food consumption group. For example, it is assumed that if the good food consumption group consumes rice six days a week, at 300g/person/day, and the poor food consumption group consumes it three days a week, the poor group consumes half as much rice as the good group.

The following data are required:

- baseline food consumption: food basket composition, frequency of each basket item, quantity consumed of each food commodity (in grams), equivalent energy intake (from food composition tables), percentage of households in each food consumption group, and percentage of food derived from own production, which is deducted from the food expenditures;

- the food expenditure quintile for each food consumption group in the baseline period, and the percentage of households in each category; the food expenditure quintiles are used as cut-offs;

- prices of the food commodities in the food basket; and

- inflation rate to calculate real prices.

First, the cost of the food basket is calculated for the baseline period by multiplying quantities by prices. The cost is then recalculated for the current period, using real price increases. If the new real cost of the basket is above the baseline cut-off food expenditure, the percentage of households in the corresponding expenditure quintile is considered affected by the price increase. The affected percentage of households that falls out of its baseline wealth group (quintile) is said to have become vulnerable.

This method was applied to data from the 2005 comprehensive food security and vulnerability analysis in Mauritania. As shown in the table on the next page, application of the cost-of-food-basket approach suggests that based on prices prevalent in Mauritania in December 2007, 6.8 percent of the rural population, or about 143,000 individuals, would not be able to afford the same food basket as in 2005.

The cost-of-food-basket approach has advantages and disadvantages. The following are some of its advantages:

- It uses existing data on food consumption and prices.

- It provides a dynamic picture of households moving from one expenditure level to another.

- It accounts for own production.

- It estimates the number of vulnerable people.

Mauritania: Estimate of total rural population affected by food price increases using the cost-of-food-basket approach

	Assaba	Adrar	Brakna	Gorgol	Guidi-makha	Hodh El Charghi	Hodh El Ghardi	Inchiri	Tagant	Trarza	Total
Poor food basket	0	0	0	2,042	488	0	0	0	938	0	3,469
Borderline food basket	16,462	202	425	10,741	19,828	0	0	0	2,317	2,969	52,945
Fairly good food basket	1,404	0	5,887	2,737	2,557	833	141	0	125	6,075	19,760
Good food basket	265	184	20,227	2,042	7,945	319	64	0	110	35,332	66,487
Total population affected (1)	18,131	386	26,539	17,562	30,818	1,153	205	0	3,491	44,375	142,660
Total population of region (2)	281,614	77,646	279,138	291,093	213,512	300,338	234,255	11,223	85,973	308,637	2,083,428
Total percentage (%) (1) (2)	6.4	0.5	9.5	6.0	14.4	0.4	0.1	0.0	4.1	14.4	6.8

Source: WFP

- It could be a monitoring tool using only food prices and food frequency and diversity data. It can also account for substitution effects, which is important when relative food price changes lead households to substitute more expensive food items with cheaper ones. This frequently used coping strategy affects the cost of the food basket. Monitoring food frequency and diversity would provide direct information on the extent of household food substitution, which is usually difficult to obtain.

The following are limitations to the approach:

- Creation of the database is demanding in terms of data and resource requirements.

- The assumption that the good food basket is nutritious has yet to be supported by evidence.

- It only accounts for shifts among food consumption groups and does not estimate increasing vulnerability within each group.

- It only addresses risks, not the actual impacts of price changes, which requires a broader perspective including income patterns and coping strategies. Combining the tool with monitoring of food frequency, diversity and prices would give some indication of impacts, but information on incomes and coping would still be required to distinguish price impacts from the other causes of changes in food consumption.

Following a different approach, WFP regularly calculates changes in the costs of food baskets in 36 countries (WFP, 2008b), based on a weighted average of price changes, using the caloric contributions of particular food basket commodities as weights. Households with diverse calorie sources are likely to be less affected by price rises than households with a single source, unless significant price increases affect all the commodities in the food basket. The method could be used for early warning. Results should be interpreted with caution, however, as they do not capture long-term and indirect impacts and the coping capacities of different households. For instance, substitution and income effects due to price changes are disregarded. The table opposite illustrates the method used in selected countries. In combination with indicators for incomes and nutritional status, this approach can be useful for monitoring the impact of the global financial crisis.

Region	Country	Main staple food	Caloric contribution (%)	Current quarter over same quarter of last five years (% change)	Contribution to the cost of the food basket	
					Individual commodity	Joint
A	B	C	D	E	F=D*E	G
West Africa	Côte d'Ivoire	Rice	22	31	7	
		Yams	13	21	3	9
		Maize	11	13	1	
		Cassava	10	−21	−2	
	Niger	Millet	48	21	10	
		Sorghum	12	23	3	17
		Imported rice	8	39	3	
		Maize	2	57	1	
	Senegal	Imported rice	32	99	32	
		Millet	10	27	3	
		Sorghum	4	6	0	
		Maize	4	37	1	
Eastern Africa	Ethiopia	Maize	21	234	49	
		Wheat	18	145	26	
		Sorghum	10	199	20	
	Madagascar	Domestic rice	49	14	7	7
	Malawi	Maize	53	206	109	
	Swaziland	Maize	25	14	3	
		Wheat	12	51	6	10
		Rice	5	14	1	
	Zambia	Maize	56	54	30	
Asia	Afghanistan	Wheat	58	172	100	
		Rice	22	35	8	
	Cambodia	Rice	69	135	93	
	Philippines	Rice	44	32	14	14
Latin America and the Caribbean	El Salvador	Maize	31	27	8	
		Sorghum	6	29	2	16
		Bean	5	44	2	
		Rice	4	91	4	
	Haiti	Import rice	21	123	26	
		Wheat flour	15	55	8	
		Domestic maize	11	92	10	

■ Low price impact on the cost of the food basket (<5%)
■ Moderate price impact on the cost of the food basket (5–10%)
■ High price impact on the cost of the food basket (10–20%)
■ Very high price impact on the cost of the food basket (>20%)

Source: WFP, based on WFP (2008b)

Part II Analysis

In pursuit of food security, households employ their assets in livelihood strategies to gain income, which enables them to buy food. Markets play a role in nearly every step between assets and food utilization, but the hungry poor are very disadvantaged in terms of benefiting from markets.

Part II introduces the framework used to analyse food security and markets, and analyses key aspects of the relation between hunger and markets. **Chapter 4** presents the framework that links a household's assets, livelihood activities and food security, highlighting the roles of various markets in these links. **Chapter 5** reviews the limited access that the hungry poor have to input and output markets. It also discusses recent moves towards concentration and consolidation in the production and distribution of food, and the implications for food security. **Chapter 6** explores the determinants of aggregate food availability – production, stocks, trade and food aid. It argues that availability of staples does not mean that households have access to nutritious food. **Chapter 7** describes how markets can increase or reduce the risks for the hungry poor. **Chapter 8** explores the impact of emergencies on food availability and access and on market performance.

"Food insecurity at household level arises from several causes, and is most devastating when more than one occurs together."

Jeremy Swift and Kate Hamilton, 2001

Households, livelihoods and food security

For most households, the pursuit of food security is the most important goal, and livelihood strategies are geared towards obtaining food or income to buy food (Stites et al., 2005). Households apply diverse livelihood strategies depending on the production systems, assets and income-generating activities they have access to. For example, WFP identified 11 different livelihood profiles in Uganda: marginal livelihoods, remittance dependents, pastoralists, agrobrewers, agrolabourers, agriculturists, agrotraders, fishers/hunters/gatherers, agro-artisans, agropastoralists and wage-labour agriculturists. Each group was identified according to its income and food sources (WFP, 2005b). In Uganda, most agriculturists are temporarily food-secure, using 60 percent of their food production for self-consumption and the rest for sale. Nevertheless, if they are unable to diversify their income sources they remain vulnerable to sudden shocks (Chapter 7). Households with marginal livelihoods are worse off. They tend to have very varied income activities, but lack access to land and productive resources, so gain insufficient income. This group spends more resources than others on food purchase – 60 percent in the Ugandan sample (WFP, 2005b).

A household also tends to have several income-earning members, and differing dynamics among its members. Modern development economics (Haddad, Hoddinott and Alderman, 1997) revokes the outdated hypothesis that a household is an undifferentiated unit – "an individual by another name" (Folbre, 1986).

Household food security is often related to gender-based labour divisions. Domestic and child-rearing tasks are generally ascribed to women and girls, which may restrict other activities, such as education, income generation or organizational work. Cropping patterns

Households

The term "household" generally refers to individuals living and eating together. "Household" and "family" are often treated as synonymous, especially in Western societies where the nuclear family has become the most common household structure. When analysing household food security, it is important to consider power and subordination, as household members may not always exhibit altruism. Households also have various compositions: nuclear families of parents with children; single-parent nuclear families of one parent with children; and extended families of a nuclear family plus other individuals, such as grandparents or other nuclear families. Household units vary from area to area; for example, where HIV and AIDS prevalence is high, there may be a significant number of child-headed households. In 2003, there were approximately 143 million orphans in sub-Saharan Africa (UNAIDS/UNICEF/USAID, 2004). In many cases, a few able-bodied adults take care of many orphans, putting significant stress on families that may also have to care for ailing victims of the disease. Increasing numbers of households in HIV/AIDS-affected areas are headed by women, children or the elderly, who often care for orphaned grandchildren. Similar situations may emerge in conflict and post-conflict areas, such as Rwanda, where the 1994 genocide resulted in 35 percent of the population being single or double orphans (WFP, 2006c).

tend to be gendered, although there are variations across societies. In households that produce cash crops and food, it is common for men to prepare the soil, cultivate basic grains, care for larger animals such as horses and cattle, and operate machinery; women care for poultry, garden plots and crops dedicated exclusively to sustaining the family. Men usually represent the household in decision forums, to authorities and in negotiations with outsiders. When cash crops require inputs purchased from the market – such as fertilizer, seeds and pesticides – it is common for men to decide what to acquire (Carr, 2008).

An important aspect of household food security is who dominates resource flows. Generally, men exercise greater control over such flows than women. The term "secondary poverty" describes the situation where unequal power relations mean that men do not spend all the household income to benefit the family (Chant, 1997).

Many development efforts promote gender equality by focusing on women, who often constitute the poorest of the poor. It is also often argued that directing resources to women maximizes household well-being, because women's control over incomes and assets generally leads to higher expenditures on food, education and health care. Such efforts start by examining the different livelihoods within a community. Who produces for subsistence? Who produces for markets? Who engages in non-farm employment? And who controls resources (Carr, 2008)?

One argument for women's empowerment and increased participation in markets and decision-making is that incomes and nutrition standards would increase if women had better access to assets. Many rural communities have highly gendered land tenure systems in which it is difficult for a woman to own land and negotiate without the aid of a man. This subordinate position affects women's access to other assets, such as credit, information about markets and transportation possibilities. However, land rights for women may increase their work burdens – with possible negative consequences on food utilization – without changing their status or decision-making authority (Rao, 2005).

Household food security depends on a range of issues, and must be studied and established within the specific socio-economic and ecological setting of household members. All food security assessments should be centred on livelihood analysis to clarify the needs of specific households and individuals. Identifying the different livelihoods and genders of community members makes it possible to establish how important markets are for each household member's food security and well-being.

The household is an important unit of analysis. Households apply various livelihood strategies to gain food security. Intra-household behaviour has a direct impact on access to food and nutrition and on nutrition status.

Markets in the food security framework

The framework depicted in Figure 4.1 shows how households employ assets in livelihood activities to gain access to food, which depends partly on food availability. It also depicts the points where markets play a role. Food availability for households depends not only on production and stocks, but also on whether markets make food available in a particular region, through flows from other domestic regions or imports from international or regional markets (Chapter 6). Adequate food availability at the aggregate level is necessary, but insufficient to achieve adequate food access for households (Bonnard, 2001). Food may be available in some parts of the country, but not to households in other parts, because of market failures or the prohibitive costs of moving food. Lack of communication and infrastructure creates high transaction costs and may undermine food availability. Other factors such as trade policies – tariffs, taxes and subsidies – competition and traders' behaviour influence market functioning and the movement of food commodities.

Many of the factors that influence livelihood strategies and market functioning are linked to the economic, institutional, political and physical context (Figure 4.1). The context is also a major source of shocks, such as natural and human-induced disasters, ranging from earthquakes, epidemics and civil strife to high food prices (Chapters 7 and 8).

Household (HH) assets are defined broadly to include natural, physical, human, financial and social capital (DFID, 2000; Davis et al., 2007). A household's assets consist of the resources it owns or has usufructuary rights over, legally or conventionally (Sen, 1981). By using these assets, a household can acquire food either directly through production, or indirectly through exchange and transfer (Figure 4.1). The richer and more liquid the asset base, the better the access to food, provided that food is available, markets are functioning and households are able to participate in them.

- **Financial assets:** cash, savings or liquid assets, such as jewellery.
- **Human assets:** skills, knowledge and health.
- **Natural assets:** natural resources, such as trees, land, clean air and water.
- **Physical assets:** agricultural tools, infrastructure – roads, sanitation, water and energy supply systems – shelter, transportation equipment, household goods and utensils.
- **Social assets:** trust, norms and values, which shape human interaction.

Figure 4.1 shows financial markets separately. Access to finance plays an important role in livelihood strategies (Chapters 5 and 7). For example, credit facilitates the purchase of production inputs and helps households cope with shocks, but needs to be repaid, hence the double arrow.

Physical inaccessibility is often a major constraint to market access (Chapter 5), as in Nepal, for example, because of its mountainous nature (WFP, 2008c). Market access can also be made difficult by violent conflict and insecurity. In rural Angola, markets suffered during the years of unrelenting warfare; only 13 percent of sampled villages had a market, and the average distance to the closest market was 30 km (WFP, 2005e). Market access in the Sudan is hindered by insecurity and isolation; households in northern Sudan are more likely to purchase roots/tubers and meats in markets, at 70 and 95 percent, respectively, than those in southern Sudan, at 24 and 66 percent, respectively. The discrepancy is partly explained by limited household access to markets (WFP, 2007e).

Markets contribute to food availability and food access at the national, regional and local levels.

Figure 4.1 – Framework for food security analysis

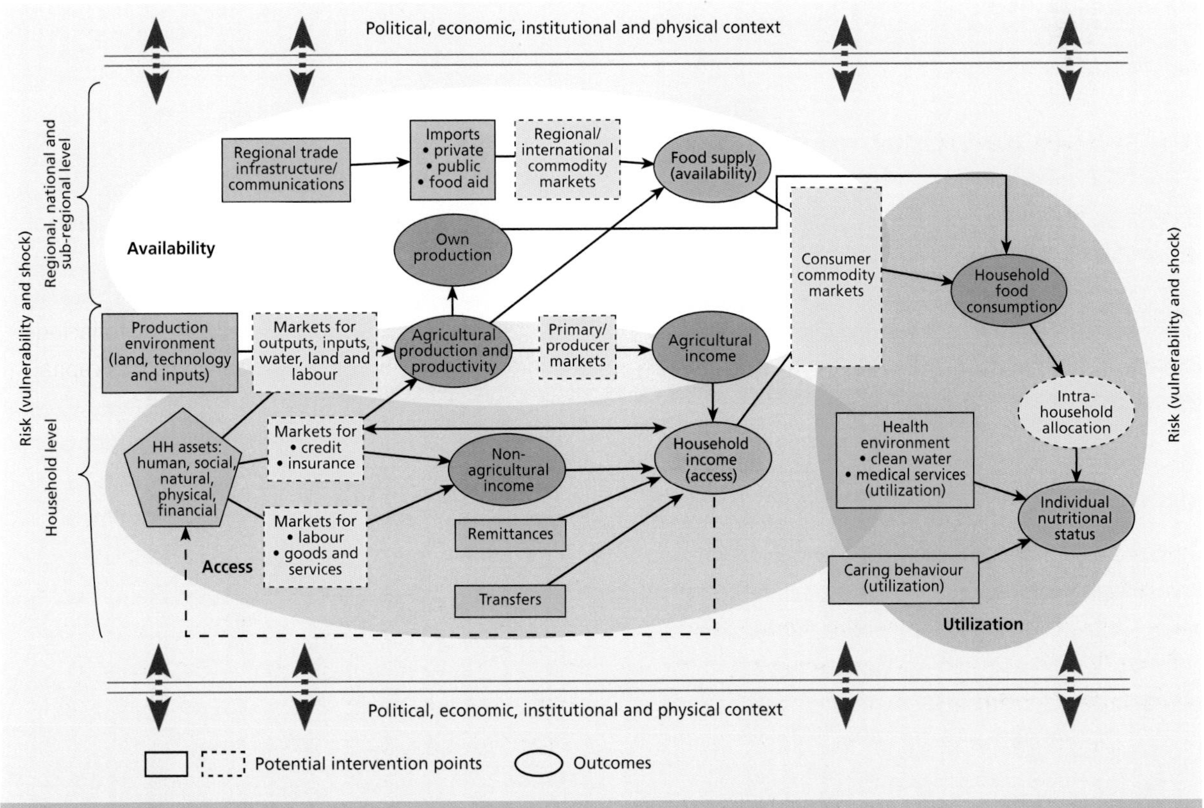

Source: WFP/Michigan State University

Figure 4.2 – Rural households' income sources by income-generating activity

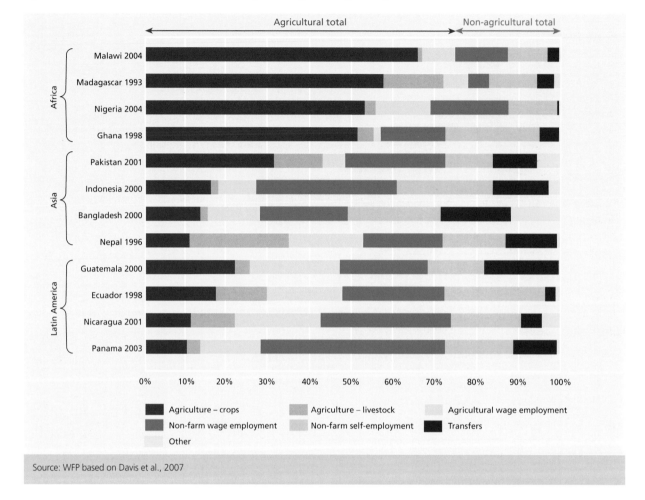

Source: WFP based on Davis et al., 2007

Household participation in markets

Food consumption is directly determined by income. Households use income to acquire food in markets, except for where households produce food commodities (Figure 4.1). Cereals are the most ubiquitous food market, and often the most important source of calories.

Income

Household incomes originate from various livelihoods. Rural income sources can be agricultural, including crop, livestock and agricultural wage activities, or non-agricultural – non-agricultural wage activities, non-agricultural self-employment, transfers and other income (Davis et al., 2007).

In Africa, the largest share of rural income comes from agricultural activities, especially crops (Figure 4.2).

Agricultural income represents an average of 50 percent of total income for the 12 countries shown in Figure 4.2: ranging from 69 percent in Africa to about 40 percent in Asia and Latin America. Non-farm wage employment is the largest income-generating activity in Asia and Latin America.

Agricultural income depends mainly on: (1) agricultural production, which is directly linked to a household's capacity to produce; and (2) prices of agricultural products, which are not under household control. Agricultural production is a function of cultivated land and inputs, such as water, labour, seeds, pesticides and soil fertility. (Input markets are discussed in Chapter 5.)

Cash crops are usually sold in markets to get income. Cereals are used for household consumption and the surplus sold on markets, but many producers are net consumers of the food commodities they produce and do not have sufficient production to sell on markets.

By 2020, more than half the population of Africa and Asia and three-quarters of Latin America's will live in urban areas. Such areas are heterogeneous, especially regarding income and nutrition aspects.

Rural households choose to leave their original settings for many reasons, ranging from push factors, such as poverty, to pull factors, such as better access to food, markets and social services. Unfortunately, although food availability is better in urban centres, food access may be worse for the urban poor.

Urban economies are often tied to rural ones, such as in the outskirts of Maputo, Mozambique, where more than half of employment is in agriculture. A large share of the labour force in urban areas are sellers, transporters or wholesalers of agricultural products. The richest urban poor may own and rent out land in rural areas. These urban–rural connections should be taken into account when designing assistance programmes and policies.

People in urban areas have to buy most food in markets. Street foods are a major source of consumption in India, accounting for 40 percent of the food budget (Dubey, 2003). Prices and incomes determine access to food. When incomes, own production or storage capacity are low, sensitivity to price changes increases. In 2002, Ghanaian households in Accra bought 90 percent of their food consumption from markets, depending heavily on unskilled labour for their incomes (IFPRI, 2002a). Urban poor households try to increase their incomes or improve their food access by growing vegetables and raising animals wherever they find space to do so. Such urban agriculture can be significant (IFPRI, 2002b). For the hungry poor, prices are on average 30 percent higher in urban than in rural areas (Ravallion, Chen and Sangraula, 2007). This could be because of higher transportation costs, richer segments of the population driving up prices, higher shares of processing and packaging, and higher real estate rents.

The urban poor generally have low and irregular incomes. They are sensitive to variations in sectors such as construction, and their jobs are often vulnerable to seasonality. They are often more affected by market shocks and price and wage volatility than the poor in rural areas, but they also have a wider range of income opportunities, allowing diversification and adaptation to changing circumstances.

Urban households might have easier access to social services, such as health care, education and food assistance programmes. Informal safety nets are still important in many rural areas, but are less relevant in cities, particularly for people who have arrived recently. Some coping strategies, such as eating wild food, may be easier in rural areas.

For smallholders, agricultural income is highly sensitive to prices, because their production level is limited by the small area of land cultivated, inputs and weather conditions.

Pastoralist households can earn income through sales of livestock products – milk, butter, meat, hides, etc. – or animals. Livestock plays a dual role as both a livelihood and savings "on the hoof", especially in areas with no functioning financial market. Livestock is commonly known as a liquid asset because it is easily transformed into income. Sale of livestock is a common coping strategy during food shortages.

Transfers in cash or kind are particularly important in complementing incomes from production. Transfers are remittances, public transfers through social protection and safety net schemes and humanitarian aid – food or cash. Formal and informal remittances are an outcome of migration, which can be international, rural–urban, regional and/or seasonal.

They refer to migrants' in-cash or in-kind transfers to resident households, usually of the same family, in their areas of origin. Poor households often consider migration a viable livelihood strategy (Black et al., 2007), and inflows of remittances usually respond strongly to signs of distress, playing an important role as a buffer to households' living standards.

Non-agricultural activities are becoming increasingly important for rural populations, and generally depend on assets available at the household level (Figure 4.1). A household's ability to get income is related to its capacity to match assets to market requirements. Training and education are key to increasing household incomes from labour markets (Chapter 5).

Cereal markets

Households' participation in cereal markets is largely determined by access to land and the geographical factors that determine agricultural potential and access

Figure 4.3 – Households' sales and purchases of maize in Malawi

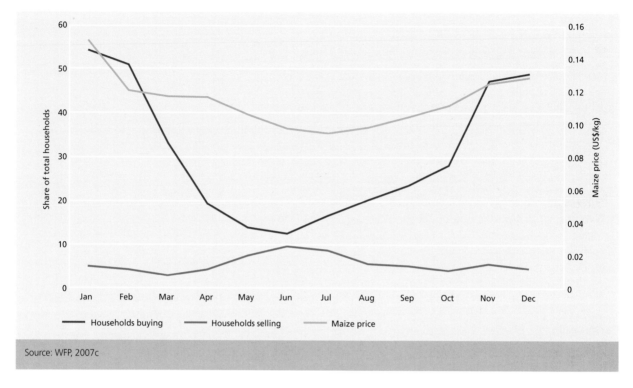

Source: WFP, 2007c

to markets. Wealthier households and those cultivating in zones of higher potential are more likely to sell to the market than other households are. Research in Zambia found strong positive correlations among households' net maize sales, incomes, landholdings, values of other crop production, off-farm incomes, values of farm assets and education levels. When households were ranked from low- to high-income, those in the top income tercile were generally sellers of maize, and those in the bottom buyers of maize (Zulu, Jayne and Beaver, 2007).

Rural households' dependence on markets typically increases in the lean season. In Malawi, for example, more households buy cereals on markets during the lean season (November to February), and the percentage of households selling cereals peaks during the harvest season (May to July) (Figure 4.3).

Farmers sell food crops even when their harvest will not be sufficient for their own consumption needs throughout the year. They sell low at harvest time and buy high during the lean season. This paradox – known as sell-low, buy-high behaviour – is common in sub-Saharan Africa; need for cash, shortage of storage capacity and lack of financial services all contribute. Households that need cash and have no access to credit have no option other than selling their only liquid asset – the cereals harvested (Barrett, 2005a).

A smallholder farmer in Iandratday, a village in a prime agricultural region of Madagascar

"A farmer sold paddy at FMG [Malagasy francs] 1,000/kg to a local collector who transports the paddy by ox cart to an urban wholesaler. Predictably, the farmer runs out of rice three months before his next harvest, and he ends up buying rice back from the same local collector using proceeds from his groundnut and maize crops.

Accounting for milling losses, he is paying FMG1,850/kg paddy-equivalent. Effectively then, he buys back in January the rice he sold the preceding June at a premium of 85 percent. This is the implicit interest rate (including storage losses) on seasonal quasi-credit obtained through the rice market. The core lesson is that when the financial market fails, people find alternative means of engaging in inter-temporal arbitrage, even when it proves very costly."

Source: Barrett, 2005a

Table 4.1 – Participation in staple food grain markets in selected countries

Country	Crop	Year	% sellers
Afghanistan	Wheat	2007	16*
Ethiopia (rural households only)	Barley	1999–2000	10*
	Maize		23*
	Sorghum		11*
	Teff		20*
	Wheat		12*
Kenya	Maize	1997	29**
		1998	34**
		1999	39**
Madagascar	Rice	2001	25**
Mali (smallholders only)	Millet	2005–2006	5**
	Sorghum		4**
	Maize		4**
	Rice		8**
Mozambique	Maize	2005	16*
Tanzania	Food	2003	33**
Zambia	Maize	2000	26**
Zimbabwe	Grains	1996	27*

Notes: * = gross, ** = net.
Sources: WFP, 2005h; FEWS NET, 2007; Barrett, 2008

The sell-low, buy-high phenomenon contributes to making many farmers net buyers of cereals. Even farmers who sell 60 percent of their harvest in weight are likely to be net buyers in value, because the 60 percent they sell is worth less than the 40 percent they buy. Although the different methodological approaches they use complicate comparisons among studies carried out in Africa, it appears that a relatively small share of rural households, or crop producers, sell staple food grains (Table 4.1). The fact that more households are net buyers than net sellers implies that the majority of small-scale farm households may be adversely affected by higher cereal prices and price and trade policies designed to raise market prices of cereals, and that these policies might work against the hungry poor (Zulu, Jayne and Beaver, 2007).

In a study of smallholders in western Kenya, nearly 30 percent of the sample were net maize sellers during the harvest period, but 62 percent became net maize buyers a few months later (Stephens and Barrett, 2008). Another study found that about 10 percent of a sample of western Kenyan maize farmers both bought and sold maize, with 83 percent of their maize sales occurring within two months of harvest, and purchases generally being made far later in the season, when households' stored maize had run out (Renkow, Hallstrom and Karanja, 2004).

WFP household surveys in selected countries suggest that most households consider markets a main source of food, especially during the lean season (Table 4.2). Households with borderline food consumption tend to devote larger proportions of their expenditures to food than those in other food consumption groups. This group is therefore likely to be more vulnerable to price shocks, and risks falling into the poor food consumption group when a price hike occurs.

The majority of smallholder and low-income farmers are net buyers of food, often selling at low prices during harvest time and buying back at high prices during the lean season. Most net sellers are wealthier households.

Understanding how households relate to markets is fundamental for understanding the nature and prevalence of hunger. Households earn income and

Table 4.2 – Households' dependence on markets for food in selected countries

Country	WFP household (HH) surveys		
	Food expenditure (% of total expenditure)	Market as a major source of food (% of HH)	Source and survey season
Mali	National average: 52% Borderline HH: 55%	70%	WFP (2005d) HH survey, post-harvest (2,074 HH)
Nepal	National average: 50% Borderline HH: —	—	WFP (2006d) HH survey, post-harvest (1,676 HH)
Niger	National average: 63% Borderline HH: 72%	> 70% (excluding milk)	WFP (2005f) HH survey, post-harvest (1,800 HH)
Lao PDR	National average: 65% Borderline HH: 68%	< 40% (cereals and pulses)	WFP (2007b) HH survey, post-harvest (3,926 HH)
Liberia	National average: 66% Borderline HH: 72%	> 80% (cereals)	WFP (2006b) HH survey, post-harvest (5,409 HH)
Rwanda	National average: 55% Borderline HH: 75%	65%	WFP (2006c) HH survey, post-harvest (2,786 HH)
Tanzania	National average: 63% Borderline HH: 64%	66%	WFP (2006d) HH survey, post-harvest (2,772 HH)
Timor Leste	National average: 55% Borderline HH: —	59%	WFP (2006d) HH survey, post-harvest (1,700 HH)

buy food through markets, which are therefore an important component of household livelihood strategies. The following chapter deals with access to markets, which is particularly difficult for the hungry poor.

"Interventions aimed at facilitating smallholder organization, at reducing costs of inter-market commerce, and, perhaps, especially, at improving poorer households' access to improved technologies and productive assets are central to stimulating smallholder market participation and escape from semi-subsistence poverty traps."

Chris B. Barrett, 2008

Market participation depends on access, and access depends partly on transaction costs, including those for transportation, storage, information gathering, trade finance and contract enforcement. High transaction costs put serious constraints on poor people, particularly by limiting production and production choices. Improving access to markets and reducing transaction costs through the development of infrastructure and institutions should be crucial elements of any food security strategy.

Physical access to markets depends not only on distances, but also the quality of roads and transportation. In developing countries, 16 percent of the rural population, 439 million people, take at least five hours to reach a town of at least 5,000 people (World Bank, 2007b). Access to markets is most difficult in Africa. In East and Southern Africa, only 25 percent of rural people can reach a town with more than 50,000 citizens within two hours (Omamo et al., 2006).

High transaction costs make it difficult for poor households to participate in markets. In Madagascar, for example, the cost of entering agricultural markets amounts to 124 to 153 percent of a subsistence producer's annual production (Cadot, Dutoit and Olarreaga, 2006). Large transaction costs also reduce sale prices, raise food prices and increase price volatility (Jayne, 1994; Minten and Kyle, 1999).

A lack of assets, knowledge and skills also results in high barriers to market entry, which are caused or enhanced by an absence of financial markets and by higher quality and safety standards.

Limited participation in markets contributes to lower incomes and increased hunger. For the hungry poor, the costs of market participation are often too high, so they remain poor and hungry. There are signs that this aspect of the poverty trap has been exacerbated in recent years by higher fuel costs and lack of investments in infrastructure. Transportation and transaction costs are a major factor in explaining comparative development. Infrastructure is a particularly important determinant of growth differences among countries (Easterly and Levine, 1997).

Market constraints in input and output markets

Input markets

Producers need access to input markets to obtain technology, buy seeds and fertilizers, buy, sell or rent land, and benefit from financial and insurance services. These input markets are often absent or work poorly – especially in remote rural areas.

Credit and financial markets

The hungry poor often lack access to financial services, such as credit, savings and insurance. There are several reasons for this. Formal financial institutions may be completely absent from rural areas of developing countries. They prefer urban areas because of higher population densities, higher incomes, the more diversified deposit base, lower costs of transport and communication, and lower risks (United Nations, 1999). Only 4 percent of the population in sub-Saharan Africa has a bank account.

It is costly for credit institutions to screen the creditworthiness of potential clients and monitor debtors' repayments, particularly for small and numerous loans in thinly populated areas. Financial markets are also plagued by market failures (Brinkman, 1999). Unlike normal markets, where an exchange takes place on the spot, in financial markets, money is offered in return for a promise to repay in the future. Banks want loans to be repaid, so they do not lend to everyone and they do not always lend all that the borrower wants. Because of asymmetric information, the bank does not know as much as the borrower about his/her capacity to repay.

Even where credit institutions exist, many households are unable to borrow, particularly the poorest ones, which generally lack land or other assets to serve as collateral. Poor rural households are therefore often excluded from official financial and insurance markets, resulting in low levels of investment and agricultural input use (Zeller et al., 1997).

Farming households face specific credit problems owing to risks inherent to agriculture and fluctuating output prices. Credit providers are generally not eager to lend for high-risk purposes. In addition, it is difficult to monitor crop management efforts. Many rural farm households therefore have to rely on informal credit sources – credit associations, moneylenders, etc. – often at high interest rates. A lack of labour markets for women explains why poor rural women are prepared to borrow small amounts of money at very high interest rates (Emran, Morshed and Stiglitz, 2007).

Lack of access to credit and insurance often prevents farmers from adopting high-quality, high-nutritional and more diversified crops, such as certain coffee varieties, vegetables and fruits that require capital inputs. Exclusion from credit and insurance also reduces households' possibilities for coping with income shocks and smoothing consumption throughout the year.

The microfinance revolution has generated a stream of innovative financial services for poor people, which address widespread market failures and reduce transaction costs. Access to financial services has increased in many countries, but hundreds of millions of people still lack such access.

Markets for inputs and technology

Farmers in developing countries are often trapped in labour-intensive agricultural activities with low productivity and low income-generating capacity. Access to input markets and agricultural technology generally benefits rural incomes (Joshi, Gulatti and Cummings, 2007), but advantages may be hampered by inadequate adaptation of technologies, fertilizers,

improved seeds and pesticides to local conditions. Private research and development initiatives usually concentrate on technological innovations adapted to wealthier regions and crops that are traded in international markets. In industrialized countries, much effort focuses on developing herbicide- and pesticide-tolerant varieties of existing crops. Developing countries would probably benefit more from seed varieties that can withstand weather-related shocks and improve the nutritional value of food (Srinivasan, 2003).

Even when appropriate inputs and technologies have been developed, rural households in developing countries cannot always afford them. Input and technology markets tend to be thin or missing in developing countries, especially in remote areas. One underlying cause of the lack of access to inputs may be the structural adjustment programmes introduced in the 1980s and 1990s. Before these reforms, state agencies frequently provided agricultural inputs and extension services at subsidized prices, but post-reform public sector withdrawal has not been replaced by private sector entry.

In low-income countries, the development of private markets is obstructed by low aggregate demand for agricultural inputs, combined with high transaction costs. To improve their access to inputs and financial and technology markets, farmers sometimes pool their interests by establishing producers' associations (Gabre-Madhin and Haggblade, 2004).

Land markets

As a result of history, power, policies and distorted markets, land is generally unequally distributed. Land productivity is often higher on small than on large farms (Chapter 6). Production would therefore increase if land were cultivated as smaller farms. Land markets, including for rentals, could play a role, but they are often absent or function very poorly.

Insecure tenure and lack of registration inhibit the development of a land market in many developing countries. Lack of clear titles to land, and heavy bureaucracy – fees, stamps, etc. – result in high transaction costs for transferring land rights, which hinder land use by the most productive cultivators.

Another market imperfection is that land may serve as collateral for credit, or be held for political power or prestige. This pushes its sales price above its productive value. Renting or buying land therefore becomes more expensive for efficient farmers, while inefficient farmers are discouraged from selling.

High food prices have driven up land prices in various locations. Higher land prices could stimulate land markets, but could also make land less accessible to poorer farmers. Smallholder rights need to be protected, especially where land titles and registration are poorly developed.

Absent or imperfect land sale and rental markets tend to impede the efficient use of scarce land resources and limit productivity. In the long run, food production may be jeopardized, while farming households' food and income-generating capacity is restricted.

Information

To take advantage of profitable market opportunities, farmers need to be well informed about market prices and conditions. Lack of information makes farmers vulnerable to exploitation by traders and buyers, decreases their bargaining power in the marketing chain, and affects their production incentives and income. Education generally improves farmers' knowledge of markets and their bargaining position.

Market information systems need to include timely and accessible information on prices, volumes, standards, trade policies, trader information and transport. Such systems are expensive and challenging to create, maintain and develop. The costs of training, capacity building, supervising enumerators, comprehensive market coverage and dissemination are significant.

With the assistance of Michigan State University, Mozambique created an Agricultural Market Information System (SIMA) in 1991. It currently covers 24 markets in ten provinces, providing weekly data on prices, flows and transport costs, which are disseminated through radio, print, e-mail, fax and a website.

The Internet and mobile telephones have created new possibilities for disseminating market information. Mobile telephone subscriptions are increasing rapidly in the developing world, especially in regions where fixed lines are rare. In Africa, 22 percent of the population had a mobile phone at the end of 2006 (United Nations, 2008b). Recent initiatives include farmers in Ghana and Kenya receiving market information through text messages on their mobile phones (World Bank, 2007c). The full potential is far from being realized, but benefits are already emerging, such as lower transaction costs, lower price volatility and disparities across markets, and higher prices for farmers (see Aker, 2008).

Sufficient and stable food availability depends on producers' access to input markets that allow increased productivity and production.

Labour markets

Rural labour markets are important for food security. Labour is often a poor household's only asset. Most rural labour markets are highly imperfect – either completely absent or very thin. Many rural people are forced to migrate to urban areas to seek employment.

Labour markets are highly segmented between skilled and non-skilled labour, with a wide wage gap between the two. Wealthier households compete better for non-farm jobs. Lack of efficient labour market information makes the search for jobs expensive in terms of money and time. Wealthier people may invest more time and money in signalling their skills and experience, and may even resort to bribes to obtain jobs. Poor people's access to labour markets is often hampered by a lack of education or skills, and their productivity may be impaired by poor nutrition.

The poor have the least access to wage employment, but often depend on their labour as a source of income and access to food. Development of rural labour markets could greatly improve the food security situation, particularly of landless and near landless households.

Warehouse receipt systems and commodity exchanges

What are they?

Warehouse receipt (WR) systems and commodity exchanges (CEs) are two information systems that can remedy market weaknesses. WRs and CEs reinforce each other, but use different avenues to realize gains.

WRs are "documents issued by warehouse operators as evidence that specified commodities of stated quantity and quality have been deposited at particular locations by named depositors" (Coulter and Onumah, 2002). A WR entitles its holder to withdraw the deposited commodity from the warehouse. WRs are transferable, and can be sold for cash, traded directly for other goods and services or used as collateral for loans. Users include farmers, producers' organizations, traders and processors. Many warehouses are operated by private agribusinesses that buy, dry, clean and store grain, but such services may also be provided by the public sector.

A CE can be thought of as a platform for organized trade among numerous buyers and sellers. CEs can also facilitate transactions among commodity producers and finance providers. The defining feature of a CE is that trade is coordinated by an independent entity, using a comprehensive framework of rules and criteria to govern the channels for trade within the CE. All agents who use the CE are required to pay fees for these services.

What is the rationale for implementing WR systems and CEs?

WR systems can empower farmers and help them end the vicious cycle of selling low and buying high. The provision of storage services allows farmers to defer the sale of their produce, smoothing seasonal price fluctuations to the benefit of both producers and consumers. Spatial price differentials and transaction costs can be reduced when the warehouse is closer than the market and farmers have to visit several markets to sell all of their crop. Lower transaction costs and enhanced access to markets reduces farmers' dependence on traders who, where there is no WR system, often exploit farmers through high trade margins.

WR systems contribute to efficient CEs. In Chicago, US, prior to the creation of the Chicago Board of Trade and the regular use of warehouses, farmers who did not find immediate buyers for their grain usually had to dump it because of high transportation costs (UNCTAD, 2005). By enforcing quality standards, a WR system can improve discipline and enhance transparency within the market, eliminating unnecessary friction in the CE and lowering transaction costs.

CEs reinforce commodity markets and improve market information. A CE market concentrates commodity trade in one place, so information asymmetry is reduced as changes in supply and demand are more rapidly and accurately reflected in price levels. All CE participants – and others – have constant access to a neutral reference price. Market centralization reduces transaction costs by making it easier to find buyers and sellers. However, no matter how efficient a CE is, it cannot override underlying market fundamentals. For instance, if there is a surplus of maize in the local market and prices are depressed, the existence of an exchange will improve prices only indirectly by encouraging more regional trade.

What are the preconditions for developing a successful CE?

CEs provide many positive externalities, which may justify public support, but ultimately an effective CE must succeed as a business. A CE's profitability depends largely on trust in its system, which is earned, for example, through well-designed contracts that accurately specify the quality and quantities of produce. The link between trade on the exchange platform and physical trade must be robust – the use of warehouses that are associated with but not owned by the exchange is crucial in this. Regulation must be tough and consistent, at storage locations and the CE itself. Trust is not the only issue, however, and it is notoriously difficult to implement a successful CE. During the last decade, more than 20 CEs have failed in Africa alone.

The South African Futures Exchange (SAFEX) is the most successful African CE (Agyeman-Duah, 2006). Infrastructure throughout most of Africa is particularly poor, storage facilities are typically lacking and production techniques are often outdated. South Africa's agriculture sector is highly mechanized and includes an effective warehouse system (Coulter, 1998). Most South African warehouses are linked directly to the national rail system, and port facilities allow grain to be shipped quickly and at low cost. The country's banking sector is relatively strong. The main challenge to the emergence of CEs in other African countries is the need for a solid institutional and legal framework and the enforcement of contracts.

A promising recent initiative is the new Ethiopia Commodity Exchange (ECX), which opened in April 2008. ECX combines a trading floor in Addis Abeba with six warehouses and a network of market information points in major market towns. Many aspects of ECX had to be created from scratch, including laws, regulations, a regulatory body, standards for commodities and a quality inspection service. The lessons from ECX will be important for other countries.

Local and regional agrofood markets

Markets help to increase farm incomes by enabling farmers to specialize in crops that yield high incomes. Markets can also help smooth consumption through exchanges between temporarily food-deficit households and food producers with sufficient surpluses. However, such welfare-enhancing channels are not always fully exploited, because of high transaction costs and imperfect financial markets, for example. These deficiencies are especially harmful to poor farmers, because risk adversity and transaction costs per unit of produce decrease with wealth, trapping farmers in value subsistence agriculture (Deaton, 1991; Fafchamps and Hill, 2005).

Products of the same agroclimatic region are exchanged in local agrofood markets, or serve the same market basins. Products of different agroclimatic regions are exchanged at regional and international markets. Food markets are commonly held once every seven days, but well-attended markets may be organized daily.

Increasing population density and the development of transport networks encourage trade among different agroclimatic regions and lower the cost of trade. When agricultural incomes remain essentially unchanged, or develop equally in the different regions, interactions among different local agrofood markets are constrained. In Rwanda, for example, falling transport costs may increase the opportunities for trading crops of high value and low bulk, such as eggplant, but trade of bulky low-value crops, such as sweet potato, may be constrained by congruent changes in local agricultural incomes (Swinnen et al., 2007).

Access to local and regional agrofood markets may be highly uneven, and agricultural income may become increasingly unequal across households and regions. Poor smallholders face a fourfold disadvantage: (1) they receive lower producer prices because lower output volumes increase unit transport costs; (2) their crop choice is likely to be motivated by safety-first considerations, because poor households are highly risk-averse, so their crops might not be well suited to the market; (3) the need for cash and the lack of storage facilities force poor households to sell at low prices during harvest season; and (4) in terms of time, the opportunity cost of reaching markets may be prohibitive for poor smallholders.

These constraints facing poor farmers are emphasized by a Rwandan widow: "I lost my husband. I don't have time to go to the market because I have to work on my land and take care of my children. When I need cash, I sell my harvest to my neighbours at a low price" (quoted in Swinnen et al., 2007). The need to acquire enough food every day may force smallholders to stop growing crops on their own land and provide off-farm labour in return for a daily wage.

Poor households are trapped in a vicious circle. Poverty limits their access to output markets, credit, insurance and agricultural inputs. Consequently, their income-generating opportunities are constrained.

International agrofood markets

Participation in international trade is generally believed to be correlated to economic growth (Dollar and Kraay, 2002). Some economists advocate participation in

Typology of smallholder markets in Rwanda

In Kibilizi, a small rural administrative sector in Rwanda, farmer households have access to ten markets and commercial centres (see the table below). Households frequently visit small commercial centres nearby to purchase household supplies, such as soap, matches, salt and sugar. Small daily markets are the main distribution points for locally grown food and staple crops. They are generally organized in the late afternoon so that casual labourers can exchange their daily wages for food.

More distant urban commercial centres and large regional markets are less frequented, despite the price advantages and larger ranges of products. Such markets attract long-distance professional merchants, dealing in high-value, low-bulk items, such as palm-oil from the Congo, beans, sorghum and maize flour from large markets in Kigali; regional traders carry bulky goods of medium value, such as bananas and Irish potatoes; and small local farmers sell their own production, which is usually bulky and of relatively low value, such as sweet potatoes and manioc. When regional crops fail, households also use two distant markets in another agroclimatic zone, which are large enough to attract both farmers and intermediary traders (Swinnen et al., 2007).

Markets visited by households in Kibilizi

Name	Type[a]	Average distance (minutes walking)	Frequency of households' visits
Gakoma	Small commercial centre	20	1–16 times/month
Kigeme	Small daily (17:00–18:30) local market and small commercial centre	30	1–20 times/month
Kibilizi	Daily local market (16:30–18:30)	30	1–16 times/month
Mushishito	Small commercial centre	40	1–4 times/month
Gikongoro	Large urban commercial centre, and large regional market twice a week	180	1–4 times/month
Gasarenda	Medium-sized urban commercial centre, and very large regional market twice a week	180	0–2 times/year
Miko	Commercial centre and periodic market	180	Only in case of crop failure in the region
Karama	Commercial centre and periodic market	180	Only in case of crop failure in the region
Ryarubondo	Large cattle market twice a week	240	0–1 time/year
Gatovu	Medium-sized commercial centre and large periodic regional market	240	0–1 time/year

Note: [a] Small commercial centres are small concentrations of shops and houses in a rural area, as distinct from concentrations in towns or cities
Source: Berlage et al., 2003

international trade and trade liberalization as major engines for growth and poverty reduction (Bhagwati and Srinivasan, 2002; Dollar and Kraay, 2004). Others are more sceptical (Rodríguez and Rodrik, 1999; Ravallion, 2006). The main areas of disagreement pertain to causality – does trade or trade liberalization cause growth, or vice versa? – and to complementarity: are other reforms or initial conditions required to make trade liberalization effective?

There has been little research into the relation between trade and food security. Whether or not imports contribute to food security depends mainly on whether food-insecure people are net consumers or net producers (Ravallion, 2006; see Chapter 4). For net consumers of food, such as urban households, food imports may enhance food availability, reduce prices and increase access. For net producers, however, the declining food prices caused by food imports have negative income effects. Subsidized food imports from

Figure 5.1 – Agricultural producer support in the OECD, 1986–2007

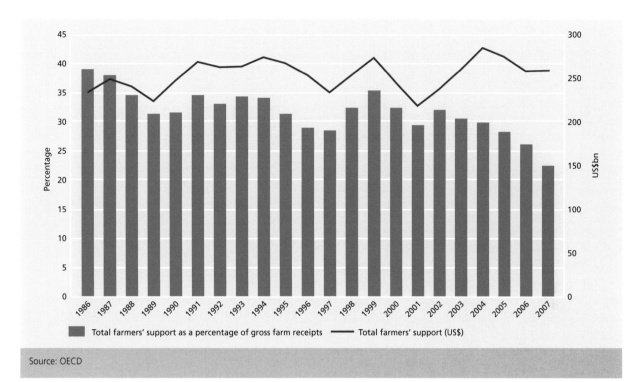

Total farmers' support as a percentage of gross farm receipts ▬▬ Total farmers' support (US$)

Source: OECD

developed countries that continue to protect their agricultural markets may distort food markets in developing countries, undermine incentives for local farmers and impede the development of domestic agrofood markets.

Agricultural protectionism in rich countries, mostly through subsidies and tariffs, makes it hard for developing countries to compete. In developed countries, the tariffs applied to agricultural goods imported from developing countries are nearly six times higher than those applied to non-agricultural goods (UNCTAD, 2008). In recent decades, barriers to trade have started to be lowered – albeit slowly – through reductions in quotas, subsidies and tariffs and preferential trade agreements for developing countries (Figure 5.1). The European Union's (EU's) Everything but Arms initiative, for example, provides duty-free and quota-free access for nearly all commodities from least developed countries (LDCs).

Agriculture is hotly debated within the Doha Round of multilateral trade negotiations, contributing to the collapse of the talks in July 2008. At the end of 2008, the prospects for concluding this round remained poor. A complete removal of developed countries'

protectionism of agriculture could generate an estimated US$40 billion a year of exports for developing countries (Watkins et al., 2003). The benefits are much smaller if protectionist measures are only partially removed, however, and this is a far more likely outcome of the Doha Round (Polaski, 2006). Few benefits are likely to go to poor households, owing to the constraints they face (Watkins et al., 2003).

Volatile world market prices for tropical exports, such as coffee, cocoa and tea, have affected developing countries' gains from international trade. This has been particularly detrimental for poor and risk-averse households, which often have major difficulties in coping with negative income shocks. Many export commodities are perennial crops, making it even more difficult for farmers to respond to changing world market prices.

The structure of world agrofood trade is changing substantially, with developing countries less dependent on traditional export commodities, such as coffee and cocoa. Many aspects of the shift towards non-traditional exports have been beneficial for developing countries (Aksoy and Beghin, 2005).

Agro-industrialization and food standards

The spread of supermarkets

Originally, supermarkets catered to the urban rich, but are now increasingly accessible to poor people (Chapter 2). For many of the hungry poor, however, supermarkets remain out of reach. Many food-insecure households use low-cost informal retail markets as the main outlet for food purchases. This is partly because supermarkets have much lower market shares for fresh fruits and vegetables than for processed, dry and packaged products, which poor households consume less of. There is also evidence that prices for fresh produce are higher in supermarkets, although prices of processed food tend to be lower (World Bank, 2007a).

Supermarkets' low prices for processed food high in fat, sugar and salt are cause for concern. In Guatemala, poor households' consumption of these items has increased, causing higher body mass index and posing a risk factor for obesity and non-communicable diseases (Asfaw, 2008).

Agro-industrialization

Private investment, resulting from privatization and liberalized investment and trade regimes, is inducing agro-industrialization, in which agro-industrial firms, agroprocessing and large-scale operations become increasingly important. Consolidation is most apparent at the retail level, but has occurred throughout the supply chain, from production to processing to distribution. Foreign investors have increased the access to international high-value food markets and introduced technology, management capacity and access to information, for example on food safety issues.

Expanding agro-industrialization is reflected in increased exports of final and processed agricultural products from developing countries. Products such as fruits, vegetables, fish and seafood are often processed and handled locally before being exported as final products. There is also evidence of expanding primary production destined for export markets, especially supermarkets. Examples from Côte d'Ivoire, Kenya and Zimbabwe suggest that horticulture exports are increasingly grown on large-scale agro-industrial farms (Dolan and Humphrey, 2000; Minot and Ngigi, 2003). The share of agro-industrial farms in Kenyan fruit and vegetable exports grew from 20 percent in the 1990s to 40 percent in 2003 (IFAD, 2003a).

Implications of agro-industrialization for market access

Agro-industrialization is providing improved technologies and increasing the supply capacity for high-value food in developing countries, in response to importers' demand for large and consistent supplies. The agro-industrialization sector is also becoming an important source of value-adding to agricultural production.

Increased agro-industrialization and concentration in food production, processing and distribution may also have negative impacts, however. Poor farmers are less likely to benefit from trends towards centralized procurement and the use of quasi-formal and formal contracts, for example because of illiteracy and lack of information. The ongoing consolidation is changing power relations in agrofood markets, with small suppliers being confronted by large multinational food companies.

Increasing food standards

Food standards are already numerous in developed countries, and are now emerging in developing ones. Increased incomes lead to a higher demand for food quality and safety, while technical and scientific knowledge is also contributing to improved food standards.

Food standards include a wide range of specifications, quality standards (technical specifications), marketing standards, sanitary and phytosanitary (SPS) measures and traceability requirements. Public standards are backed by private standards and national and international legislation. The growing importance of international food standardization is reflected in the sharp increase in new notifications of SPS measures to the World Trade Organization (WTO) (Figure 5.2).

The tightening of food standards in developed markets may diminish the export opportunities for developing countries (Unnevehr, 2000), but can also act as a

Figure 5.2 – Notifications of new SPS measures to WTO, 1995–2007

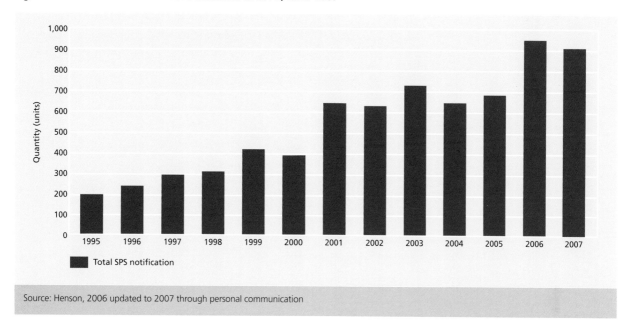

Source: Henson, 2006 updated to 2007 through personal communication

catalyst for upgrading and modernizing developing countries' food supply systems, thus improving market access and export growth (Jaffe and Henson, 2005; Henson, 2006). However, small and poor farmers do not have the financial capacity to invest in upgrading their production, and developing countries generally lack the institutional and infrastructure capacity for food quality and safety, which further hampers farmers' compliance with stringent standards in overseas markets (Reardon et al., 1999; Dolan and Humphrey, 2000; Farina and Reardon, 2000). Several empirical studies indicate that small farmers in developing countries do not have access to international markets because of increasing food standards (Key and Runsten, 1999; Kherallah, 2000; Gibbon, 2003; Reardon et al., 2003; Weatherspoon and Reardon, 2003).

Agricultural exports and small farmers

High-value international and domestic markets tend to exclude small and poor farmers. For example, the number of sub-Saharan small-scale vegetable farmers producing for the UK market fell from about 11,600 in 2002 to about 5,500 in 2006. This is attributed to the increased dominance of supermarket food retailers and food quality and safety requirements – 60 percent of all vegetable exports from sub-Saharan Africa to the UK were destined for supermarkets (Legge et al., 2006).

There has also been a sharp decrease in pineapple exports from small farmers in Ghana since the 1990s, when pineapple production became increasingly concentrated in large-scale industrial plantations, even though small farm production costs are estimated to be 22 percent lower. This is also the result of quality and safety demands in overseas markets and increased processing of produce (Takane, 2004; Danielou and Ravry, 2005).

A recent survey concluded that companies tend to favour larger farmers over small farmers in the same area. Where small farmers dominate the agrarian structure, companies tend to source their supplies from those with access to such assets as irrigation, farm equipment and paved roads (Reardon et al., forthcoming). These thresholds reinforce the hunger–poverty trap.

Increasing agro-industrialization and the emergence of supermarkets have created opportunities for developing countries, but low-income and small farmers are less able to take advantage of these trends as they lack the assets and capability to meet quality and safety standards and quantity and delivery requirements.

Vegetable exports, labour markets and poverty in Senegal

Exports of fruits and vegetables from Senegal have increased sharply over the past 15 years – from 2,700 metric tons (MT) in 1991 to 16,000 MT in 2005 – and play a central role in the country's export diversification strategy. Most exports are destined for EU markets and have to satisfy stringent quality and safety standards.

Food standards have induced consolidation and increased vertical coordination in vegetable export supply chains in Senegal. Most notable is the shift from smallholder contract-based farming to large-scale vertically integrated estate production on bought or rented land.

These developments have had major implications for small farmers and rural households. The proportion of local farm households with export agro-industry contracts is decreasing (see the figure below), but more local households are working in export agro-industry. These households obtain about one-third of their total income from agro-industry wages, and earn an average of 60 percent more than the average income in the area. Increasing vegetable exports have a major impact on rural poverty reduction, especially through creating agro-industrial employment. The incidence of poverty in the area is estimated at 14 percent lower than the national average.

Participation of local households in vegetable export chains, 1991–2005

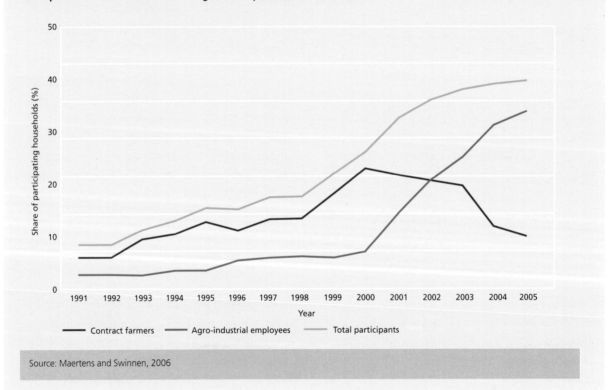

Source: Maertens and Swinnen, 2006

Institutional innovations

Vertical coordination can help farmers to overcome their capability and capital constraints and produce high-standard foodstuffs. Most vegetable exports from Madagascar to EU supermarkets are sourced from small land-poor farmers (see the box on page 73). A predominance of small farms in high-value supply chains has also been reported from South and Southeast Asia (Gulati et al., 2005).

Vertical coordination is a private institutional initiative to address market constraints. Innovations have been introduced to overcome financial constraints, difficulties in input markets and lack of technical and managerial capacity. Foreign investment may overcome financial constraints, and foreign investors often initiate institutional innovations. The need for high-quality, reliable and timely volumes for agroprocessors, supermarkets and traders has been a main driving factor for increasing vertical coordination.

The importance of vertical coordination and its implications for small farmers

Vertical coordination and contract farming are increasingly important in many developing countries, particularly for such commodities as sugar, cotton, coffee, cocoa, rubber, palm-oil, tea, horticultural products and tobacco (Swinnen and Maertens, 2007). In sub-Saharan Africa, vertical coordination has become an important source of rural financing (IFAD, 2003a). In Mozambique, an estimated 12 percent of the rural population is engaged in contract farming (Table 5.1).

Many sub-Saharan African governments are involved in vertical coordination schemes, through minority or majority shareholdings in privatized processing companies, financing and the provision of extension services. In general, however, the private sector takes the lead in supply-chain governance and vertical coordination (Humphrey, McCulloch and Ota, 2004; Maertens and Swinnen, 2006; Minten, Randrianarison and Swinnen, 2006).

Most studies of the welfare implications for poverty reduction and increased food security have reached positive conclusions. Emerging evidence shows that contract farming helps lower production and marketing costs and raise farm productivity and rural incomes (Birthal, Joshi and Gulati, 2005; Minot, 2007;

Table 5.1 – Contract farming in sub-Saharan Africa

Country	Commodity	Number of contracted smallholders
Kenya	Tea	406,000
	Sugar	200,000
	Horticulture	15,000–20,000
	Tobacco	>10,000
Zambia	Cotton	150,000
	Tobacco	570
	Horticulture	13,500
Mozambique	Cotton	270,000
	Tobacco	100,000

Source: IFAD, 2003a

Swinnen and Maertens, 2007). Through contract farming, farmers can improve their access to inputs, working capital and technical assistance, which are often provided as part of the contract. Vertical coordination also provides farmers with an assured market outlet, often with a guaranteed price, thus decreasing the risks. Contractor firms share the production risk through providing inputs and credit. Reduced production and marketing risks improve the stability of farmers' incomes and are a significant advantage for those operating in high-risk environments with no insurance markets.

Production of vegetables for EU supermarkets in Madagascar

In Madagascar, the production of vegetables for export to EU supermarkets has grown rapidly over the last 15 years, despite stringent public and private safety and quality requirements and the disadvantages of geography, bad local infrastructure, low rural education levels and high compliance and transaction costs.

The vast majority of high-value vegetable exports from Madagascar go through one company, which has contracts with five supermarket chains in Europe. This firm has to meet requirements regarding quality, ethical standards – no use of child labour, for example – employment practices and hygiene in the processing plant. The company buys vegetables from more than 9,000 small farmers, each with an average land area of 1ha, which is about the national average farm size. As part of the contract, the firm supplies seeds, fertilizer and pesticides on credit at the beginning of the growing season. It monitors farmers to ensure correct production management and prevent "side-selling".

Farmers benefit from contract production through improved access to inputs, credit, extension services and technology. Another benefit is the firm's teaching on better technologies and management practices, such as the use of compost. This has spill-over effects on other crops, and rice productivity is 64 percent higher on plots under contract. Smallholders participating in contract farming have higher welfare, greater income stability and shorter lean periods. Farmers' income from the contracts represents an average of 50 percent of total monetary household income.

Source: Minten, Randrianarison and Swinnen, 2006

Agro-industries generally find it more advantageous to work with a small number of large suppliers than a large number of small farmers; small farmers also generally require more assistance. On the other hand, using a large number of suppliers can lower the risk of supply failure, and production costs can be lower on small farms because family labour is used (Minot, 2007). Empirical observations show a mixed picture: in some schemes, small farms have a smaller share than large farms; in others, the reverse is true. Shifts from small to large farmers, or vice versa, have also occurred (Minot, 2007).

Contract farming has benefits, but it "cannot serve as a broad-based strategy for rural development because it only makes sense for certain commodities in certain markets" (Minot, 2007).

Increased industrialization, liberalization and vertical coordination in international agrofood markets create opportunities for producing and exporting higher-value crops. When small farmers have access to such markets, the benefits can be significant, but few small farmers have access. They lack access to essential inputs and finance, have few capabilities and are far from the nearest road.

The hungry poor have limited access to input, output and labour markets and financial services. To benefit from institutional innovations, growing export markets and agro-industrialization, the hungry poor have to overcome a wide range of obstacles that deny them full participation in markets. Otherwise, they are likely to endure continuing food insecurity. The following chapter deals with two aspects of food insecurity: availability and access.

Intermezzo 5.1: Purchase for progress – innovations to connect low-income farmers to markets

WFP's Purchase for Progress (P4P) initiative aims to boost the incomes of smallholder and low-income farmers through leveraging the procurement of food commodities in developing countries and creating sustainable market access. P4P shows how one innovation can address several of the structural constraints faced by smallholder farmers. P4P is likely to have important spill-over impacts on the surrounding communities, as well as direct positive outcomes for participating farmers.

P4P builds on WFP's extensive experience with local procurement. Globally, local procurement has increased over the last two decades (see the figure below). Between 2001 and 2007, WFP purchased about US$1.5 billion (2007 prices) of food commodities in Africa alone.

During its initial stage, P4P will concentrate on Burkina Faso, the Democratic Republic of the Congo, Ghana, Kenya, Liberia, Malawi, Mali, Mozambique, Rwanda, Sierra Leone, the Sudan, the United Republic of Tanzania, Uganda and Zambia in Africa; Afghanistan and Lao People's Democratic Republic in Asia; and El Salvador, Guatemala, Honduras and Nicaragua in Latin America.

Market failures, risks and lack of access to inputs, information, technologies and infrastructure create significant barriers to market entry for subsistence farmers in remote rural areas. As a result, "there is a need for specific policy attention to improving coordination of market activities to overcome 'low-level equilibrium traps'" (Poulton, Kydd and Dorward, 2006: 243), a process in which low investment leads to low production, low revenue and back to low investment.

By creating a platform of demand for food staples grown by small farmers, P4P aims to increase farmers' income and boost their incentives to invest in inputs and technologies that improve production. The strategy is multifaceted and uses several tools simultaneously. P4P can have a specific role in mitigating market failures caused by transaction costs, risk and lack of market information.

P4P can *reduce transaction costs.* Pilots for direct procurement from smallholder farmers' associations can eliminate potentially costly market intermediaries, allowing farmers to receive higher prices for their goods, at lower risk. Where infrastructure is weak and volumes traded are low,

Triangular and local purchases, 1990–2007

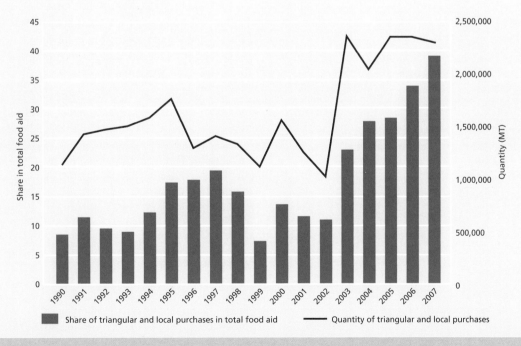

Source: WFP/INTERFAIS

75

P4P: two scenarios

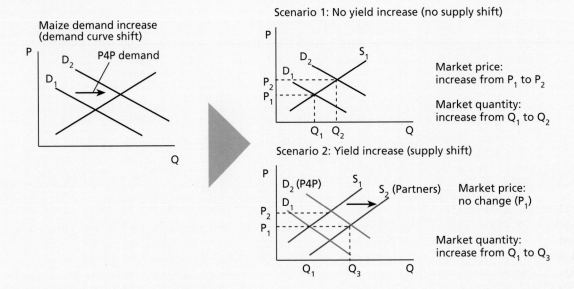

Maize demand increase (demand curve shift)

Scenario 1: No yield increase (no supply shift)

Market price: increase from P_1 to P_2

Market quantity: increase from Q_1 to Q_2

Scenario 2: Yield increase (supply shift)

Market price: no change (P_1)

Market quantity: increase from Q_1 to Q_3

a market outlet will be created through special provisions that facilitate procurement from smallholders, such as tendering for smaller amounts, arranging transportation from farms and setting up collection points close to producer areas. This will allow the aggregation of supply from thin markets.

P4P can *increase market information.* P4P will link small farmers to commodity exchanges, where they exist or are being developed, such as in Ethiopia and Uganda. These exchanges enhance market transparency by generating and disseminating information on supply and demand conditions and allocating set volumes of food purchases to the commodity exchange. WFP will also improve information flows to small farmers by disseminating market availability and price information through its network of sub-offices and during monitoring visits to remote areas.

P4P can *mitigate and reduce risk,* including through forward contracting and existing warehouse receipt systems, which WFP will leverage. The warehouse receipts obtained by farmers attest to the quantity and quality of grain stored, reducing the information asymmetry faced by smallholders, and enhancing access to credit. Warehouse receipts also smooth prices by facilitating sales throughout the year, reducing market-related risk and providing smallholders with greater bargaining power. These advantages can also be achieved through forward contracting, which WFP will use in its procurement systems with smallholder farmers and farmers' associations.

P4P should provide farmers with skills that enhance their participation in markets, including those with quality, quantity and timeliness requirements. WFP and partners will provide training. P4P will also procure processed commodities, especially where there is demand for fortified and blended foods.

WFP will work with partners to ensure that the increased demand for food commodities is matched by interventions that boost productivity. Without simultaneous yield increases, P4P runs the risk of pushing up prices (Scenario 1 in the figure above), but if WFP and partners help increase yields, prices will be affected less (Scenario 2 in the figure). Higher productivity will enhance the income impact on farmers and reduce the possibility of unintended negative consequences through higher food prices.

Farmers' incomes are expected to increase through multiplier impacts, beyond the direct benefit of higher prices at the farm gate. P4P will reduce risks and enhance incentives to engage in higher-value income-generating activities by providing greater market information and stability through forward contracts, leveraging warehouse receipt systems and developing commodity exchanges.

P4P is expected to have a significant direct impact on farmers' incomes through procurements that aim to constitute the first steps out of the hunger–poverty trap. In Uganda, for example, there is evidence that farmers' associations participating in WFP procurement activities have benefited directly in terms of revenue (see the figure on page 77).

WFP farmer groups: net revenues (2005)
(000s USh/ha)

Non-WFP farmer groups: net revenues (2005)
(000s USh/ha)

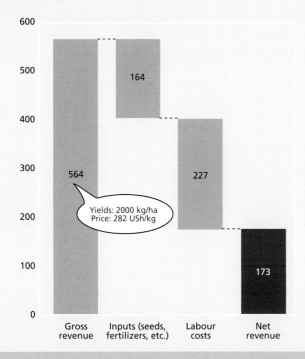

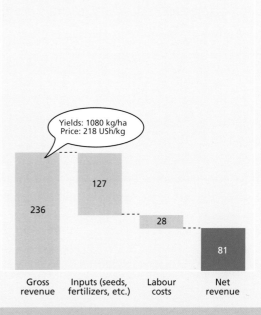

Note: US$1 = 1,781 Ugandan shillings (USh).
Source: Farmer Survey in Sserunkuuma & Associates Consult: *Local and Regional Food Procurement in Uganda – An Analytical Review,* Kampala, June 2005

"[T]he persistence of malnutrition as a global health concern despite the successes in increasing agricultural production belies any notion that malnutrition and undernutrition can be solved entirely from the supply side by increasing agricultural production."

World Bank, 2007a

Lack of food in the markets or on-farm can be a major cause of chronic and acute hunger. Food availability is secured in several ways, including domestic production, international trade, food aid, and the ability of food marketing chains to move food from the farm gate and from regional and international markets to local markets, where it can be bought by households for consumption.

Access to and availability of food of sufficient quality and quantity depend on the proper functioning of markets and on adequately formulated and managed government food policies. Policies concerned with aggregate food availability have focused on protein-energy rather than micronutrient availability (Underwood, 2000; Welch and Graham, 2000). Although there has been significant liberalization of food policies and markets (Chapter 2), there is no guarantee that markets will ensure food and nutrition security for all. This has become even more evident in the current food crisis, in which households' access to quality diets has been reduced by high food prices (von Braun, 2007; FAO, 2008c; Chapter 3).

Aggregate food availability – production, stocks, trade and food aid

Agricultural production, the availability of food in the markets, and households' own-production and vegetable gardens are essential for supplying both macro- and micronutrient needs. Agricultural production and productivity create income, jobs and economic growth, and reduce inequality (Haddad, 2000; Timmer, 2000). Such indirect effects have

consequences for food security because they increase household purchasing power (World Bank and IFPRI, 2005). Some 86 percent of rural populations depend on agriculture for their livelihood (World Bank, 2007c).

Despite a shift in focus towards food access during the past decade, food availability remains an important dimension of food and nutrition security.

National food production and productivity

The institutional and food policy environment in which farmers operate has direct influences on whether or not they will be able to produce sufficient amounts of nutritious food. As well as the hazards of weather variability and price volatility, farmers' agricultural activities are also determined by shifts in policies, which can change farmers' incentives (Timmer, Falcon and Pearson, 1983).

The green revolution

The most important feature of the Asian green revolution was probably increased productivity and food availability. Favourable initial conditions, such as equitable access to land and infrastructure, combined with the adoption of high-yielding varieties (HYVs) doubled yields in Asia between 1970 and 1995. In spite of a 60 percent increase in population, calorie availability per person rose by 30 percent (Hazell, 2003; Rockefeller Foundation, 2006). Progress in Asia is in sharp contrast to sub-Saharan Africa, where there has been little increase in kilocalorie availability (Figure 6.1).

The green revolution successfully overcame an era of acute food shortages and famines, such as those in China and India. It had a positive social impact by decreasing the prevalence of absolute poverty, which in India decreased from 50–65 percent in 1960–1965, to about 30 percent in 1993 (Hazell, 2003). There is contention regarding the impact on equity, however, and larger farmers may have benefited more than smaller ones (Freebairn, 1995).

Figure 6.1 – Daily per capita calorie availability, 1979–2003

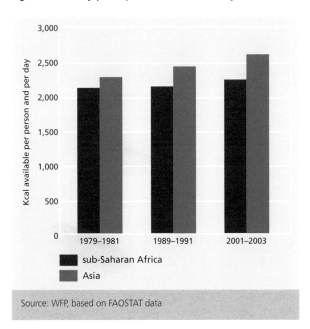

Source: WFP, based on FAOSTAT data

The green revolution had positive effects on the hungry poor in areas where it was implemented (Conway, 1997; Lipton, 2007). It increased productivity, including among poorer farmers. Small farmers usually face significant barriers to the adoption of new technologies, because of their limited access to irrigation water, fertilizers, HYV seeds and credit, and because technologies are rarely designed with poor farmers in mind (Lipton and Longhurst, 1989; Rao, 1989). However, small farmers did benefit, because of government actions prior to the introduction of green revolution technologies, including investments in irrigation and roads, provision of seeds and dissemination of market information (Rockefeller Foundation, 2006; Lipton 2007).

The green revolution also increased the availability of cheap food and the demand for on-farm labour (Meier, 1984; Hayami and Ruttan, 1985; Rao, 1989). As such, it was a pro-poor revolution, even if the issue of access was not resolved (Evenson and Gollin, 2003).

The green revolution did not ameliorate micronutrient deficiencies (Lipton, 2007). In countries such as Bangladesh, agricultural policies focused on increasing the land area dedicated to staple crops have led to reduced production of other types of food, such as fish, pulses, vegetables and fruits. Households' dietary diversity has declined, and micronutrient deficiencies persist, limiting human growth, development, health and productivity.

Given the declining investment in agriculture and agricultural technology over the past ten years, it is estimated that global production of grains will have to increase by nearly 50 percent in the next 30 years, to meet all the food needs of the world's population (World Bank, 2007c). Attaining adequate food availability requires complementarity and coordination among land, labour, technology, credit and insurance markets, and the establishment of a proper institutional legal and policy context (Poulton et al., 2006a). Efforts to launch a green revolution in Africa

Land distribution and productivity

Unequal land distribution often has myriad negative consequences. Equity of land ownership and use is often stressed in developing and transition economies, and land distribution can be politicized.

There is a well-documented inverse relationship between farm size and land productivity, which persists even when country-specific variables such as land quality and human capital are controlled for (Vollrath, 2007). The main factor is that smaller farms operate with family labour, using more labour, but requiring less supervision (Johnston and Kilby, 1975; Berry and Cline, 1979; Deininger, Zegarra and Lavadenz, 2003; Vollrath, 2007). When large farms are more productive than small ones, it is usually because policies favour large farms and market failures give them easier access to credit.

Land inequalities can compound income inequalities. Land can be used as collateral to generate investment capital for off-farm businesses (Reardon et al., 2000; Jayne et al., 2001). The strength of the correlation between large landholdings and off-farm incomes varies among countries, which has important ramifications for policy (Jayne et al., 2001).

There is growing evidence that land-use distribution enhances productivity when it is shaped by land sale and rental markets that are controlled and monitored, and accompanied by measures that ensure access to extension services, inputs and credit (Deininger, Zegarra and Lavadenz, 2003; Vranken and Swinnen, 2006; Deininger and Jin, 2008).

Figure 6.2 – Food consumption diversity in developing countries: kcal share by source

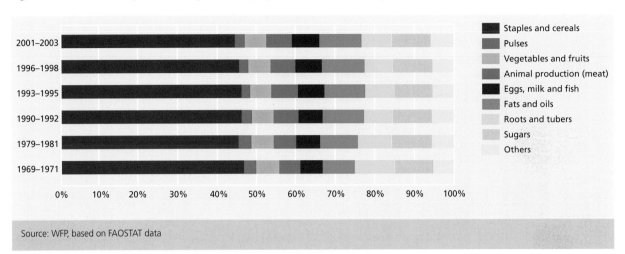

Source: WFP, based on FAOSTAT data

should focus on the conditions of smallholder farmers, who produce approximately 80 percent of the food in sub-Saharan Africa (Jayne et al., 2001), on the crops they grow, such as coarse grains, roots and tubers, and on efforts to increase access to nutritious foods.

Production decisions and dietary diversity

Several market factors have impacts on farmers' production decisions regarding amounts and varieties of crops. These factors include "appropriate and high-yielding agricultural technologies; local markets offering stable output prices that provide reasonable returns to investment in 'improved' technologies; seasonal finance for purchased inputs; reasonably secure and equitable access to land, with attractive returns for operators (whether tenants or landowners); and infrastructure to support input, output and financial markets" (Dorward et al., 2004).

Owing to the risks farmers perceive in both consumer and producer markets, many households produce their own food to insulate themselves from price fluctuations. Barriers to entry to higher-value and more nutritious agricultural production, or even surplus production of staple grains, have a definite impact on food availability and nutrition at the aggregate level. With limited access to finance, poor farmers are unable to opt for higher-value agricultural products, such as fruits, vegetables and legumes, which are particularly high in micronutrients (Kurosaki and Fafchamps, 2002). Dietary diversity and quality have evolved particularly slowly in the developing world, despite the progress in poverty indicators (Figure 6.2).

Household food production is very important in improving dietary diversity and nutrition. Production of fruits, vegetables, dairy foods, eggs, fish and meat can have significant impacts on micronutrient deficiencies (World Bank, 2007a; de Pee, Talukder and Bloem, 2008). Household production is not limited to rural areas. It can generate additional income through sales of surplus production, and save money that would have been spent on food.

Limited availability of and access to nutritious food remain a problem, particularly for smallholder farmers, even in countries where a green revolution has increased the availability of calories.

Food reserves and stocks

National governments, private traders, processors and farmers store food, smoothing over inter-annual and seasonal variations in food availability. Recently, the use of physical food stocks and strategic grain reserves has been steadily declining. Global stocks were in recent years at their lowest levels since 1981 (Figure 6.3). The relative decrease in the importance of strategic food reserves is a result of the costs and difficulties associated with maintaining physical food stocks, especially for governments and poor farmers, and of increasing reliance on trade to cover shortfalls.

Increased market liberalization and improved information and transport technology, infrastructure and ports have reduced bottlenecks in the movement

Figure 6.3 – Global cereal stocks and stock-to-utilization ratios

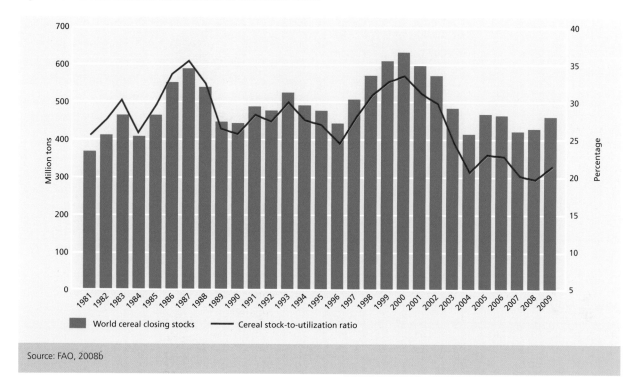

Source: FAO, 2008b

of food. There is therefore less need to keep physical stocks. Governments may avoid having to manage physical food stocks by increasing the cash reserves with which food can be bought on the international market (WFP and NEPAD, 2004; Byerlee, Jayne and Myers, 2006).

The management of food reserves is costly and requires an excellent market and production information system. The quality of food stocks needs to be sustained. When stocks are released, there is a risk of crowding out the private sector and creating disincentives for traders to import food. Large food reserves also have strong signalling effects on world and/or regional markets, which can have positive or negative influences on prices and trade volumes. To be cost-efficient and effective, food reserves must be consistent with national and international food and trade policies. Although stocks can help solve seasonal and inter-annual changes, they are less likely to be a solution to long-lasting price shocks. It is also difficult and costly to create reserves when prices are high and availability is limited, as happened in 2008.

Physical food stocks can play important national and regional roles in emergencies and in increasing price

stability. Government food reserve systems may also be valuable in situations where private traders could start speculating, as happened recently with rice stocks in the Philippines, where already high food prices were driven even higher, and during the Bangladesh famine of 1974 (Ravallion, 1987; Devereux, 2001).

Reserve systems can be particularly useful for countries facing chronic vulnerability to food crises, such as Ethiopia and those in the Sahel. A food reserve in a disaster-prone country can mitigate food emergencies and stabilize prices. Countries in Southern Africa are considering the creation of regional food reserves to avert food shortages similar to that of 2002 (WFP and NEPAD, 2004).

Indonesia's successful food reserve system assigns sufficient space to private trade and provides a good example of striking a balance (Poulton et al., 2006b). The Indonesian Logistic Bureau (BULOG) maintains food prices within a certain band around world prices, allowing private traders to continue trading, and facilitating the functioning of commodity exchange markets while avoiding excess volatility.

The issue of global reserves has recently re-emerged in response to high food prices, partly because the prevalence of export restrictions has made it more difficult to use trade to cover availability gaps. The International Food Policy Research Institute (IFPRI) has proposed a two-prong approach (von Braun and Torero, 2008). The first prong is a physical emergency grain reserve of 300,000 MT, managed by WFP, which would help address the procurement problems WFP faced in 2008. The second prong is a virtual reserve and intervention mechanism with a fund of US$12 billion to US$20 billion. This would be guided by a high-level technical commission, using information provided by a global intelligence unit, to maintain prices within a dynamic price band and to counter speculation.

Maintaining some form of storage can be important in mitigating shocks and maintaining a stable supply of food to markets at the national, regional, local and household levels. However, the costs of the reserves should be weighed against the benefits, and alternatives should be considered.

Trade

When local production is insufficient to meet demand, international and domestic trade may expand food availability. The driving forces behind international and domestic trade are similar, but international trade also depends on trade barriers, exchange rates and foreign exchange reserves, which are earned through exports or capital inflows.

Traders have an incentive to move food from surplus to deficit regions when price differences among regions exceed the costs of doing so (Chapter 2). Physical infrastructure and market information systems are important in minimizing transaction costs. Domestic trade depends on several factors, including the existence of a marketable surplus, transport costs and price differentials between surplus and deficit regions. Ultimately, marketing margins determine whether or not traders have an incentive to move food from one place to another (Baulch, 2001).

Certain regions of a country may be better integrated with neighbouring countries than with

Figure 6.4 – Rice imports and domestic and imported rice prices in Bangladesh, 1997–2008

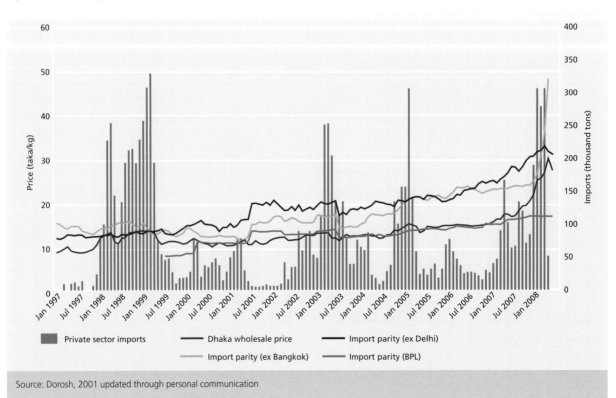

Private sector imports
Dhaka wholesale price
Import parity (ex Delhi)
Import parity (ex Bangkok)
Import parity (BPL)

Source: Dorosh, 2001 updated through personal communication

the rest of the country. For example, prices and marketing margins in eastern Ethiopia are more closely related to markets in Somalia and Kenya than to those in the rest of Ethiopia (Dorosh and Subran, 2007; Intermezzo 6.1).

A country might rely on international markets to make up for an aggregate production shortfall in staples, such as during the 1998 floods in Bangladesh (Dorosh, 2001). In 1996/1997, Bangladesh had three consecutive good rice harvests, which pushed prices below import parity level – the prices paid for imported Indian perimal rice at the border. There was therefore no incentive to import rice. However, floods then destroyed large quantities of crops, leading to sharp rises in wholesale rice prices. Domestic prices exceeded import parity prices, providing the private sector with an incentive to import rice. As a result, imports surged (Figure 6.4).

Government interventions in the domestic rice market were far smaller than private sector rice imports, at 399,000 MT and 2.42 million MT, respectively, from July 1998 to April 1999. The private import of rice following the 1998 floods averted a major humanitarian disaster.

In November 2007, however, Cyclone Sidr had a different impact on the critical boro rice harvest in Bangladesh. Rice prices had exceeded the import parity level since early 2007 (Figure 6.4). By October 2007, wholesale rice prices in Dhaka were about 3 taka/kg above import parity for Indian below-poverty-line (BPL) rice. Private imports increased, but by less than expected given the historical pattern, because India imposed an export ban on non-basmati rice in October 2007, later converting it to a minimum export price of US$425/MT. This export price translated to an import parity price of 27.9 taka/kg, 53 percent higher than the BPL import parity and also above parity levels for imports from Thailand.

Global cereal trade accounts for a small share of requirements. Only 7 percent of global rice production is traded, 18 percent of wheat and 10 percent of coarse grains (FAO, 2008a). Net cereal imports amount to less than 30 percent of domestic production (Figure 6.5) in most major developing regions except the Middle East and North Africa, where imports have typically amounted to more than 50 percent of production. However, the dependence on imports seems to be increasing in sub-Saharan Africa and Latin America and the Caribbean.

Figure 6.5 – Net imports as percentages of production, 1961–2005

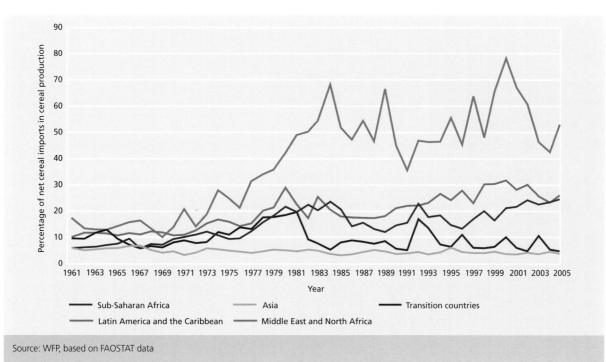

Source: WFP, based on FAOSTAT data

The staples of many LDCs, such as sorghum, millet, sweet potatoes and cassava, are hardly traded internationally, which makes domestic production important. Thus, despite the liberalization of international agricultural markets, close attention must be paid to domestic agricultural production.

As well as being small, the international cereals market is also concentrated. As Figure 6.6 shows, the ten largest exporters of cereals still account for more than 90 percent of global cereal exports, with three countries accounting for more than 50 percent, despite a reduction in the concentration over the last two decades. This makes markets vulnerable, as a production failure in one country affects millions of people in dozens of other countries.

International trade can play an important role in mitigating domestic production shortfalls, but international food markets are vulnerable because of a concentration of exporters.

Food aid

When domestic production, stocks and international trade fail to make up for a shortfall in consumption,

Figure 6.6 – The shares of the largest three and ten cereal exporters

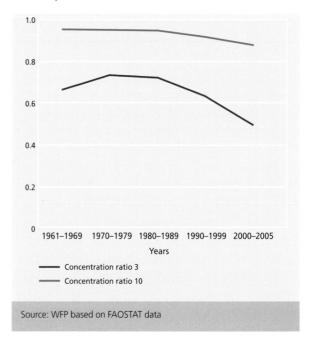

Source: WFP based on FAOSTAT data

the last resort is to rely on international aid. Food aid declined from about 15 million MT in 1999 to about 6 million MT in 2007 (Figure 6.7), the lowest level since 1961, amounting to 0.3 percent of global cereal production.

Figure 6.7 – Global food aid deliveries, 1990–2007

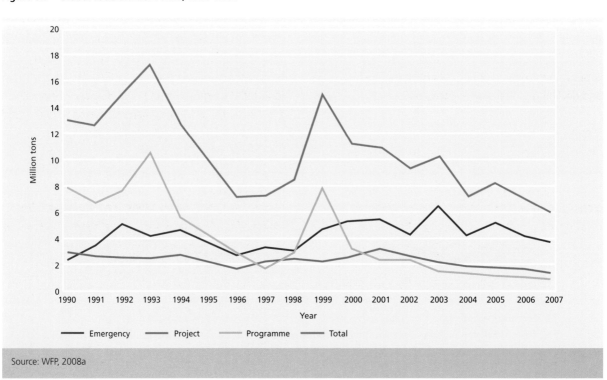

Source: WFP, 2008a

Figure 6.8 – Wheat prices and direct transfers of wheat food aid, 2000–2007

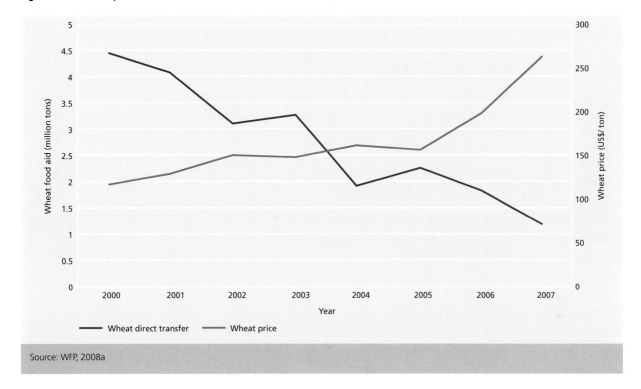

Source: WFP, 2008a

The food aid regime that emerged in the 1950s was largely a system to redistribute developed countries' food surpluses to developing countries with deficits. Over time, such in-kind donations have declined in importance. Contributing factors include the budgeting of food aid in value terms since the 1970s, the decline of government-held surplus stocks since the 1980s, increased purchasing of food aid in developing countries since the 1980s, declining farm support in developed countries since the mid-1990s, and declining global stocks since 2000.

High food prices are partly to blame for the recent decline in global food aid flows. Food aid actors buy their donations on markets, so their budgets buy fewer tons of food aid when food prices rise (Figure 6.8). As a result, food aid becomes less available when it is most needed – when food prices are high.

Food aid can have a negative impact on markets in recipient countries (Intermezzo 6.2), but unintended effects on prices, production incentives, trade and labour markets can be minimized through proper timing and targeting. Possible negative effects are of particular concern in countries where commercial imports are not affordable, increasing the likelihood of dependency on long-term food aid, at both the household and national levels. Ethiopia has often been cited as an example of both micro- and macro-level dependency, but studies (Barrett and Maxwell, 2005; Lentz, Barrett and Hoddinott, 2005; Little, 2008) have found that irregularly timed deliveries and the small contribution that food aid actually makes to household consumption provide little scope for long-term dependence.

Food aid remains an option of last resort for addressing food insecurity crises. However, the food aid system depends on markets, and food aid's potential negative impacts on markets should be avoided.

Turning availability into access: purchasing power, the food price dilemma and nutrition

Purchasing power, or household income, provides the key to access (Webb et al., 2006). Food availability is a necessary but insufficient condition for access, which is in turn a necessary but insufficient condition for utilization, or access to nutrition. Amartya Sen's entitlement approach has become central to the concept of food security. Its focus on markets and household incomes has revolutionized the way in which governments and international organizations deal with protein-energy malnutrition in chronic and acute hunger (Lipton, 2001), shifting attention from investment in food production to a complementary approach that also considers the sustainability and sufficiency of household livelihood strategies – the capabilities, assets and activities required for a means of living (Chapter 4).

However, income and markets are not sufficient. Malnutrition exists even among the non-poor, partly because of a lack of knowledge. Markets fail because of information asymmetries: people cannot tell when their children are malnourished or do not know how to prevent it (World Bank, 2006). Beyond a medical model for food supplementation, access to nutrition remains an under-explored issue (Underwood, 2000).

Food price dilemma

The food price dilemma describes the intrinsic difficulties in increasing both domestic food availability and food access. High prices for staple foods provide incentives to producers, but consumers may lack the purchasing power for adequate food access. If prices are too low, producers will not be able to cover their costs, or make agricultural investments that lead to increased food supply. Many food security policies are driven by the search for ways to encourage production while keeping food within the reach of the (urban) population.

The food price dilemma is complicated by two factors. First, many small producers are consumers and net purchasers of food (Chapter 4). They might sell some of their harvests, but buy food during the hunger season, at high prices. Higher prices could harm them part of the year, but may benefit them during harvest periods (Jayne and Jones, 1997; Barrett, 2002). Second, intermediaries transport, process and package food, so there must be a difference between what producers receive and what consumers pay, to provide incomes for traders and processors.

Another aspect of food price policy is volatility. Sharply fluctuating prices suggest weak underlying food storage and marketing systems, and can be a proxy indicator of food insecurity (Timmer, 1989; Barrett, 2002). Volatile prices cause economy-wide disincentives and have adverse impacts on both consumers and producers. Unstable prices create uncertainty and risks, and discourage investments by producers.

Access to nutrition

Food prices become even more important in relation to purchasing power, because changes in food prices or household budgets have real impacts on access to food and nutrition. Engel's Law states that as budgets expand, the fraction of income dedicated to food declines. This implies that growing incomes provide a buffer against vulnerability and rising and volatile food prices (Timmer, 2000). An empirical corollary to Engel's Law indicates that increasing a household's income will also improve its dietary diversity. Instead of spending more of its budget on cereals or staples, households will be able to afford meats, pulses, fruits and vegetables; this is generally referred to as Bennett's Law (Timmer, Falcon and Pearson, 1983; Webb and Thorne-Lyman, 2006).

The relation between incomes and dietary diversity is illustrated in Figure 6.9, with an example from Cameroon. However, very different levels of income can achieve the same food consumption score, which measures the diversity and frequency of food consumed within a seven-day recall period. Dietary diversity is increasingly becoming an indicator for the nutritional adequacy of household diets, but it is still far from detecting a lack of access to specific nutrients (Webb and Thorne-Lyman, 2006).

Figure 6.9 – Relation between the food consumption score and expenditures in Cameroon

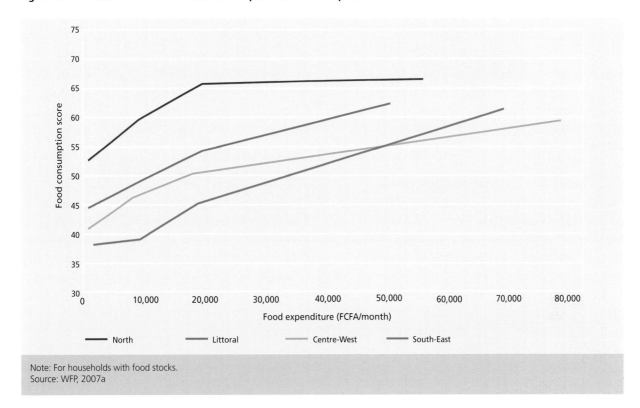

Note: For households with food stocks.
Source: WFP, 2007a

Although there is a link between incomes and dietary diversity, it is unclear whether the causality is due to factors associated with income, such as education and access to health care and sanitation (Block, 2004; Webb and Thorne-Lyman, 2006; Ray, 2007). Poor households spend a large portion of their incomes on food, but they may also spend on luxuries such as alcohol and tobacco (Banerjee and Duflo, 2007).

The relation between access to food and access to nutrition does not always depend on the same factors. Incomes depend on markets, so access to food is largely a market-based phenomenon. Access to nutrition is also determined by market forces, although possibly to a lesser extent. Access to nutrients is through food, but foods rich in micronutrients tend to be more expensive, and hungry poor households often have limited access to them. Large proportions of the population in developing countries cannot afford a healthy diet (Chastre et al., 2007).

Household budgetary allocations are not determined by market forces alone, but also by knowledge and cultural and social norms, which also determine intra-

household allocations of resources and food (Block, 2004). For example, in India, Deaton and Subramanian (1996) found that even though millets were the best buy in terms of rupees per calorie, households spent only about two-thirds of their food expenditure on these grains, dedicating 20 percent to rice and 10 percent to wheat, which were 70 percent more expensive per calorie. Furthermore, the poor spent almost 7 percent of their total budget on sugar, which is expensive and holds no nutritional value. Similar patterns exist in the Sudan, where tea and sugar are important food expenditures.

Maternal nutrition knowledge influences households' budgetary allocations, the composition of household food expenditures, and decisions on intra-household food allocation. Access to nutrition usually increases when women control food expenditures. Utilization of nutrients can be maximized through proper access to health care centres and more effective information systems (Block, 2004; UNICEF, 1990).

Food markets alone do not guarantee adequate access to nutrition, but market analysis can help determine whether certain foods are within the scope of poor household budgets. In recent years, the potential for market-based access to nutrient-rich food has increased through the expansion of (bio)fortification, micronutrient powders and other food commodities addressing the nutrition needs of certain population groups. Governments have an important role in many of these initiatives, including through public–private partnerships (Chapter 9).

Vegetable gardens can promote under-exploited traditional crops with high nutrition values (Moron, 2006). Vegetables are typically expensive on the markets, so rural households are likely to produce them for sale, while urban households with access to land tend to grow them for their own consumption. In greater Monrovia, for example, only 8 percent of households produce crops, compared with 50 percent producing vegetables. These households are not part of the hungry poor, and own their land, 44 percent of which is tended by landless workers who receive a share of the produce (WFP, 2006b). This has a direct impact on the mix of foods consumed in a household and an indirect impact on the incomes of households engaged in these activities. Continued investment in the production and marketing of nutrient-rich foods – such as fruits, vegetables, roots and legumes – is essential.

The distinction between access to food and access to nutrition is illustrated by an example from Bangladesh.

In 1998, imports of rice from neighbouring India prevented protein-energy malnutrition in flood-affected areas. However, among mothers in these areas, the prevalence of night blindness caused by vitamin A deficiency increased to four times the national average (Webb and Thorne-Lyman, 2006). Food security can coexist with nutrition insecurity, at the same time and in the same place.

The terms of trade for nutrients

The terms of trade give indications of how markets influence household access to food in relation to livelihood strategies. The terms of trade are the ratio of the prices of two items, indicating how much food can be bought with one unit of something else. Terms of trade are useful in analysing the level of access to food for cash crop producers, pastoralists and wage labourers.

In Darfur, for example, daily casual labour was an important income source for about half of the households WFP interviewed during its emergency food security and needs assessment in 2007. In El Fasher, daily wages increased between 2005 and 2007, and cereal prices fell. As a result, the terms of trade between wages and sorghum increased. A day of casual labour could buy a little more than 8 kg of millet in June 2007, up from 2.5 kg in May 2005. One day of casual labour could feed one adult for about 20 days with millet. Finding work was difficult,

Table 6.1 – Terms of trade for nutrients

	Price Nyala, May 2007 SDG/kg	Nutrient content						
		Kcal kcal/kg	Protein gram/kg	Iron mg/kg	Niacin mg/kg	Calcium mg/kg	Vit C mg/kg	Folic acid mg/kg
Sorghum food aid	0.40	3,350	110	45	50	260	0	110
Millet	0.73	3,350	110	207	67	220	30	320
Sorghum food aid/millet	0.56	1.00	1.00	0.22	0.75	1.18	0.00	0.34

	Cost per nutrient						
	SDG/kcal	SDG/g	SDG/mg	SDG/mg	SDG/mg	SDG/mg	SDG/mg
Sorghum food aid	0.000	0.004	0.009	0.008	0.002	NA	0.004
Millet	0.000	0.007	0.004	0.011	0.003	0.024	0.002
Sorghum food aid/millet	0.56	0.56	2.56	0.75	0.47	NA	1.62

Note: SDG = Sudanese pound
Source: WFP, 2007d

however, and 56 percent of households cited the lack of employment opportunities as the major constraint to income generation. Such obstacles are the main rationale for income diversification (Chambers, 1995).

Cultural practices should also be considered. For example, in Darfur, sizeable amounts of sorghum food aid is sold to buy millet, which is the preferred cereal. In 2007, households in Nyala exchanged 1 g of sorghum food aid for 0.56 kg of millet. This rate of exchange is worrying in terms of kilocalorie content, which is the same for both commodities, but the terms of trade for micronutrients give a more positive picture. Millet is richer in micronutrients than sorghum, and some micronutrients cost less from millet than from sorghum (Table 6.1). Thus, the exchange of millet for sorghum is not as bad as the price ratio or kilocalorie ratio would suggest – 0.75 for niacin compared with 0.56 for calories.

Some micronutrients are so much more prevalent in millet that it becomes a cheaper alternative. A milligram of folic acid in sorghum costs 0.004 SDG, compared with 0.002 SDG in millet. Thus, 1 mg of folic acid from sorghum can be exchanged for 1.6 mg of folic acid from millet (Table 6.1). It was not knowledge of the nutritional benefits of millet that motivated this change, however, and certain micronutrients, such as niacin, could have been more cheaply obtained from many other types of food, possibly even corn–soya blend (CSB), which

was being sold at a particularly low price on the market.

Selling food aid sorghum provides internally displaced people (IDPs) with access to essential nutrients, such as vitamin C (Reed and Habicht, 1998). For households that lack other income sources, selling food aid is an important strategy for obtaining access to a diverse diet. It is not always as bad an exchange as prices might suggest, but there are often more cost-efficient ways of addressing micronutrient deficiencies among beneficiaries.

Household incomes and food prices have a direct impact on access to food and protein-energy kilocalories, and an impact on access to nutrient-rich food. However, the extent to which market forces determine the nutrient sufficiency of a household's diet is less clear, and nutrition knowledge is important.

Access to and availability of nutritious food depend on markets, but are also influenced by cultural preferences and practices and nutrition knowledge. Markets are unlikely to provide adequate nutrition for all. In every society, marginalized and poor people are the most likely to be vulnerable and exposed to inadequate nutrition. They are also victims of a wide array of other perils, some of which emanate from markets. The following chapter discusses the strategies poor people apply when trying to mitigate risks.

Intermezzo 6.1: Informal cross-border trade – ensuring availabilty, access and stability by bags on bikes

Trade in staple food commodities is critical to food security, as it contributes to national food availability by compensating for shortfalls in domestic production. By limiting price escalations, trade increases consumers' access to affordable food. Underestimating commercial trade's ability to supply national food deficits may lead to poor decision-making on the use of publicly funded food imports and food aid.

However, statistics on the trade in food commodities are incomplete, and cover only formal food flows. Formal trade typically consists of large quantities transported by road, rail or ship, and inspected, taxed and reported in official statistics.

Analysts are increasingly aware of the scale of informal trade in food commodities in Southern Africa. Informal trade usually involves small quantities in individual transactions, typically a few bags of maize on the back of a bicycle, but the aggregate quantities may be very substantial. Informal trade is believed to have been a major factor in averting a widespread crisis during the 2001–2003 food emergency in Southern Africa. In some cases, a lack of understanding of this type of trade may have led to an overestimation of food aid needs, oversupply of food aid, low prices and reduced incentives for farmers to produce locally and for private sector trade.

Studies on cross-border trade in the region confirm the significance of informal trade (Whiteside et al., 2003). However, these one-off studies cannot capture the volatility of this trade, where large changes in volumes and direction can occur quickly, depending on production, price differentials and the policy environment, including the imposition of export bans. It is therefore important to establish systems that continuously monitor food trade.

In March 2004, WFP and the Famine Early Warning System Network (FEWS NET) established a system for monitoring informal cross-border trade in Southern Africa, drawing on experience in East Africa with the Regional Trade Information Network (RATIN) and its component for monitoring informal cross-border trade. A Technical Steering Committee (TSC) of regional representatives of WFP and FEWS NET was established to oversee project implementation. The system's overall aim was to collect, analyse and disseminate data on volumes, prices and directions of trade, in order to

understand cross-border food trade and provide information for decision-making on response strategies to food emergencies and food import needs. Positive feedback from the users of this information – ranging from governments to private sector traders, policy analysts and humanitarian agencies – demonstrates the system's value.

An initial survey led to the establishment of key points for monitoring significant commodity flows across the most active borders shared by the Democratic Republic of the Congo (DRC), Malawi, Mozambique, South Africa, the United Republic of Tanzania, Zambia and Zimbabwe. Border monitors were recruited to collect daily source and destination prices and volumes of informal trade in maize, rice and beans. Monitoring started in July 2004 and continues. The monitors submit their data to a central processing centre, managed by the Malawi FEWS NET office, using mobile phones, faxes, ordinary mail and e-mail for data transmission. The data are analysed and disseminated through monthly reports and postings on the FEWS NET, RATIN and other websites.

On the most active Malawi–Mozambique borders, maize is transported almost exclusively on bicycles, after being purchased and collected by traders, who hire the cyclists. Three or four 50–90 kg bags on a bicycle are regarded as petty trade or for personal consumption, and are therefore exempt from formal export licences in Mozambique. Large consignments are taken across the border in this way, and assembled for dispatch to the main markets in Malawi without attracting duty and without being recorded. During peak season, many tons can be moved across in a single day. The border monitors recruited by the monitoring system record the amounts that go through, including the prices at the source and destination.

Informal cross-border trade trends

The system has captured data for part of the 2004/2005 marketing year, and the three full marketing years 2005/2006 to 2007/2008. A series of at least four to five years of data is needed before statistical inferences can be made and likely flows modelled, but the data collected so far demonstrate the importance of monitoring informal trade and understanding its role in filling staple food deficits. As shown in Figures 1 and 2, volumes of informal trade in maize, rice and beans

Table 1 – Informal maize imports and exports by country (MT)

	2005/2006		2006/2007		2007/2008	
	Imports	Exports	Imports	Exports	Imports	Exports
Malawi	156,499	1,158	79,660	3,721	59,651	7,115
Mozambique	273	71,272	887	80,748	3,884	58,202
DRC	4,682	0	9,486	0	33,424	0
Tanzania	944	98,418	2,928	8,148	1,581	6,053
Zambia	13,686	5,338	7,731	10,167	9,038	36,361
South Africa	0	1,688	0	49	0	47
Zimbabwe	1,875	85	2,435	294	495	295
Total	**177,959**	**177,959**	**103,127**	**103,127**	**108,073**	**108,073**

Source: Informal Cross-Border Food Trade Monitoring System

are significant, varying according to availability in each marketing year. The monitored countries have had one year of significant food shortages (2005/2006) and two of favourable harvests, except in Zimbabwe.

Table 1 and Figure 1 demonstrate that trade was particularly vibrant during 2005/2006, when shortages were acute in most countries, except Tanzania. Informal imports of maize reached a high of 178,000 MT, mainly from Tanzania to its southern neighbours, and from Mozambique to Malawi. Trade with Tanzania was aided by the absence of trade restrictions until near the end of the season, when the vuli harvest failed, supplies quickly dwindled and the government imposed an export ban, which curtailed most informal exports. Figure 2 illustrates the high volumes of imports

from Mozambique to Malawi throughout the three years, accounting for a large proportion of the total captured from all border points.

The importance of informal flows is demonstrated in Table 2, which gives the maize balance sheet for Malawi for the three years under review. During the 2005/2006 deficit year, informal imports into Malawi were almost as large as formal imports. Table 2 also shows that the remaining import gap – requirement minus imports – for that year is about halved when informal imports are included. In the two successive years of bumper harvests, informal imports contributed 48 and 76 percent, respectively, to total imports. The formal export programme in 2007/2008 ran concurrently with informal imports, which were directly supplying food needs in the border areas, but also being sold

Figure 1 – Informal maize cross-border flows July 2004–March 2008 (MT)

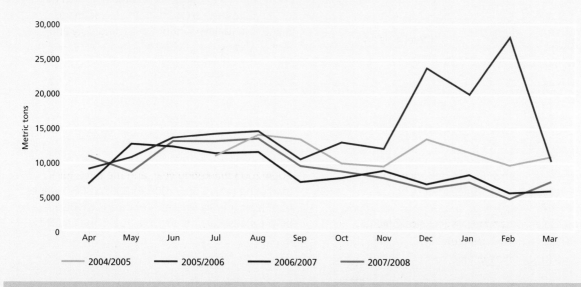

Source: Informal Cross-Border Food Trade Monitoring System

Figure 2 – Informal maize cross-border flows by source and destination (MT)

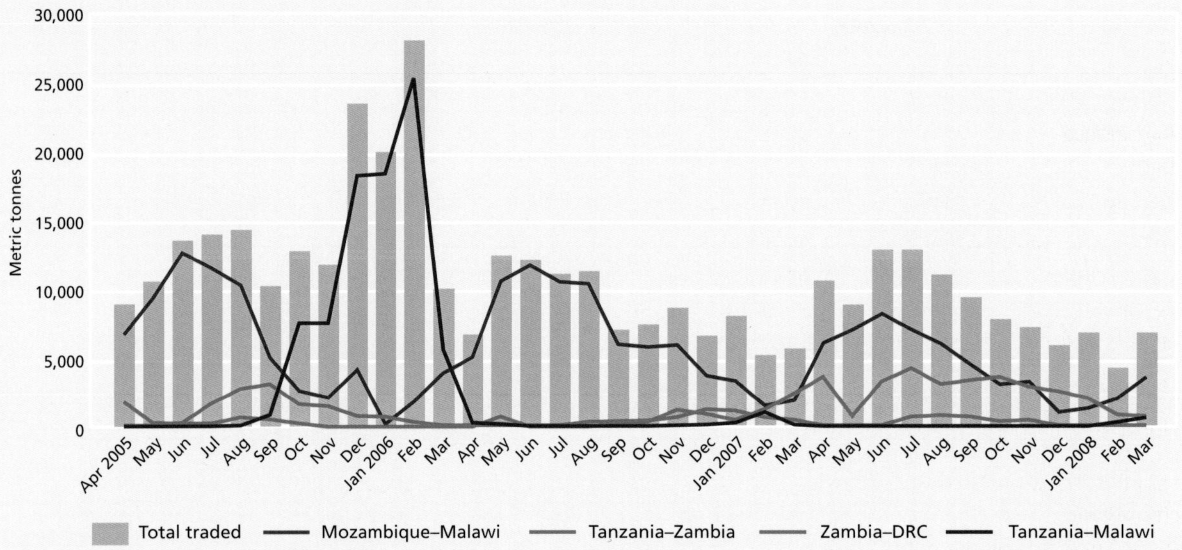

Source: Informal Cross-Border Food Trade Monitoring System

to traders supplying the formal export programme, mainly because of favourable price differentials. Import data for Malawi indicate that 60,000–100,000 MT of maize is imported informally into Malawi in an average year.

Informal imports in 2005/2006 enabled WFP and other agencies to adjust their estimated food aid imports. Studies along the busiest Malawi–

Mozambique borders also underline the importance of this type of trade for livelihoods, as it provides an income for those involved in moving the food across the border.

The system also captured informal trade in rice and beans and significant flows of other staple foods including cassava; volumes of these are not as substantial as for maize.

Table 2 – Malawi maize balance sheet (thousand MT)

Maize	2005/2006	2006/2007	2007/2008
Deficit/surplus	−905	130	933
Cross- substitution	293	184	−396
Import requirement	**−612**	**314**	**538**
Total imports	**456**	**166**	**79**
Formal imports	176	31	3
Informal imports	165	80	60
Food aid	115	56	17
Total exports	**1**	**4**	**341**
Formal exports	0	0	334
Informal exports	1	4	7
Net imports	**455**	**162**	**−262**
Remaining gap (import requirement + net imports)	**−157**	**477**	**276**
Remaining gap (without informal)	**−322**	**397**	**216**
Informal imports as % of total	**36**	**48**	**76**

Sources: Malawi National Early Warning Unit, FEWS NET and Informal Cross-Border Food Trade Monitoring System

Intermezzo 6.2: Food assistance and markets

A sound understanding of markets is essential for analysing hunger, malnutrition and food security, and market analysis is vital to the design, programming and implementation of interventions. Market analysis can provide information for:

- food security analysis;

- response options;

- amount of food aid needs;

- targeting;

- local procurement possibilities; and

- minimizing possible adverse effects of food assistance.

A food security analysis is not complete without an assessment of markets. Access to markets might be limited, and markets can increase households' vulnerability. Higher food prices and lower cash crop prices can be especially compromising to food security, and vulnerability is high when food expenditure accounts for a large share of total expenditure. Markets can also be an instrument for reducing vulnerability and coping with a crisis. Households diversify their income sources to reduce their vulnerability – through markets, households can avoid putting all their eggs in one basket.

Recommendations on responses to food insecurity are informed by knowledge of how markets function. Markets play a role in food availability and access, and several response options should be analysed, including production support, facilitating trade among regions and improving access to markets. For food access, cash or voucher transfers might be a more appropriate response to a food crisis than food transfers, as long as markets are integrated, food is available in markets, prices are stable and households have access to markets. Whether cash or vouchers is the appropriate response also depends on other factors, such as security, local capacities and recipients' preferences.

If food aid is among the response options, the amount needed depends on the functioning of markets. For example, a drought may lead to higher food prices, providing traders with incentives to move food from surplus to deficit areas, including from neighbouring countries.

These food flows would bring prices down in deficit areas and raise prices in surplus ones. International trade is often important in smoothing price fluctuations, but trade barriers tend to hamper the functioning of this buffer. Generally, the better markets function, the less food aid needed.

Targeting mechanisms sometimes rely on markets. For example, a good understanding of the market for and consumption patterns of less-preferred food commodities is important in strengthening the self-targeting characteristics of food aid commodities. Food-for-work schemes often use self-targeting of people in need by setting the reward below the current market rate, so that only those truly in need join the scheme. Geographical targeting can also be partly determined by market analysis, as areas where markets are poorly functioning are likely to have higher food assistance needs. Market analysis can also influence the timing of food assistance. If prices show a strong seasonal pattern, food assistance is most likely to be needed during the lean season, when food prices are relatively high.

Market information is important in maximizing the positive effects and minimizing unintended negative effects of food assistance on markets. When there are supply constraints, cash or vouchers can push food prices up. Food aid may depress market prices, which can be intentional, as in Darfur in 2005. The risk of negative effects is greater when markets are not integrated. Food aid's negative effects on the prices can be minimized through proper timing and targeting, but even when there are negative effects on prices, there is little evidence that food aid has negative effects on local agricultural production (FAO, 2006c).

Cash, vouchers and food aid can have positive effects on markets. In Darfur, for example, food markets are surviving partly because of the influx of food aid commodities. Food aid "has kept the market functioning and has maintained prices at affordable levels" (Buchanan-Smith and Jaspers, 2006). There are other examples where food aid has stimulated market development in more or less hostile environments (Abdulai, Barrett and Hoddinott, 2005).

Cash and vouchers can also stimulate local markets. A study in Malawi found that one unit of cash transfer stimulated demand in local markets by an amount more than twice as large (Davies and Davey, 2008).

A decision to purchase locally depends on a market assessment. What food crops are available and in what quantities? What are the price trends and fluctuations? Is there a risk of procurement pushing prices up? What is the scope for procurement contributing to market development? Through procurement in developing countries, WFP has reduced transportation costs and delivery times, promoted markets and opportunities for local farmers, and provided food aid that is closer to local preferences.

"The revolutionary idea that defines the boundary between modern times and the past is the mastery of risk: the notion that the future is more than whim of gods and that men and women are not passive before nature."

Peter L. Bernstein, 1996

Markets may worsen the risks that households face, but they can also be instrumental in reducing risk and in coping with a crisis, because they offer possibilities to find other jobs, sell assets or borrow money. They may transfer risks from vulnerable people to others who can cope with them more easily.

In developed countries, most people are protected from market-related vulnerabilities and risks. They are usually shielded by, for example, high incomes, insurance systems, fairly efficient labour markets, social protection schemes and access to credit. In every society, however, marginalized and poor people are vulnerable and exposed to a wide array of hazards, including market-related ones. Even if they employ mechanisms for managing risk, insufficient income often makes it impossible for these people to eliminate their vulnerability.

Inadequate risk management and response to disasters led Amartya Sen (1981) to describe "droughts as human failures". Others have suggested that a new paradigm has emerged in which famines result from "acts of man", rather than "acts of God" – natural disasters. Famines can be prevented, even when production and markets fail, unless political actions or inactions yield response failures as well (Devereux, 2007b).

Market-related hazards, vulnerabilities and risks

Not all households are equally affected by a shock, such as high food prices. Whether the shock results in food insecurity depends on a household's vulnerability, which is determined by its exposure and coping capacities (see the box on page 96). Shocks tend to have the largest impacts on the poorest segments of the population, because of increased exposure, vulnerability and limited capacity to manage and cope with risk.

Weather-related shocks are probably the most common hazards faced by the hungry poor. Table 7.1

Table 7.1 – Shocks in rural Ethiopia, 1999–2004

	Households reporting the shock (%)	How widespread was the shock?				
		Only affected this household (%)	Affected some households in the village (%)	Affected all households in the village (%)	Affected this and nearby villages (%)	Affected areas beyond the kebele (%)
		Idiosyncratic ←			→	Covariate
Drought	52	6	15	32	26	21
Pests or diseases affecting crops or livestock	38	20	29	25	18	8
Input shocks: price increase or access difficulties	35	13	18	27	23	18
Output shocks: price decrease or difficulty making sales	29	6	12	36	33	14
Victim of theft or other crime	22	77	14	4	3	1
Death of husband, wife or other person	35	80	10	5	4	1
Illness of husband, wife or other person	39	83	9	5	3	0

Source: Dercon, Hoddinott and Woldehanna, 2005

Table 7.2 – Understanding risk to hunger through markets

Market-based risk	
Market-based vulnerability	**Market-based hazard**
Food price volatility	High food prices
Low and unstable income	Terms of trade decline
High unemployment rate	Policy changes, e.g. in taxes or tariffs
High dependence on markets for food	Financial crisis
Market failure (fragmentation)	Market failure (collusion)
Absence of social protection	Propagation of production shock
Lack of access to credit, savings and insurance	

lists the shocks that created hardship for rural households in Ethiopia between 1999 and 2004. After drought, pests and diseases, market-related shocks were the most prevalent, but even shocks that do not originate from markets may have consequences for them. The hungry poor face a wide range of market-based risks (Table 7.2).

Markets can increase risk

Markets can increase household vulnerability or relay a shock. Pastoralists in the Horn of Africa and the Sahel are net buyers of food and sell part of their livestock to buy food. When pastures are deteriorating, livestock markets experience a supply shock, putting downward pressure on prices. Lower livestock prices mean that pastoralists have to sell more to buy the same amount of food, reducing livestock prices even more. Market dynamics worsen the situation. Distress sales can constitute a harmful coping strategy, because prices may collapse when an abundant supply enters the market, deepening the hunger–poverty trap.

Definitions and concepts

Risk to food security (R): The probability of food insecurity resulting from interactions between natural or human-induced hazards and vulnerable conditions.

Hazard (H): The probability of damaging phenomena in a given period and area. Can be expressed as the probability of the incidence of a harmful event at a specific site during a given period.

Shock: Disturbance caused by a hazard.

Individual or idiosyncratic shock: Affects an individual or household, for example, sickness or death of either humans or animals.

Common or covariate shock: Affects all members of a community, region or country. It is not always easy to distinguish idiosyncratic from covariate shocks, for example, in the case of contagious diseases.

Vulnerability to food insecurity (V): Vulnerability is a function of a household's exposure to a hazard and its capacity to mitigate and cope with the hazard's effects.

Risk = f(hazard, vulnerability) = f(H, V)

Vulnerability = f(exposure to hazard, ability to cope with risks)

Hazard = f(probability, intensity, coverage)

If a hazard, such as a flood, is likely to occur but a household is not vulnerable because it is not on a floodplain or because it has built flood walls, the risk of a decline in food security is low. In another scenario, the risk of food insecurity is significant if the probability of increasing food prices is high (hazard) and a poor household spends 70 percent of its income on food (exposure) and lacks the capacity to cope with high food prices, because it cannot increase its income or obtain credit, and has few assets to sell.

"Markets have to respond to demand not to needs."

The Economist, 1 September 2005

As a result of a locust invasion and drought, Niger faced a drop in production in the 2004/2005 agricultural year – 7.5 percent below food requirements (FAO/WFP, 2004). This drop was not exceptional (Mittal and Mousseau, 2006). The government and media blamed grain traders for the crisis, arguing that the removal of government regulations had led to market failure. Econometric analysis refutes this hypothesis by stressing the market integration that exists in the Kano-Katsina-Maradi basin, especially during drought years (Aker, 2008). "West African grain markets are generally working very well, and perhaps too well. The high cereal price levels found in the Sahel are being driven by strong demand for Sahelian cereal production, and greater purchasing power in coastal West African countries" (FEWS NET, 2005).

There was no reason for regional trade to ensure an adequate food supply in Niger. Niger's purchasing power was too low to cover households' basic food needs. Food was present in markets, but not accessible. Research indicates that during 2004, up to 200,000 MT of millet – 10 percent of Niger's total net supply – was exported from Niger as traders were getting higher prices in Nigeria (World Bank, 2008d).

As well as food and trade policies for regional integration, and market-based food security policies, the 2005 crisis emphasized the need for West African early-warning systems with integrated price and food security monitoring (WFP, 2005e, 2005f).

Two examples where complex entitlement-related risks were exacerbated by markets are the 2005 food crisis in Niger (see the box above) and high food prices (Chapter 3).

Markets can reduce risk

When markets work well, they self-correct, which can benefit the hungry poor. The deeper the market, the smaller the impact of the shock on that market. Rising prices provide traders with incentives to move food from surplus to deficit areas. Such food flows bring prices down in deficit areas and raise them in surplus ones. Examples are private sector imports of rice during the Bangladeshi floods in 1998 (Chapter 6), and market recovery in urban and semi-urban areas after the 2005 earthquake in Pakistan (WFP, 2005c).

This can happen only if markets function well: prices rise as a result of scarcity, traders receive correct information, transportation costs are not prohibitively high, and markets are competitive. When all these "ifs" are fulfilled, markets become integrated and a shock might be disseminated.

Four examples of market-based risks

Fluctuating food prices: In many developing countries, food prices often fluctuate significantly within a year because of seasonality, and between years because of weather-related production shocks, combined with inelastic domestic supply and demand responses and high transaction costs (Figure 7.1). Where transport and storage facilities are good, and markets are functioning, traders can use arbitrage to reduce price differences over time and space. However, price volatility remains high in several developing countries, despite market-oriented reforms. After price liberalization in Madagascar during the 1980s, for example, the rice price rose by 42 percent and the variance increased by 52 percent. Two-thirds of rice farmers were hurt because they consumed more rice than they produced (Barrett and Dorosh, 2006).

Instability and risk are not synonymous, because some price fluctuations are predictable. Seasonal price patterns reflecting food availability between harvests are generally predictable and motivate the private sector to invest in storage. Eliminating all price variability might be neither feasible nor desirable. Efforts to eliminate seasonal price fluctuations, such as through pan-seasonal pricing policies, have usually shifted the burden of seasonal storage on to state marketing agencies, often imposing costs beyond their capacity and reducing incentives for private sector participation (Byerlee, Jayne and Myers, 2006).

Figure 7.1 – Burkina Faso: a price pattern like that in many other African countries

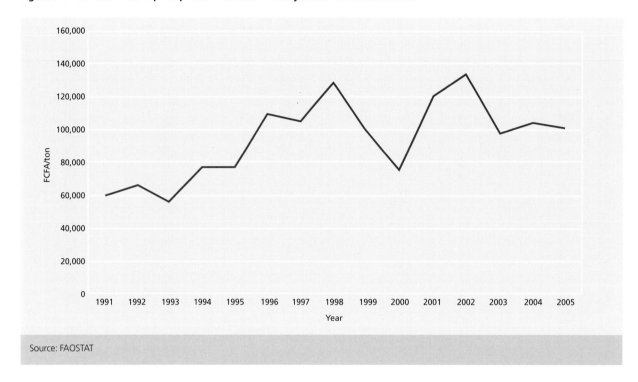

Source: FAOSTAT

Seasonal and unpredictable price fluctuations can be a major cause of market-related food insecurity. Many famines, such as that in Bangladesh in 1974 (Ravallion, 1987), have been caused by the poor being priced out of the market. Food price increases should be limited, their impact mitigated, or safety nets provided to the hungry poor if necessary.

Unemployment and terms-of-trade shocks: Labour market risks include unemployment, falling wages and compulsion to take precarious and low-quality jobs. During the East Asian financial crisis, for example, real wages and non-agricultural employment fell in all affected countries (World Bank, 1999). Fluctuations in labour demand often affect young workers and women disproportionately (Horton and Mazumdar, 1999).

As incomes fall, poor households often try to increase their labour market participation. Recent food price hikes in Afghanistan predominantly affected the urban poor. To afford an increasingly expensive food basket, more household members had to find jobs, but an exceptionally harsh winter reduced job opportunities and, subsequently, real wages (Forsen and Subran, 2008).

In 2000/2001, bad weather caused a coffee harvest failure in several areas of Central America. Small farmers who relied largely on coffee for their incomes might have been able to cope had coffee prices not declined in the second half of the 1990s (Maluccio, 2005), as exemplified by the terms of trade between maize and coffee in Nicaragua (Figure 7.2).

Market failure: Market failures can have various consequences. Price differentials may exceed transaction costs in fragmented markets. Price seasonality may be large, reflecting a lack of storage and inter-temporal arbitrage. Access to finance may be curtailed. Precautionary or speculative hoarding may create artificial scarcities by withdrawing food from the markets, turning a minor production shortfall into a major crisis (Devereux, 1988; Ravallion, 1987). Such hazards and vulnerabilities affect food security, particularly if combined with unstable livelihoods.

Policy failure: Government responses to a shock can make matters worse. A simulation of a drought in Zambia demonstrated that food aid, announced government imports that do not materialize, and controls on private sector trade, rather than improving domestic supply, can inadvertently exacerbate price

Figure 7.2 – Terms of trade between maize and coffee in Nicaragua

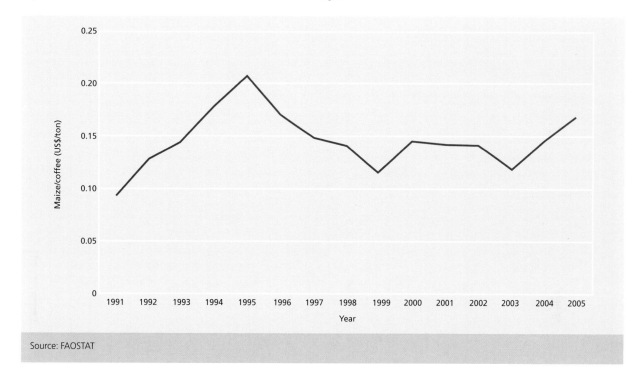

Source: FAOSTAT

instability and food insecurity (Dorosh, Dradri and Haggblade, 2007; and Table 8.1). Another example concerns trade barriers for maize in El Salvador; lifting tariffs may lead to increased maize imports from the US, translating into lower costs for consumers (Angel and Subran, 2008).

Shocks have both market and non-market origins. However, the impact of any shock can be mitigated and relayed by the market mechanism.

Before a shock: risk management

Risks are pervasive for the hungry poor and determine their livelihood choices. There is a difference between coping practices and risk management. Risk is managed before a shock, and coped with after it. Through risk management, households reduce the exposure to hazards and mitigate the impacts of shocks. Coping strategies employed after a shock reduce its impact. Markets can help households to manage risk and cope with shocks, but at a cost.

Risks can deepen the hunger–poverty trap

Shocks can deplete the capacity to manage future risk because they can have long-term impacts. A shock can push poor households into a hunger–poverty trap, for example, by wiping out assets. In Zimbabwe, children under 3 who were exposed to the war in the late 1970s or to the 1982–1984 drought suffered negative effects on height and educational attainment, which translated into a 14 percent reduction in lifetime earnings (Alderman, Hoddinott and Kinsey, 2006). Ethiopian households that were affected by a drought, illness or price shocks between 1999 and 2001 still had significantly lower consumption levels in 2004 (Dercon, Hoddinott and Woldehanna, 2005).

The presence of risk, even without a shock, can deepen the hunger–poverty trap. The hungry poor are rational economic actors who generally allocate resources wisely, compare risk profiles and expected returns and weigh trade-offs (de Janvry, Fafchamps and Sadoulet, 1991; Barrett, 2008). Risk aversion is common among the hungry poor (Binswanger, 1981; Newbery and Stiglitz, 1981). It can be interpreted as the behaviours through which people opt to pay for

The food and fuel price risk index

To prioritize responses to high food prices, WFP used a risk decomposition approach (Husain and Subran, 2008), linking baseline in-country vulnerability information to high food prices. Two indices were developed to address the underlying vulnerability and high food prices.

A The global vulnerability index (GVI) is a composite of five indices:

(i) National response capacity: This index assumes that a country classified as low-income, food-deficit and severely indebted and receiving no debt relief assistance, such as from the Heavily Indebted Poor Country (HIPC) Initiative, will get the lowest index values.

(ii) Socio-economic situation: This index is similar to the Human Development Index (HDI) developed by the United Nations Development Programme (UNDP) and includes GDP per capita, health status, education and life expectancy. Health is derived from four variables: per capita national health expenditures, doctors per thousand population, percentage of population with sustainable access to improved sanitation, and percentage of population with sustainable access to improved water.

(iii) Child vulnerability: This index assumes that child vulnerability will be more severe in countries with relatively high overall child and adolescent populations and a high percentage of underweight children cared for by an undernourished adult population with high HIV/AIDS prevalence. Calculations for this index therefore involve the percentage of population under 15, the percentage of children underweight for age, the percentage of adults undernourished, and the prevalence of HIV/AIDS.

(iv) Income poverty and distribution: This index ranks countries in terms of both absolute income poverty and income distribution. It is derived from four variables: percentage of population living on less than US$1/day, percentage of population living below the national poverty line, percentage share in consumption of the poorest 10 percent, and the Gini coefficient. The first two variables capture income poverty, and the last two income distribution.

(v) Dietary consumption: This index represents total energy as a function of average per capita cereal and non-cereal (fats and protein) consumption.

The GVI is created from an average of these indices, weighted by the difference from the mean of each index. Each index is compared with its mean for all countries, and weighted, with the worst country below the mean weighted as 0, the best country above the mean as 1, and other countries falling between 0 and 1. This means that a country's good performance in one index is not cancelled out by a poor performance in another.

B The high price risk index (HPRI) uses four variables to capture current domestic inflation trends, dependence on international food markets and a coping indicator:

(i) The extent of the price shock: The actual, and partly projected, headline inflation rates between 2005 and 2008, estimated by IMF.

(ii) The country's dependence on imported food and fuel: The food and fuel import bill as a percentage of total imports, to capture both the value and the volume effects of openness.

(iii) Household dependence on imported staple cereals: Combines imports' contribution to in-country net cereal availability and the composition of the food basket (cereal energetic contribution).

(iv) Household resources for coping: Captured through per capita GDP in 2008 purchasing power parity and included negatively in the HPRI as it correlates negatively with the other variables.

Weights: A simple signed average – using equal weights, but with the sign of the contribution based on the correlation with the intensity of the hazard – gave similar results to a principal components analysis (PCA) so was used for the sake of interpretation.

C Combining the two indices into a food and fuel price risk index (FFPRI): The scores were averaged, at 60 percent for the GVI and 40 percent for the HPRI, to obtain a final food and fuel price risk index embedding both the vulnerability status of a country (with country and household components) and the severity of the high food prices. Rankings were then derived, based on quintiles. Map B at the end of this publication shows the outcome of this endeavour.

In sharecropping systems, tenant farmers keep a contractually predetermined proportion of their harvests and give the remainder to the landowner in lieu of money-rent. The landowner may share some or all of the non-labour costs. Since Adam Smith, many economists have condemned sharecropping as inefficient, because sharecroppers would make more effort if they could keep all of their harvests. Nonetheless, sharecropping continues to be prevalent.

Sharecropping helps solve the problems associated with market and weather-related risks where there are no financial markets. A tenant paying a fixed rent bears all the risk associated with production, while a sharecropping tenant shares this risk with the landowner because the rent varies with the harvest size. Relative to a fixed-rent tenant, a sharecropping tenant's return is lower when the harvest is large, but increases when the harvest is small. Sharecropping reduces the farmer's risk where other risk management mechanisms, safety nets or coping strategies are not viable or absent.

Working for a wage would shift all the uncertainties and risks to the landowner, who would also have to bear monitoring costs.

Sharecropping is an imperfect but functional institution. It has adapted to constrained environments, and enhanced land access for the risk-averse and vulnerable poor, by compromising between the rental system of production incentives but no risk sharing, and the wage system of no risk exposure but no production incentives, plus monitoring costs for the landowner.

Source: Stiglitz, 1989

less risky choices (Dercon, 2005). Risk-averse households may forgo profitable opportunities by clinging to lower-return and lower-risk alternatives. Farmers use few or no purchased inputs, such as fertilizer and seeds, to avoid losing money if crop prices decline or the rains fail; using only their own labour input reduces the risks, but crop yields are also smaller. For example, asset-poor households in India grow more traditional varieties of rice, while those in the United Republic of Tanzania grow more sweet potatoes, which have low returns and low risks (Dercon, 2002).

Households sometimes have to weigh market risks against other risks. In southern Zambia, for example, rural households cultivate maize as a cash and food crop, even though it is vulnerable to drought. Adopting drought-tolerant food crops would insulate households from drought effects, but would also generate less income for other needs (Murray and Mwengwe, 2004).

The poor are most affected by the trade-off between risk and average return, which is a significant feature of the hunger–poverty trap. In a risky environment, poverty compels households to be risk-averse, keeping them in poverty. Among other measures, insurance products and safety nets can help solve this problem.

Using markets to reduce risk

The hungry poor often lack the assets that make people resilient to market shocks. They often grow their own food to avoid the risk of food price rises, and diversify their incomes by using markets (Reardon, 1997; Dercon, 2002). Non-farm income accounts for 30–45 percent of rural household income in developing countries, and this share is increasing (Haggblade, Hazell and Reardon, 2007). Households with less than 0.5 ha of land earn 50–90 percent of their incomes from non-farm activities, which may allow them to smooth income throughout the year and cover food purchases during the lean season (Banerjee and Duflo, 2007).

The hungry poor employ various mechanisms to reduce and share risks. Many of these use markets, such as for flexible and contingent contracts, and for developing networks and trust (Fafchamps, 2004). A common risk-reduction system for smallholder farmers is sharecropping (see the box above). Warehouse receipts and commodity exchanges can also reduce risk (Chapter 5). Cooperatives that enable cash crop growers to pool their resources to reach bigger and more diverse markets with better, more stable prices also help manage risk.

Risk analysis in Lao People's Democratic Republic

Over the last 30 years, the main hazards reported for the lower Mekong have been floods, droughts, epidemics and windstorms.

Households can reduce risks by reducing their exposure to a shock and by coping, often using markets. Regardless of the shock, the most common coping strategies employed are changes in food consumption, borrowing and help from relatives and friends, consumption of wild foods, and the use of credit. Savings are less commonly used for slow-onset covariate shocks, such as droughts, crop pests and regular floods, than for flash floods and landslides (see the first figure below).

Households' vulnerability to shocks, such as droughts, floods, inaccessible markets and price increases, can be assessed across livelihoods and food consumption groups. Unskilled labourers are the most vulnerable to an increase in the rice price; in March, six months after the harvest, 68 percent are vulnerable, increasing to 73 percent in August, 11 months after the harvest. Households that depend on farming are most vulnerable 11 months after the harvest. Petty traders remain largely food-secure throughout the year. Overall, 21 percent of households suffer cyclical food insecurity due to price increases (see the second figure below).

Shocks and related coping strategies in Lao PDR

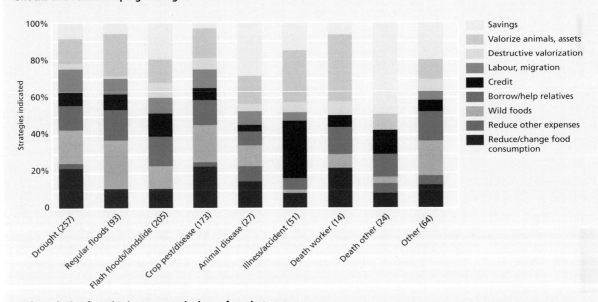

Risk analysis of a price increase and a loss of market access

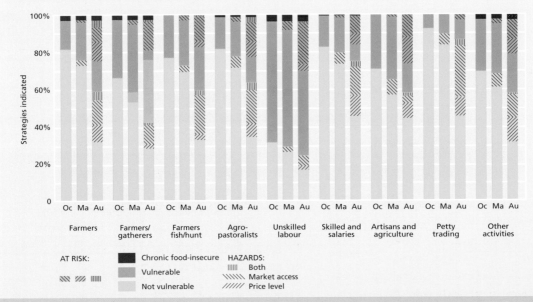

Source: WFP, 2007b

Poor households can also reduce their vulnerability by accumulating financial, physical and social assets. Assets can be risky, however, as their prices may collapse if everybody sells them at the same time. Some are bulky – nobody can sell half a cow, for example (Dercon, 2002).

Using markets to transfer risk

Vulnerable households have limited capacity to smooth their consumption or income over time. Income shocks put consumption at risk. Financial markets are among the most important markets for transferring risk, but they are poorly developed in many developing countries. Volatile prices may provoke inefficient production decisions, especially in the absence of credit, insurance and forward contracting (Newbery and Stiglitz, 1981). Lack of insurance and credit markets also makes it difficult to recover the assets lost to cope with a shock or destroyed by it. In China, for example, access to credit was instrumental in reducing poverty and inequality (Guabao, 2006).

Various efforts have been made to develop insurance schemes, for example, to mitigate weather-related events. WFP has developed index-based insurance products that could be a valid option for many countries (Hess, Robertson and Wiseman, 2006; Lacey, 2006; Intermezzo 9.1). Social protection schemes, including disability, sickness and unemployment insurance, can also be effective market-based instruments for reducing risks, but they are not widely available.

Futures and options are another set of instruments for transferring risks. Hedging mechanisms based on futures or options spread import costs over time, reduce variability and possibly lower average costs (Dana, Gilbert and Shim, 2006). However, they have less potential for small farmers and traders than for large traders and governments (World Bank, 2005); for example, Malawi's maize imports were hedged on the South African Futures Exchange.

Risks can cause long-term and deep vulnerability to food insecurity and hunger, and deepen the hunger–poverty trap. Insurance, credit and other mechanisms may help manage risk, but are not always available to the hungry poor. If risk management schemes are well implemented, reliable and sustainable, households may not need to engage in harmful coping mechanisms.

After a shock: household coping strategies

Coping strategies are the behaviours households adopt when they do not have access to enough food after a shock (FANTA, 2003; Maxwell et al., 1999). Households' coping aims to reduce fluctuations in income and consumption. In general, the more effectively a household diversifies its income and risk management, the better it can withstand or adjust to shocks. During crop failure, the shock to a household's income can be at least partially absorbed if a portion of the household's labour time is dedicated to activities other than agriculture, such as handicrafts or a job in the public sector. A household's asset base is a fundamental element of its capacity to smooth its consumption. A household with several assets may maintain its consumption level by selling some of these assets. Its ability to do so increases according to the proportion of assets held in liquid form. Thus, the value and liquidity of its assets are important determinants of a household's ability to cope with food access shocks.

If a food-insecure household suffers a temporary food shortage or lack of money it may use one or several of the following strategies:

- changing the diet to less costly, less preferred and less nutritious foods – dietary change strategies;

- increasing food access through food-seeking strategies, such as borrowing money, buying on credit, consuming wild foods and seed stocks, and diversifying income sources, including begging;

- decreasing the number of individuals being fed by the household through household structure strategies such as migration;

- rationing available food by reducing meal size or frequency; and

Figure 7.3 – A household impact framework: from more expensive foodstuffs to child malnutrition

Livelihood	Diversify/change livelihood activities	Reduced expenditure on non-essential or luxury items Beginning to sell non-productive/disposable assets	Children drop out of school Migration: rural to urban moves	Increased use of child and women's labour Beginning to borrow/purchase on credit, become indebted	Selling productive assets Depletion of natural resource base, e.g. cutting trees, etc.	Selling all assets	Reduced expenditure on essential items: food, water, etc.	Engaging in illegal/health-threatening activities as last resort coping
Food-related – nutrition	Change to cheaper, lower-quality, and less preferred foods	Reduced diversity of food – poor nutrient intake Favouring certain ill members over others for consumption	Reduced size/number of meals	Consuming wild foods/immature crops/seed stocks	Begging for food	Skipping entire days without eating	Eating items not eaten in the past/not part of normal diet, e.g. plants and insects	Child malnutrition

Source: Adapted from Maxwell and Caldwell, 2008

- spending less on health and education, including taking children out of school.

The sequence and impact of these strategies varies depending on the context. Figure 7.3 shows a possible sequence following a shock.

A household close to the hunger–poverty trap employs different coping behaviour. It might reduce food consumption, rather than sell assets, to avoid falling into the poverty trap from which it is difficult to escape. In Zimbabwe, for example, farmers with more than two oxen were three times more likely to sell an animal than households with one or two. As a result, loss of body mass was greater among women in households that did not sell oxen, and young children in households with few oxen were permanently stunted (Hoddinott, 2008). In Pakistan, having more than a certain amount of land was critical in avoiding declined food consumption (Kurosaki, 2006).

Figure 7.4 illustrates the difference between a poor household that reduces its food consumption to preserve its asset base and avoid falling below the asset threshold for the hunger–poverty trap, and one that smoothes consumption by selling assets, but falls into the hunger–poverty trap. The former is able to recover after the shock; the latter is not.

Markets play a critical role in triggering behavioural changes among households. If the price of maize increases because of a drought, households will switch to cheaper food staples, such as cassava, mitigating the price rise. This substitution effect also reduces the demand for maize, and brings down its price. For example, the model developed for Zambia (Dorosh, Dradri and Haggblade, 2007; Table 8.1) predicts that food consumption among poor households that substitute will fall by 84,000 MT, compared with 140,000 MT among those that do not.

Food-seeking strategies that aim to increase households' access to food have clear links with markets. For example, a study in Ghana found that

Figure 7.4 – Avoiding the poverty trap by reducing food consumption

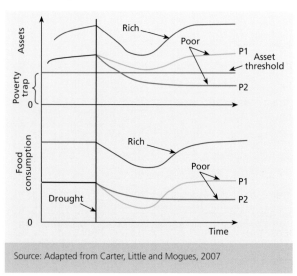

Source: Adapted from Carter, Little and Mogues, 2007

female-headed households often rely on short-term strategies to increase food availability. When normal coping and response strategies are exhausted, many such households are forced to use negative crisis strategies, such as selling productive assets. Repeated shocks and the use of crisis strategies to manage their effects may increase vulnerability, decrease food security and force households into the hunger–poverty trap. When vulnerability is extreme, selling land may become the only option for securing food. Land is a major asset in rural areas, but it is also a low-liquidity asset. Sale of land can be interpreted as a household's resignation of future production opportunities in favour of immediate food purchase (Maxwell and Wiebe, 1999). Timely food assistance could help prevent these negative consequences.

Reducing risk: the role of social protection

Compared with the narrower "safety net" discussion of the 1990s, current social protection debates are returning to the focus on innovative *ex-ante* measures to reduce risk, such as through insurance, in addition to more traditional *ex-post* safety net transfers in food, cash or vouchers. There is growing evidence that social protection is not a palliative to food insecurity, but an investment in economic growth (Devereux and Sabates-Wheeler, 2007).

Many of the countries that are introducing social protection systems, such as Ethiopia, Kenya and Malawi, have been hit by emergencies almost every year, implying that the level of need is to some extent predictable. Rather than responding to recurrent needs, the rationale behind social protection is to meet core needs predictably over many years.

Guaranteeing stable support over time may decrease the risks perceived by households, thereby reducing the adoption of negative risk management and coping strategies and fostering more entrepreneurial behaviours and activities. For example, about 75 percent of its beneficiaries reported that they consumed more or better quality foods because of Ethiopia's new Productive Safety Net Programme

(PSNP), and 62 percent were able to retain more of their own food production to eat rather than selling it for other needs (Devereux et al., 2006).

Social protection can reduce risk and promote growth through four key channels: investments in human capital, improved risk management, addressing (some) market failures and reduced inequality (Gentilini and Carucci, 2008).

Investing in human capital: Recent evidence indicates that better nutrition among children can lead to higher earnings and income streams when they become adults, because nutrition affects cognitive development, educational attainment and productivity, which contribute to higher incomes (Behrman, Alderman and Hoddinott, 2004; Hoddinott, 2008).

Managing risks: Higher income opportunities are often associated with higher risks; risk aversion prevents people from investing to gain higher incomes from endeavours that involve higher risks, such as introducing new plant varieties. Studies in south India and the United Republic of Tanzania show that because poor households deploy their assets more conservatively, their return on assets is generally 25–50 percent lower than wealthy households' (Alderman and Hoddinott, 2007). By externalizing some of the risks, predictable social protection can provide poor people with the confidence and security to engage in potentially risky income-generating activities. Social protection can also prevent the selling of assets after a shock, keeping vulnerable households out of the hunger–poverty trap.

Addressing (some) market failures: Safety nets may reduce the transaction costs faced by farmers by, for example, creating infrastructure through food-/cash-for-work programmes. Insurance products can reduce uncertainty about the future, hence allowing better allocation of resources. The provision of regular social protection transfers may also help alleviate some household liquidity constraints, thereby partially addressing credit market failures (Dercon, 2004).

Inequality reduction: The trade-offs between equity and efficiency are less pronounced than often perceived (Ravallion, 2003, 2007). More equality can help boost growth, as demonstrated in East Asia (Birdsall, Ross and Sabot, 1995). Inequality can result in policies that favour a small elite, rather than the general population, and a lack of social capital. There is a distinction between inequalities that are good for sustainable growth and those that are bad. "Good" inequalities may provide incentives for innovation and investment, while "bad" ones prevent access to markets and limit investments in human and physical capital (Chaudhuri and Ravallion, 2006). Maximizing the good inequalities and minimizing the bad are key ingredients of an inclusive and pro-poor growth strategy.

Developing countries have different capacities for introducing and scaling up social protection systems (Chronic Poverty Research Center, 2008; WFP, 2004). Diverse models could be developed to capture different stages of development of social protection systems, ranging from the absence of such systems, such as in Somalia or the Sudan, to consolidated systems, such as in Mexico or South Africa (Gentilini, 2009). Social protection issues in low-capacity, post-conflict countries are different from those in countries with institutionalized and domestically financed systems. There is a need to overcome the policy and capacity constraints that prevent the most vulnerable and food-insecure countries from introducing and scaling up formal social protection systems.

The way in which markets influence the prevalence of hunger, despite risks, depends on whether markets are functioning well, and whether the hungry poor have access to risk reduction instruments, such as insurance, and are supported by social protection.

Markets are risky. Market-based vulnerabilities and hazards can have severe impacts on food security. Shocks emanating from other sources can also affect market functioning, compounding the impact on food security. If markets were poorly functioning before a disaster, its effect on hunger can be particularly fierce. An emergency's impact on markets depends on its duration, intensity and frequency, and the underlying vulnerability of the victims. The following chapter highlights the impacts of emergencies on markets.

"Most decisive was the collapse of commercial circuits. Settlers, shopkeepers, wholesale merchants and transporters departed en masse in the period 1974–1976... The flows of goods and services for rural households began to dry up as distribution systems collapsed and factory output and imports fell. This was the beginning of the 'goods famine' in Angola's countryside, a condition persisting to present... These processes were driven by war."

David Sogge, 1994

The term emergency can refer to a wide variety of unfavourable and harmful conditions that affect food security. Disasters and crises that may affect markets range from droughts to violent conflicts. The onset of the HIV/AIDS pandemic, for instance, has radically changed the world's emergency landscape over the past 20 years. It is a global disaster contributing to food emergencies. Chapter 7 looked at risks that emanate from markets and could lead to a food emergency. This chapter discusses the impact of food emergencies on markets and food systems.

Impact of emergencies on food availability and access

Emergencies may be defined as "urgent situations in which there is clear evidence that an event or series of events has occurred which causes human suffering or imminently threatens human lives or livelihoods and which the government concerned has not the means to remedy; and it is a demonstrably abnormal event or series of events which produces dislocation in the life of a community on an exceptional scale" (WFP, 2005b).

The event or series of critical events may comprise one or a combination of the following:

- sudden calamities, such as earthquakes, floods and locust infestations;

- human-made emergencies resulting in an influx of refugees, internal displacement of populations, or the suffering of populations affected in other ways;

- food scarcity owing to slow-onset events, such as drought, crop failures, pests and diseases that erode the capacity of communities and vulnerable populations to meet their food needs;

Figure 8.1 – Emergencies and markets: an overview

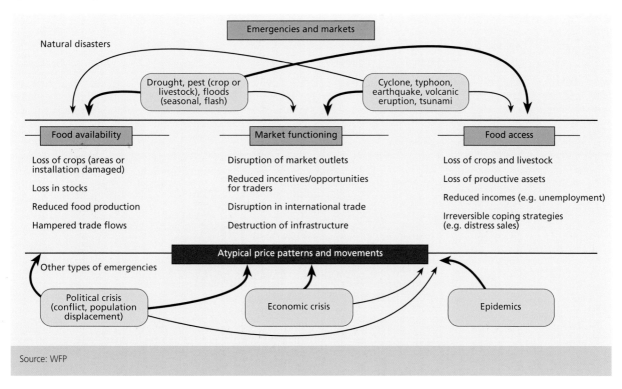

Source: WFP

- severe difficulties in food access or availability, owing to sudden economic shocks, market failure or economic collapse that erode the capacity of communities and vulnerable populations to meet their food needs; and

- complex emergencies for which the government of an affected country has requested assistance.

Emergencies can severely impair food security through their impacts on market functioning and food availability and access, which are determined by incomes and prices (Figure 8.1).

Food production

The most direct impact an emergency can have on food availability is destruction of standing food crops and existing stocks, such as by flood, drought and pests. For example, the 1998 flood in Bangladesh destroyed production equivalent to 10 percent of annual consumption (del Ninno, Dorosh and Smith, 2003). The risks of these kinds of impacts are increasing, as the number of natural disasters in developing countries is rising (Figure 8.2).

In conflict situations, food stocks, crops and livestock are often deliberately destroyed or looted. Food production generally diminishes because it is too risky for farmers to reach, cultivate or harvest their plots, or too difficult to purchase inputs and/or sell the output. In Darfur, for example, the area planted in 2004/2005 was only 30–40 percent of the previous five-year average, and only half of this planted area was harvested, because many communities had evacuated to IDP camps and insecurity prevented farming operations. Sorghum and millet yields were, respectively, 36 and 54 percent of the average (Hamid et al., 2005).

Impact on incomes

Emergencies can affect agricultural incomes through the destruction of crops and livestock. They may also lead to the loss of on- and off-farm work opportunities and decreasing wages. Lost crops, fewer employment opportunities and deteriorating terms of trade tend to accompany emergency situations, and may deepen the crisis. In Kenya, Rift Valley fever frequently causes deaths and/or forced slaughter of cattle. The subsequent income loss is a common cause of household food insecurity.

The impact of emergencies on informal transfers depends on how resilient existing social networks are. When an emergency hits all the households in a village, transfers among households cannot make up for the income loss. Public assistance can also crowd out informal private arrangements (Dercon, 2002).

Figure 8.2 – Increasing frequency of natural disasters

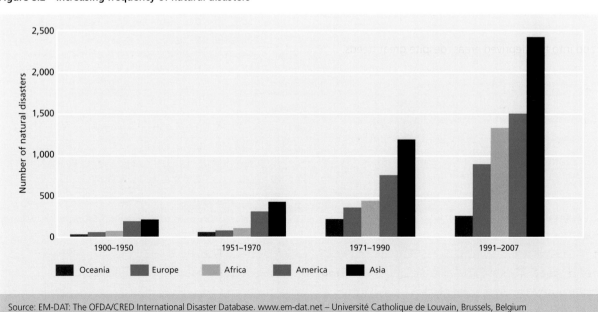

Source: EM-DAT: The OFDA/CRED International Disaster Database. www.em-dat.net – Université Catholique de Louvain, Brussels, Belgium

To respond to a shock, family members may send more remittances from abroad, but households' access to remittances might be hampered if the emergency has affected the functioning of the financial system.

Human epidemics can have an impact on markets. HIV/AIDS affects a third of the population of Southern Africa. Many of these people are unable to work, particularly if the disease is combined with tuberculosis or malaria. Incomes are seriously reduced, and traders have few incentives to move food to areas where people's ability to buy is low. In other words, "people weakened by HIV and AIDS find it harder to access food, because they are often not strong enough to work or to walk long distances to the market" (Oxfam, 2002).

Impact on food prices

An emergency's impact on food prices depends on supply and demand in the affected area. If food production, stocks and transport channels are affected, prices are likely to rise. If transport systems are not destroyed, high prices in the shock-affected area may induce movement from unaffected regions, eventually dampening prices.

For such a mechanism to work there must be effective demand. If people have lost most of their assets and income-earning opportunities, food will not be imported from elsewhere. Lack of demand causes prices to fall, and traders have no incentive to move food into the deprived areas, despite great needs.

Even in situations where demand is high, expectations of future price rises might lead to withholding of stocks, which is likely to fuel price increases (Ravallion, 1997). Such speculative behaviour can exert major inflationary pressure in an emergency-affected area.

Emergencies affect agricultural production, incomes and trade by damaging crops, livestock and infrastructure. Markets respond to demand, not to need. If demand decreases, prices fall and traders have no incentive to move food into deprived areas.

Impact of emergencies on market performance

Linkages between markets and emergencies go beyond food availability and access. Other, often overlooked aspects of market performance are also affected – the actors, price-setting mechanisms and distribution of goods. Most natural and human-made disasters have a significant impact on the structure, conduct and performance of markets, especially those for food, cash crops and livestock. The underlying role of markets – to match demand (not needs) and supply – may be severely hindered by emergencies, and market malfunction can have fierce effects on hunger (Sen, 1981).

The impact of an emergency depends on its duration, intensity, frequency and the underlying vulnerability of the affected society. Most emergency shocks have direct and indirect impacts on trade, which could harm vulnerable households. Earthquakes, seasonal floods and long-lasting droughts have diverse influences on markets, from slight changes to complete closure. After a low-intensity earthquake, market recovery may be quick, whereas persistent drought, entailing low production and reduced effective demand, affects market performance for longer (WFP, 2006d). Figure 8.3 summarizes the aspects of markets that might by affected by a shock. The structure and functioning of markets determine market resilience. If markets are deep and well integrated before a disaster, they are more likely to recover quickly, but disaster-prone areas do not attract private sector investment in uncertain market endeavours.

Trade flows

Food availability depends on food production and flows among regions. When local food production and stocks have been destroyed by an emergency, food inflows from other unaffected regions can make up the shortfall. However, such inflows can take place only when infrastructure has not been destroyed and the transportation of food is not too dangerous. Data from Bangladesh in the mid-1970s and Ethiopia in the mid-1980s indicate that emergencies led to decreased market integration (Ó Gráda, 2007). On the other hand, efficient

Figure 8.3 – Oxfam's market analysis tool for emergencies

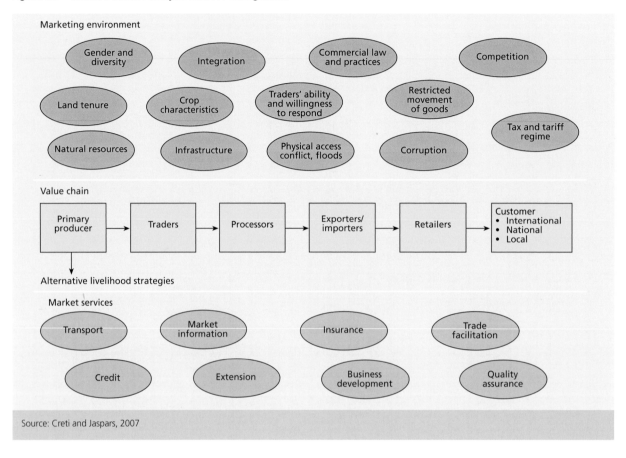

Source: Creti and Jaspars, 2007

market linkages in Southern Africa – where cross-border informal trade is prevalent – contributed to trade activities in flood-affected areas of Mozambique (Dradri, 2007; Intermezzo 6.1).

Countries often introduce protectionist measures when a food emergency strikes a neighbour. For example, the steep food price increases in 2008 were partly the result of export restrictions (World Bank, 2008a; and Chapter 3).

As well as the breakdown of infrastructure, food availability may also be affected by political, religious and ethnic strife. In an armed conflict, warring parties might hamper physical access to markets. For example, in the Sudan, only people with a certain ethnic background were able to transport and sell livestock, making livestock markets inaccessible to other groups (Buchanan-Smith and Jaspars, 2006). After an emergency, the restoration of physical access to markets is essential for the resumption of normal food consumption patterns.

Natural disasters such as storms, earthquakes and volcanic eruptions usually destroy infrastructure and cause supply shortfalls, but these types of emergencies are mostly localized. The destruction of infrastructure and harvests through conflict tends to be more complex, and is sometimes due to deliberate attempts to cut off opponents' supplies. Even when infrastructure is not affected, it might be too risky for traders to move food, owing to dangers of cargo looting or the hijacking of trucks. Between early 2004 and early 2005 in Darfur, transport costs between Omdurman and El Geneina increased by 150 percent, and fuel prices by more than 130 percent. The protection payments demanded at frequent roadblocks added to these costs (Hamid et al., 2005). In South Sudan, a devastated road infrastructure, coupled with insecurity and depressed grain production pushed prices to twice as high as those in the rest of the Sudan (FAO/WFP, 2008a); this difference persists and will probably continue as long as transportation costs remain high. Figure 8.4 gives sorghum prices for Juba (South Sudan) and three cities in Darfur.

Figure 8.4 – Sorghum price differences between South Sudan and the rest of the Sudan

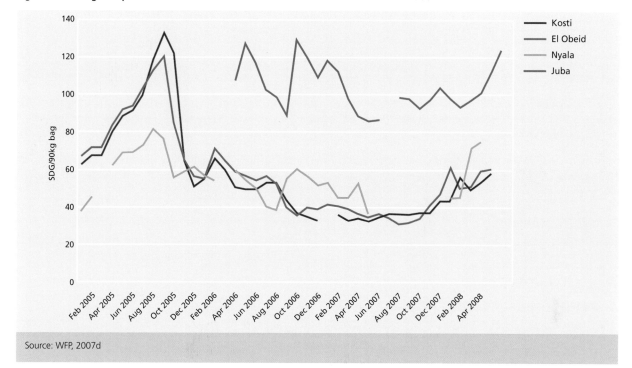

Source: WFP, 2007d

Hampered market functioning and traders' aversion to risk

Devereux (1988) highlights three sets of factors that influence traders' response during famines: (1) logistics constraints, from the costs of redirecting distribution channels and the small surpluses available; (2) limited rewards, from the small size of famine markets and the opportunity cost of losing other customers; and (3) risk and uncertainty, such as the risk of being undercut by other traders, and the uncertainty caused by limited information about famine markets.

Market functioning depends on legal and institutional systems. When these are disrupted by a complex emergency, markets stop working altogether or work differently, generally by switching to informal channels to make up for the failure in formal markets. Deficient legal frameworks may enable the mushrooming of unnecessary intermediaries, increasing transaction costs.

Market actors play multiple roles because of the complementarity of markets and market actors and because specialization is underdeveloped. Therefore, even localized emergencies tend to affect various levels of the marketing chain (see the upper box on page 112).

Traders' stocks may be destroyed by natural disasters, looting and other incidences. Traders may also be denied access to supplies, or suffer from lower demand. In addition, they might lack cash or access to credit for restocking.

Access to credit is often essential for traders and households recovering from an emergency, because assets and production have been lost, and cash holdings might be insufficient to buy food and material for rebuilding, or to replace productive assets. Emergencies can affect access to formal credit by destroying financial infrastructure, such as bank buildings and records. For example, in areas of Pakistan affected by the 2005 earthquake, banks remained closed because data on accounts had been lost. This hampered access to credit and bank savings, which limited shopkeepers' and traders' possibilities for replenishing stocks (WFP, 2005c). Traders are often the main providers of credit in developing countries, so credit to households tends to be limited after a shock. An emergency can also interrupt credit provision among relatives and within social networks, because

111

A flood causing a ripple throughout the marketing chain in Haiti

"A few local wholesalers … purchased goods directly from Port-au-Prince, getting zero-interest loans (acquaintance and trust-based), used to supply goods to middlemen with limited transport facilities [such as donkeys and mules. The middlemen/intermediaries then sold] the commodities to numerous retailers on a daily credit basis… Alternatively, Madame Saras [women who transport and trade goods between rural areas and the capital] would [buy and sell] directly from general market suppliers and supply the retailers in the local markets. As a result of the floods, wholesalers lost their transport and storage facilities (damaged trucks, storehouses destroyed) [and were left with debts to pay]. Middlemen and retailers, including Madame Saras were affected both in terms of transport and stocks… The general market suppliers were not affected."

Source: Creti and Jaspars, 2007

all members of a community are simultaneously in need of money.

Competition, information asymmetries and other market failures

Most emergencies increase the likelihood of market failures because the number of sellers declines and transaction costs, risks, uncertainty and information asymmetries increase. Increased information asymmetries mean that traders might know more about prices or availability than their customers, and might use this information to their own advantage.

When the number of traders servicing an affected area decreases, those who remain might gain market power or collude and obtain higher sales prices and profit margins. This is particularly likely during armed conflicts, when markets are prone to interventions from traders associated with warring factions, who benefit from their connections with people in power. For example, during the late 1980s conflict in southern Sudan, traders who delivered goods by train were able to maintain high prices by restricting the quantities

delivered. Benefits from excessive pricing were restricted to a few well-connected and wealthy traders (Keen, 1994; see the box below).

Emergencies are likely to benefit those traders who possess food stocks, transportation and storage capacity, and access to finance. In conflicts, markets can be manipulated to benefit politically influential groups, or to suppress people by limiting their access to food.

Emergencies may create information asymmetries among market participants, because people have different perceptions about the consequences of the emergency, and objective information about damages might not be available. This can be a problem if food availability is perceived to be lower than it actually is. If farmers and traders anticipate a price rise, they may opt to withhold their stocks to sell them later at the expected higher prices.

In the aftermath of an emergency, governments and international agencies are compelled to make complicated policy decisions. When assessing needs

Markets feeding violent conflicts

Violent conflict has played a significant role in many famines and food emergencies during the last few decades, including in Ethiopia in the mid-1980s, the Sudan in 1987–1991 and Somalia in 1992. Markets are often severely affected by violence. Some argue that dysfunctional markets are not an unintended consequence of violence, but a deliberate result of market manipulation – "forced markets" (Keen, 1994) – to yield economic benefits that may help finance the violence and create incentives to keep it going. Economic incentives have been an important impetus for several conflicts (Collier and Hoeffler, 1998; Berdal and Malone, 2000). Natural resources, such as diamonds, have been particularly significant in creating these incentives. In some instances, food aid has played a similar role. Violence has been used to trigger relief, creating opportunities for looting (Berdal and Malone, 2000).

Table 8.1 – Impact of a drought on food security: simulations for Zambia

Simulated percentage change after a maize production decline of 30%	Autarky		With imports		
	Without substitution of cassava for maize (%)	With substitution of cassava for maize (%)	Small public imports (including food aid) (%)	Large public imports (including food aid) (%)	Small public imports announced but not fulfilled (%)
Maize prices	150	150	36	2	104
Total consumption: maize plus cassava in maize equivalent	−24	−15	−7	−1	−12

Source: Adapted from Dorosh, Dradri and Haggblade, 2007

and recommendations, it is important to analyse markets and discern how they may determine food availability. Simulations of policy responses to a drought in Zambia showed that food aid needs must take private imports into account, to prevent a price collapse and the flow of food out of the country, fuelling an ensuing crisis (Dorosh, Dradri and Haggblade, 2007). Unfulfilled government announcements of large public imports may also discourage private traders from importing, thus widening the food gap and hurting the most vulnerable households (Table 8.1).

When local food production and stocks have been destroyed, food may be brought in from unaffected regions. Food markets are hampered during and after emergencies, because risks and uncertainties are high, information is limited, protectionist measures are common, transaction costs are increasing, surpluses and stocks are often limited, and famine markets are too small.

Mitigating emergency impacts on markets

The impact of disasters on markets must be prevented and mitigated to protect vulnerable households' food security (Vincent, Tanner and Devereux, 2008). Establishing emergency-specific interventions to do so is difficult. Support to households in an emergency aims to provide enough food, water, sanitation and health care to preserve people's lives and safeguard their livelihoods by protecting and replacing their assets. Addressing these needs depends partly on

market performance (Intermezzo 9.2). The extent to which markets function and the quantities that traders are able to import also influence the amount of food assistance needed.

Paving the way for recovery and development after a humanitarian food emergency is of fundamental importance. It is also crucial not to harm markets, as they could support recovery. Market-friendly interventions during an emergency include:

- *increasing availability and stabilizing prices*, through encouraging private imports with tax and tariff cuts, releasing government food stocks, or supplementing government imports;

- *facilitating or supporting the transport of goods*, through repairing damaged infrastructure;

- *supporting complementary markets access*; traders whose stocks have been destroyed and who lack the financial resources to restock could benefit from loans, grants or loan guarantees that enable them to borrow without collateral; and

- *providing clear messages*; governments and aid agencies must give private traders clear messages about the volumes of in-kind or cash interventions, so that traders can adapt to expected market demand.

Rebuilding markets

Humanitarian relief programmes address the immediate needs of affected populations. The urgency to save lives, often combined with short-term and inflexible funding, may impede the need to focus on rebuilding markets and the in-depth analysis necessary for understanding how markets function within specific contexts.

Relief staff are not always well informed about economics and the functioning of food markets. They may be reluctant to pursue commercial solutions to market constraints. Opinions and misconceptions often emerge in relief environments, with elites taking advantage of the situation to maximize business opportunities, create distortions, co-opt relief resources and try to consolidate their own market positions. Strife over economic resources and endemic inequalities underlie many conflicts, and tend to be more pronounced when a humanitarian crisis is at hand.

It is necessary to assess local markets at the onset of a crisis; humanitarian relief should aim to sustain food security, or even to "build back better", to quote a slogan for the post-tsunami reconstruction efforts in Sri Lanka (Kennedy et al., 2008).

Market development should be supported soon after a crisis, or during low-intensity crises. Essential conditions for reconstructing damaged markets are reasonable security and stability. To prevent relief funds from undermining development initiatives, it may be vital to collaborate with private sector businesses, rather than creating parallel supply channels (The SEEP Network, 2007).

Implementing market development strategies requires flexible donor funding with integrated relief and development goals. Programme goals, performance criteria and staff/recipient incentives should be more closely tied to outcomes than they have tended to be in relief operations (The SEEP Network, 2007).

To kick-start production and restore markets after an emergency, infrastructure may need to be restored, rebuilt and constructed. However, it is difficult for poverty-stricken communities hit by an emergency to dedicate themselves to rebuilding infrastructure for redevelopment, because community members are busy looking for food for their families.

Food- or cash-for-work programmes aim to help people take the first steps out of the hunger–poverty trap. Workers are paid in money or food rations for building vital infrastructure, such as dams, roads, swamp reclamation structures, hillside terraces, water facilities and catchment areas. In war-torn countries, WFP offers food assistance as an incentive for ex-combatants to learn new skills and abandon their weapons.

To reduce the cost of transporting food and other humanitarian supplies, WFP has been involved in a massive road project in South Sudan since 2006. Some 3,000 km of roads have been rebuilt and cleared of mines, improving links between the Sudan and Kenya and Uganda, and between the Nile River and a network of feeder roads. The project is not only benefiting WFP's food transports, but also revitalizing trade and facilitating the return of displaced people. In one year, vehicle movements on the road connecting Juba to Uganda shot up from zero to 200 a day. According to a recent WFP survey, the roads built so far have halved the average travel time to markets, schools and health centres and reduced cereal prices in locations with road access.

The extent to which markets functioned before and during an emergency has important implications for the emergency response, so assessments must include market analysis. Interventions have to be flexible and geared to the local context, and should use, support and rebuild markets, as appropriate.

Any emergency can have a large impact on markets. In-depth understanding of the linkages between a shock and food security is essential for an effective and efficient response. Markets can help the hungry poor not only to sustain their livelihoods, but also to safeguard their food security, but interventions are sometimes necessary to manage vulnerability and address food insecurity. State interventions are needed to support markets with infrastructure and institutions. The following chapter describes why, when, how and what interventions can be made.

Intermezzo 8.1: **Market analysis in WFP**

In recent years, WFP has significantly improved its capacity to conduct market analyses, particularly through the Strengthening Emergency Needs Assessment Capacity (SENAC) project, funded by Canada, Denmark, the European Commission, Germany and Citigroup. About 20 market profiles have been produced, several desk reviews on a range of topics published, and three workshops organized. The workshops move beyond the market profiles and aim to strengthen the connections among market analysis, recommendations and decisions by integrating market analysis into assessments.

WFP has developed good practices for integrating market analysis into food security and needs assessments. New guidance materials for crop and food security assessment missions, comprehensive food security and vulnerability assessments and emergency food security assessments include comprehensive guidance on market analysis.

WFP has also developed tools and guidance that make the work of assessment officers easier. Tools have been developed for:

- analysing prices, import parity prices, marketing margins and terms of trade;
- analysing the effects of high food prices on food security;
- analysing seasonality, and forecasting prices;
- estimating the effects of market shocks on the food security of various household groups;
- determining and using elasticities;
- determining the degree of market integration; and
- estimating shock impacts, food aid and policy options using a multi-market model.

Standard questionnaires have been developed for household, trader and focus group surveys that pay specific attention to markets. The multi-market model has been developed as an Excel spreadsheet to estimate the impact of shocks on food prices and simultaneously to evaluate the effect of these price changes on consumers, producers and traders. The model can predict these effects for various shocks, such as a drought; policies, such as import/export bans; and programme interventions, such as food aid, cash transfers and local procurement. It can also estimate the quantity of food aid that can be imported without disturbing the market. The spreadsheet was developed for

Zambia and has also been applied to Ethiopia and Niger.

Market analysis has made a difference. For example, the 2007 emergency needs assessment in Darfur argued that large-scale replacement of food aid with cash transfers was not an option, but cash or vouchers complementing food transfers could be considered as a pilot, to prevent food aid sales to cover milling costs and repay debts. Milling vouchers were explored in 2008, but depend on security. Large-scale cash or vouchers were not possible, because import parity prices were so high that private traders had no incentives for bringing cereals into Darfur from abroad or eastern Sudan. However, bringing cereals from eastern Sudan was cheaper than importing, which provided opportunities for local procurement.

In Bangladesh, following Cyclone Sidr in November 2007, food assistance was extended for several months, partly based on the market analysis included in the emergency needs assessment. This analysis concluded that rising rice prices were having negative effects on household food security and malnutrition and that food availability could be a problem because of export restrictions imposed by India, which had been a major source of rice imports for Bangladesh in times of domestic production shortfalls.

After the earthquake in Pakistan, WFP food aid was targeted to rural areas because the assessment had concluded that markets were recovering in most urban and semi-urban areas. Of a total of 2.3 million in need of food assistance, the needs assessment identified only 230,000 people in the worst-affected urban and semi-urban areas, focusing on those areas where market recovery was slowest. In the other less-affected urban and semi-urban areas, where markets were integrated, cash-based interventions were recommended.

WFP has also conducted assessments – such as in Darfur, Georgia and Malawi – to determine whether and where cash or vouchers could be appropriate and feasible. Market analysis was central to these assessments, but other aspects such as implementation capacity were also considered (Intermezzo 9.2).

High food prices have put the importance of market analysis centre stage in WFP. A specific tool kit has been developed to assist assessments of the impact of high food prices on food security. Assessments have included analysis of food prices and their impact on food security. Market analysis is also critical in analysing the impact of the global financial crisis, for example on incomes, employment, exports and exchange rates, and how they, in turn, affect food security.

Part III Actions and the Way Forward

Markets offer great potential for the hungry poor, but markets need to be supported by institutions and infrastructure. They also need to be supplemented by social protection systems and nutrition interventions.

Part III outlines policy options and actions that various actors, including governments, can take to ensure that markets function to the benefit of the hungry poor. **Chapter 9** outlines why, how, when and what actions should be taken, and by whom. It reviews the pros and cons of a variety of actions in staple food, international and complementary markets, which should be supplemented by social protection systems and interventions focusing on nutrition. **Chapter 10** highlights ten priority actions to help markets break the vicious cycle of hunger and poverty.

"The important thing for government is not to do things which individuals are doing already, and to do them a little better or a little worse; but to do those things which at present are not done at all."

John Maynard Keynes, 1926

There are moments when markets provide the best playing field for the hungry poor to sustain their livelihoods and safeguard food security. However, government actions are *often* necessary to manage vulnerability and address food insecurity, and always desirable to guide and discipline markets, particularly during the first stages of economic and agricultural development or in transition situations (Timmer, 2008). One of the key ingredients for China's remarkable progress in reducing poverty was that "China did not make the mistake of believing that freer markets called for weakening [state] institutions… It is plain that the combination of sound policy-making practices with strong state institutions was a key factor in China's success against poverty. And it is also clear that the two ingredients are complements, not substitutes" (Ravallion, 2008). However, inadequate actions can be worse than no action, and there are often trade-offs.

Markets, market failures and interventions

Why intervene in markets?

Markets "fail" for several reasons: externalities, market power, public goods and imperfect information (Chapter 2). If markets send incorrect price signals to producers, traders and consumers, these groups are likely to misallocate scarce resources, thus contributing to food insecurity. Actions to enhance market functioning may prevent or mitigate the effects of market failures and improve households' access to food, local food availability and, in some cases, food utilization.

As well as addressing market failures, there are other motivations for intervening in markets, including fighting hunger, improving political support, stabilizing prices and ensuring domestic food self-sufficiency.

Even Adam Smith, the father of the free market argument, "did not hesitate to investigate economic circumstances in which particular restrictions may be sensibly proposed, or economic fields in which non-market institutions would be badly needed to supplement what the markets can do" (Sen, 2000). During 2007 and 2008, governments implemented a wide range of policies to dampen the impact of high food prices.

However, just as interventions can alleviate market failures, they can also cause distortions that have negative impacts on decisions concerning short- and long-run resource allocations. Governments need to strike a balance. A "need to pay attention *simultaneously* to efficiency and equity aspects of the problem remains, since equity-motivated interference with the working of the market mechanism can weaken efficiency achievements even as it promotes equity" (Sen, 2000).

Public goods, institutions and market functioning

The success of market interventions depends on several factors, including the quality of the design and implementation of interventions. The response to interventions depends partly on public goods, such as local infrastructure, market information systems, research and development, agricultural extension and contract enforcement. Providing public goods and improving market performance may decrease transaction costs, information asymmetries and coordination failures, indirectly enhancing both food availability and food access. "Where markets and food production systems are weak, the most effective strategy is therefore not to abandon them (to states that are likely also weak), but rather to build them up through necessary investment" (Barrett, 2002).

Providing public goods may lessen or obviate the need to intervene in markets. "The very important role that these public goods played in Asia's green revolution … underscores the need for African governments and donors to make a major commitment to improving the provision of these goods. It is becoming increasingly clear that the dearth of investment in public goods during the last two decades is now constraining the expansion of agricultural intensification beyond the high-potential zones and export sectors" (Crawford et al., 2003).

Who should take action?

Nowadays, state involvement is generally smaller than and different from what many development economists argued for in the 1950s, but it is nonetheless critical. Rather than being directly involved in producing goods and services, governments have an important role in implementing constructive policies, creating a regulatory environment, developing institutions and providing public goods.

Governments have access to numerous policy levers. They set tariff rates, implement trade policies, and establish expenditure levels and exchange rate regimes. All these measures have impacts on national and international food availability. Actions to improve food security locally and nationally can have consequences for regional trading partners and, in some cases, international markets. Governments may not have the capacity to act effectively, however, and their interferences may fail, or weaken markets (Barrett, 2002). Budgetary shortfalls, lack of information or capacity, internal shortcomings and corruption may all limit the efficacy of government actions.

Although non-governmental organizations (NGOs), the private sector and other actors, such as United Nations agencies, may not have direct access to national policy levers, they can influence local or regional markets and advocate for government policy changes that may eventually enhance food security, such as lifting trade barriers. Beyond this, the private sector has applied innovations that have improved access to various markets and products (Mendoza and Thelen, 2008), such as contract farming (Chapter 5) and making durable and affordable mobile phones accessible to illiterate people.

The role of non-state actors in development has increased dramatically in recent decades as a result of globalization, technological innovations and political and economic liberalization. For example,

public–private partnerships have become increasingly prominent in recent years, partly because the markets-versus-governments divide has evolved into a markets-*and*-governments approach. Public–private partnerships have become particularly important in the fields of nutrition, microfinance and market information systems. Opportunities are plentiful.

Public–private partnerships recognize that many of the world's problems are too big, too complex and too interdependent for one actor to solve alone and that actors can be more effective when they join forces. Various forms and divisions of labour among partners exist regarding financing, risk sharing, standard setting and production. Critical factors for success include common objectives and indicators against which joint performance can be measured, clear roles, expectations, capacities and decision-making among all partners, and open communication and accountability.

Governments are still ultimately responsible for ensuring food security and the right to adequate food, but they can be more effective if they work with partners. Where national governments are unable or unwilling to ensure food security, the international community can assist.

How to take action in markets

Actions depend on the contexts and capacities of local markets and households. Policies may be relatively easy to define, but they can be executed in numerous ways, leading to very different outcomes. Some incentives are directly operationalized in food markets; others indirectly influence complementary markets and even non-market arenas. Direct actions that modify the supply and prices of food can address access, availability and utilization failures. Indirect actions in complementary markets include strengthening markets, adjusting trade policies, supporting access to agricultural inputs and improving purchasing power through minimum wage laws and access to credit. Such actions are "indirect" because their impact on food security tends to emerge through the improved performance of market forces. Safety net programmes to enhance food utilization/access are often important components of food security strategies and can be targeted to reach needy households.

A single action may have impacts on several aspects of food insecurity. In particular, actions to strengthen markets through improved infrastructure, institutions and competition may simultaneously improve access, availability and utilization. In other cases, several policy levers may need to be coordinated to nudge markets to respond and to ensure that households receive what they need.

To minimize the potential negative effects of government actions on the private sector, governments should follow a number of principles (see the box above).

When to take action in markets: improving information about food insecurity

In remote or poorly integrated areas, information about possible food availability shortfalls or weakening household access may be slow to reach outsiders. It is often necessary to improve the information flow to and from remote areas, to determine when and where to take action.

Journalism

It has been argued that famines do not occur in places with a functioning democracy and a free press (Sen, 1989). However, famines in Bihar, India in 1966–1967 and the Sudan in 1986–1989 occurred in areas referred to as having active democracies and a free press (Myhrvold-Hanssen,

2003). "Free press" is a relative concept, and the role of a free press is limited in nations and regions with low literacy rates (Baro and Deubel, 2006). Nevertheless, the media can play an important role in raising policy-makers' awareness of impending food security problems.

In Bangladesh, WFP currently trains journalists on food insecurity and advocates for them to take a proactive approach to reporting hunger. In general, the media is a last resort that springs into action when food insecurity and famines are imminent, often long after notice about impending dangers has been given; this indicates that early-warning systems (EWS) are an essential complement to journalism (Buchanan-Smith, 2002). Developing an effective EWS is particularly necessary in places that do not have a functioning free press (Barrett, 2002).

Early-warning systems

EWS can provide information on crop cover, climate and weather patterns, prices, terms of trade and disease. They can trigger food security responses before livelihoods are damaged and people become destitute. Data analysis can identify changes in food availability or access. Most data are open to different interpretations, however, and failure to deliver clear and consistent messages may delay timely responses (Buchanan-Smith, 2002).

Among the various reasons for governments to intervene in markets, the most important is to fight hunger and improve food security.

Table 9.1 – Consequences and issues of common food security actions

	Intended consequences	Issues to watch
Direct market actions: Price actions		
Stabilizing producer prices, including through state marketing boards	Encourages production by stabilizing prices and providing subsidized inputs or other assistance	• May discourage innovation and market development in the long run • Unpredictable measures could discourage the private sector in the short run • Marketing boards are often costly because of subsidies, inefficiencies and/or corruption • Does not encourage private sector involvement in stock holding
Stabilizing consumer prices, including through subsidies or ceilings	Keeps prices low and increases household access	• If prices are kept too low, may create disincentives to agricultural production in the longer run • Is costly, burdening government finances • When interventions are not targeted, households that do not need them receive lower prices
Posting prices	Keeps prices stable Provides market information and facilitates price discovery	• Requires a stable macroeconomic environment • Needs to reflect cost increases
Direct market actions: Non-price actions		
Decreasing staple food tariffs	Lowers the relative prices of imports and potentially increases their inflow	• If governments depend on such tariffs in their revenues, there may be fiscal losses • If rapid and substantial, can disrupt domestic production
Removing import barriers	Lowers the relative prices of imports and potentially increases their inflow	• If rapid and substantial, can disrupt domestic production
Imposing export restrictions	Keeps food supplies within the country	• In the longer run, may provide production disincentives, especially for export-dependent producers • Can be inefficient because not targeted • Has a negative impact on food security and availability in neighbouring and net food-importing countries • May be ineffective as a result of porous borders and market power
Releasing strategic grain reserves	Increases the supply of food when there are unforeseen shortfalls Can be used for targeted consumer subsidies	• Reserves may be costly to manage and maintain • May dampen private sector involvement in food marketing and storage
Releasing strategic cash reserves	If used to purchase and import food, increases supply	• Can be a fiscal burden to governments • Susceptible to corruption, especially in countries where governance is weak
Monetization	Selling food aid in local markets, increasing supply	• Can provide production disincentives locally as it may depress food prices • Timing might be wrong
Futures and options	Protect governments, importers and NGOs from future price changes Eliminate price risks and make decision-making more efficient	• A complex tool requiring extensive knowledge and effective institutions
Complementary market actions		
Enhancing public goods, including infrastructure and market information	Improves market functioning to encourage investment, production and access to markets	• Needs careful planning, coordination and implementation
Investing in agricultural research and extension	Encourages productivity and potential increase of supply	• Needs local capacity, particularly for adaptation to local conditions
Improving labour markets and creating employment	Increases household purchasing power	• Needs careful planning, coordination and implementation
Protecting productive assets	Keeps households, traders and producers from engaging in damaging coping strategies	• Best as part of a government social protection strategy

Table 9.1 – *continued*

	Intended consequences	Issues to watch
Improving access to finance: credit, savings and insurance	Improves access to food and allows recipients to buy inputs and invest in productive assets, or to avoid divesting productive assets	• Innovations must be adapted to local context • Poorest of the poor require special attention; a push for financial sustainability would exclude them
Insuring against weather variability	Mitigates weather-related risks associated with food production	• Insurance must be structured so that payouts are timely • Problems of moral hazard could result from inappropriate insurance policies
Subsidizing inputs	Encourages production	• Can be a fiscal burden to governments • Can discourage the private sector • Benefits may partly accrue to wealthier farmers • Once established, might be difficult to eliminate
Establishing producer marketing associations	Supports local producers, potentially leading to increases in production	• Could be difficult and costly to establish and maintain
Social protection instruments		
Establishing ration shops	Gives recipients access to staples from fixed-price shops	• If wrong commodities are subsidized, ration shops may attract non-poor instead of poor households • Administrative costs
Delivering food transfers, including fortified food products	Increases recipients' access to food	• If not properly timed and targeted, can have unintended negative effects on markets • Can be relatively expensive
Delivering cash transfers	Allows recipients to purchase necessary items	• Markets need to function • Requires implementation capacity • Can compromise food security and nutrition-related objectives • Susceptible to corruption • Security risk in unstable and insecure environments
Delivering vouchers	Allows recipients to redeem vouchers for food items at local shops	• Markets need to function • Requires implementation capacity • Involves suppliers' cooperation
Nutritional actions		
Fortifying foods	Provides necessary micronutrients	• Public–private partnerships are important • May need relatively large milling facilities and distribution systems to ensure sustainability • Foods being fortified should be consumed by the majority of the population
Providing specific fortified food products or supplements to address nutrition needs of target population	Provides necessary macro- and micronutrients	• Pilots for specific products are in progress e.g. corn–soya blend (CSB), iodized salt and vitamin A and D-fortified oil • Multi-nutrient supplements (micronutrient powders) are relatively new but promising
Vouchers and cash transfers	Can foster dietary diversity Provide market-based access to food	• Cash could compromise food security and nutrition-related objectives • Commodity-based vouchers could be linked to the provision of fortified foods (see Intermezzo 9.2) • Impact on long-term child nutrition and uptake of micronutrients needs further investigation
Providing nutrition education	Helps households make informed decisions about nutrition needs	• Takes a long time to change people's habits, especially those that are embedded in traditions and culture • Needs multiple contacts and persuasion methods
Labelling and quality assurance	Assures safety of foods and informs consumers	• Needs strong monitoring and enforcement

Availability

Availability interventions aim to increase the food supply through production or trade. Measures used to improve short-run supply availability to households include strategic releases of grain reserves, export bans, monetization of food aid, and decreasing tariffs to encourage traders to import. If food availability is increased enough to depress local prices, food access will improve. Actions in complementary markets, such as to increase access to credit and inputs and enhance agricultural extension, research and technology, can also improve productivity and longer-term availability. Interventions to improve market functioning, such as stabilizing macroeconomic conditions and investing in public goods – market structures, institutions, transportation and storage infrastructure – will enhance access and availability.

Access

Access interventions tend to focus on increasing income or removing non-market barriers. When low income leads to access-based food insecurity, access constraints may be ameliorated by enhancing productivity or asset creation, increasing income-earning opportunities, and safety net transfers. Some availability interventions that increase supply and decrease staple food prices improve purchasing power, and therefore access.

Utilization

When availability or access is hampered, utilization is almost certainly also adversely affected. Interventions may improve utilization by: (1) fortifying food with micronutrients or special blends of amino acids, vitamins, grains and pulses: (2) improving food quality through better storage or processing, or changing consumption and preparation patterns; and (3) protecting or improving non-food factors – water, sanitation, health – that have an impact on the body's ability to utilize food. Long-term investment in basic services, including access to health care for the poorest, can substantially enhance the effectiveness of food. Combining utilization interventions with safety net programmes focusing on access can be a cost-effective means of improving food security (Barrett, 2002).

Direct action in staple markets

To influence prices, governments can enact price floors to protect producers, establish price ceilings to shield consumers, and provide subsidies to decrease the purchase prices of food or inputs. Such interventions are often combined. Price floors are the minimum prices producers receive for their goods, price ceilings are the maximum amount paid by consumers, and subsidized prices are generally lower than market prices. Although these types of actions are still very common, their importance and effectiveness are disputed.

Price interventions

Some economists argue for removing all price controls and privatizing staple markets to encourage traders to "get prices right"; others claim that without adequate

Table 9.2 – Direct actions in staple markets through prices

	Effect on food security			Time frame between intervention and effect	
	Availability	Access	Utilization	Within 1 season	Longer than 1 season
Stabilizing producer prices, including through state marketing boards	X				X
Stabilizing consumer prices, including through subsidies or ceilings		X	X	X	
Posting prices		X		X	

Note: This table is a heuristic device. The information may not apply to all cases in all markets.

infrastructure and efficient institutions, traders will be unable to fill the gap left by liberalizing policies (Dorward and Kydd, 2004). The focus on getting prices right has generally been at the expense of other necessary interventions, such as infrastructure developments (Kelly, Adesina and Gordon, 2003).

It has been claimed that maintaining prices at 10 percent higher than world prices would allow importing countries to support domestic agricultural incomes, while minimizing the price impact on the poor (Timmer, 2002). However, price stabilization efforts, including defending a price band, are problematic. Determining the correct trend price can be difficult – particularly in the current environment of high food prices – and long-term stabilization can lead to rent seeking that discourages innovation and market development. Price stabilization schemes are "inherently devastating" for a government's budget and tend to damage the credit sectors (Timmer, 1989). Many short-run stabilization policies for fixing prices tend ultimately to clash with longer-term goals of market development (Byerlee, Jayne and Myers, 2006).

The Asian green revolution was successful partly because of grain price stabilization policies that encouraged the adoption of innovative techniques, while minimizing price variability (Cummings, Rashid and Gulati, 2006). Grain price stabilization can increase agricultural growth and overall economic development, given the low risk-bearing capacity and incomes of both farmers and consumers, but interventions should be limited to cases of market failure. Intervening in prices is less effective if it is not combined with measures to improve price stability, infrastructure, incentives and investment. Price stabilization policies are expensive and sticky; when conditions change, stabilization policies have to follow. Getting markets right should be the main task for any government interested in supporting food markets, so a government involved in grain support must constantly adapt its policies to changing marketing situations. They should consider revoking price stabilization policies, unless market failure is apparent and/or poverty has become endemic. Governments should intervene only when domestic prices move outside a band, using international prices as a

reference point (Timmer, 2002; Cummings, Rashid and Gulati, 2006). In the long run, stabilizing macroeconomic conditions, enhancing market information, reducing transaction costs, improving credit and insurance markets, and developing safety nets may be more beneficial than price stabilization schemes (Gabre-Madhin, 2005).

State-run marketing boards

State-run marketing boards implement a variety of policies, such as encouraging production increases through price supports, stabilizing prices by determining the prices received by producers and paid by consumers, establishing a supply for strategic reserves, and supplying inputs at subsidized prices. Marketing boards have long been associated with disincentives to the private sector and high costs, including for subsidies and through losses to inefficiency and corruption (Jayne and Jones, 1997).

During recent periods of structural adjustment, marketing boards in developing countries have often been reorganized to lessen their influence on markets, but many remain active, with varying degrees of involvement and success. For example, the Malawian Agricultural Development and Marketing Corporation (ADMARC) sells maize at subsidized prices. This is intended to smooth price volatility, but has had only relative success. Malawi's maize prices are generally more volatile than those in neighbouring South Africa, which is a regional exporter, or than the international Chicago Board of Trade prices (Chilowa, 1998; USAID, 2005; Dana, Gilbert and Shim, 2006).

Marketing boards may provide targeted support to producers of key staples, for example by guaranteeing minimum prices (Poulton et al., 2006b). Additional services or support are bundled with such price floors to help smallholders overcome coordination failures and to mitigate their risk. Other cost-effective price supports include announcing a pre-cultivation price, for instance based on export parity prices, with a final price determined after the harvest. A marketing board may also defend a large price band through purchases or sales (Byerlee, Jayne and Myers, 2006).

Posting prices

Posting prices at entrances to local markets, labelling products with maximum retail prices (MRPs), and broadcasting and/or printing local staple prices may reduce information asymmetries between consumers and sellers. A stable macroeconomic situation is necessary for successful maximum retail pricing policies, and MRPs should reflect market-related cost increases. They are therefore better suited to limiting price variability and fixing prices during festival or holiday periods, than to functioning as longer-term interventions. MRPs can be coordinated with labelling and quality control.

Direct price interventions are controversial; although their use has diminished over the years, they still feature in government efforts to maintain food security. The costs can be significant, however, and alternative measures might be more effective and less costly.

Regional trade and international commodity markets

It may take years of investment to strengthen markets and stabilize prices. Stocking policies and variable tariffs aim to stabilize prices and increase availability with as little distortion to the local economy as possible (Byerlee, Jayne and Myers, 2006). When world prices rise above acceptable domestic prices, governments may restrict trade or impose tariffs to minimize the harmful effects of short-term price fluctuations. Many countries used such measures to mitigate the impact of high food prices in 2007–2008. Policy-makers may also seek to smooth prices by influencing the supply. Buffer stocks create minimal disincentives, but are expensive to operate. Relying on international trade is often a preferred strategy, which tends to be cheaper than stocking strategies, as long as the international supply is adequate (Barrett, 2002).

Adjusting trade barriers and tariffs

If international staple prices drop rapidly, variable tariff rates can be increased to protect producer prices from a flood of cheap imports. However, raising tariffs can potentially hurt poor households' access to food. As food access declines because of rising import prices, variable tariffs can be adjusted downwards to lower the total price of imports, thereby making food imports more attractive to traders (Byerlee, Jayne and Myers, 2006).

If traders expect the government to change tariff rates during a supply shortage, they may wait until the government decreases rates before they import commodities. This may result in an undersupply of commodities and a possible worsening of price instability. A more effective way of improving food security might be to encourage small traders by simplifying customs and trade policies. Such measures can be effective, particularly if they are combined with investments and transparent government efforts to support marketing along the supply value chain (Jayne, Zulu and Nijhoff, 2006). Establishing clear rules regulating when and how governments intervene may

Table 9.3 – Direct actions in staple markets through non-price measures

	Effect on food security			Time frame between intervention and effect	
	Availability	Access	Utilization	Within 1 season	Longer than 1 season
Decreasing staple food tariffs	✗	✗		✗	
Removing import barriers	✗			✗	
Imposing export restrictions	✗			✗	
Releasing strategic grain reserves	✗			✗	
Releasing strategic cash reserves	✗			✗	
Monetization	✗	✗		✗	
Futures and options	✗	✗			✗

prevent negative reactions from the private sector. Removing restrictions on movements of grain both within a country and across borders can encourage market development and stabilize prices (Byerlee, Jayne and Myers, 2006).

By mid-2008, high food prices had induced about 40 countries to impose export restrictions. Countries generally introduce such measures when they face food deficits. Export controls may increase supply in the short run, but they are inefficient because they are not targeted and in the long run they tend to have disincentive effects on producers and traders, and may encourage traders to move food illegally to neighbouring countries and charge higher prices.

Following the 2006/2007 growing season, fertilizer subsidies and ideal growing conditions in Malawi generated a 73 percent increase in output compared with the previous five-year average. The government removed export restrictions so traders could export maize to Zimbabwe. However, 34 percent of the population remained malnourished, suggesting that food insecurity in Malawi extends beyond availability and that access is of critical importance. Improved access might lower the incentives to export (WFP, 2007c).

Strategic reserves

Strategically storing and releasing stocked food or cash for purchases may increase food availability and access. Releasing stored food for sale increases availability, and may smooth supply and stabilize prices. If the food is targeted to poorer households, or is of a quality that wealthy people will avoid, the release of stored food may also increase access. Strategic grain reserves can be especially useful in areas facing regular seasonal shortfalls. In areas prone to recurring food security crises, aid agencies and governments may develop stocking strategies. One example of this is the Ethiopian Emergency Food Security Reserve (EFSR), which is financed by international donors and managed by a committee of government officials and donors (Buchanan-Smith, 2002). Having readily available surplus food reduces response lags; depending on the local marketing context and household needs assessments, the food can be

released to the market or distributed directly to targeted households. A strategic reserve programme may support producer prices by restocking reserves when prices are seasonally low.

Holding strategic stocks can be expensive and is less necessary when markets are open to trade and imports are easily accessible, which was not always the case during the food crisis in 2008 (Byerlee, Jayne and Myers, 2006). A government with strategic cash reserves can procure stocks, either independently or through private trader tenders. The latter allow governments to capture some of the efficiency of, and provide incentives to, private traders. If a government intends to maintain an EFSR, it should engage in additional storage only if it faces lower purchasing, transportation and delivery costs than private traders (Dana, Gilbert and Shim, 2006). Government storage may crowd out private sector storage and discourage traders from storing. Releasing stocks may also be politicized and dissuade importers and local traders from bringing food to shortage areas, potentially harming longer-run supply chains (Dana, Gilbert and Shim, 2006). Discussions with traders about the timing and amounts of stock sales or transfers can help them to plan so they avoid importing food at a loss. In some cases, releasing stocks to stabilize prices can end speculative hoarding by traders (Ravallion, 1997).

Because of the costs and the potential negative effects on the private sector, reserves were often regarded as less attractive than trade. High food prices have put reserves back into focus, however, as several countries faced difficulties or very high costs when importing food in 2008. Among several proposals, is a scheme for creating a minimum physical reserve for humanitarian assistance, and a virtual reserve and intervention mechanisms to calm markets under speculative stress (von Braun and Torero, 2008). A virtual reserve is a set of commitments to supply funds for buying grains on futures markets at prices lower than spot prices, thus increasing the supply of future sales and lowering spot prices when grain might be needed to avert a crisis similar to that of 2007–2008. These proposals require careful analysis and comparisons with alternatives. For example, stronger coordination and agreements among importers and exporters and averting export restrictions can also play important roles in avoiding the shortages that emerged in 2007–2008.

Monetization

When food availability is poor and prices high, the sale of food aid can relieve market pressure and lower consumer prices. When food aid is monetized in places with adequate food supplies, the potential decrease in prices can harm local producers (Faminow, 1995; Clay, Dhiri and Benson, 1996). The impact of monetized aid on local market prices is determined by several factors, including elasticities of supply and demand, the relative quantity of monetized aid, local storage capacity, trade policies, import parity prices and the economies of neighbouring countries.

Selling small quantities of food aid to village-based traders can support local markets and help traders develop marketing chains (Abdulai, Barrett and Hazell, 2004), but monetization often does not benefit the poorest of the poor. If food security deteriorates rapidly, transoceanic food aid may arrive too late, such as during harvest time (Barrett and Maxwell, 2005). Monetization may not be an effective short-run intervention unless food aid is stored nearby, or NGOs and governments react quickly to early warnings.

In an interesting recent innovation implemented in Zimbabwe since 2003, food aid is sold through market channels, but targeted to low-income urban neighbourhoods using commercial millers. The project was funded by the US Agency for International Development (USAID), with programme staff estimating an affordable price and collaborating with millers to sell packages of milled sorghum.

Futures and options

The trading of futures and options by governments and NGOs may protect them from future price risks. Such contracts are particularly useful where seasonal shortages and rising prices are fairly regular. Futures and options are most effective if combined with access-based safety net programmes, as it is unlikely that organizations or governments will be able to trade futures and options in quantities sufficient to improve population-wide food availability. However, hedging does not protect against price changes related to transportation, storage or financing costs, which may amount to a large portion of total costs.

Trading futures and options requires technical knowledge, institutions, access to credit, timely information and adequate financial resources. Most traders in developing country markets are excluded from such financial instruments. One solution could be to establish a public agency that handles futures and options. If such an agency relies heavily on futures and options, private traders will be crowded out, but a public agency could facilitate the use of financial instruments by larger traders, or bundle small producer

---

Future contracts in Malawi

In Malawi, a drought-related production shortfall during the 2004/2005 season culminated in rising prices and general food insecurity, which at its peak made nearly 5 million people food-insecure. Early in 2005, the Government of Malawi, with technical support from the World Bank, entered into a six-month option contract that fixed the price for 60,000 metric tons (MT) of maize from South Africa (Slater and Dana, 2006). The cost of the option was a premium based on the duration of the contract, the price differential and market vulnerability. If prices were below the price stipulated in the option, or if private traders and donors covered the expected food gap, the Government of Malawi could choose not to exercise the option (Slater and Dana, 2006). Maize prices increased by 37 percent in the months following the poor spring harvest, and the government marketing board instituted rationing of its subsidized stored maize (USAID, 2005). The government exercised its option at the end of 2005, using the 60,000 MT of grain to improve food access for a targeted population. It also made its call option public, ensuring that traders could anticipate government interventions. This is a promising method of stabilizing prices, but alone it was not enough to keep maize prices within reach of poor households, although maize remained available in local markets. In early 2006, global acute malnutrition rates exceeded 10 percent in three districts.

Source: USAID, 2006b

contracts for minimum prices (Byerlee, Jayne and Myers, 2006).

Some NGOs have successfully used forward contracting to lock in the purchase price of food baskets. For example, the Cooperative for Assistance and Relief Everywhere (CARE)-Zimbabwe contracted six months of food basket delivery with traders who had ties to South African wholesalers and paid in a stable currency (the South African rand). The traders purchased food from Zimbabwe or South Africa, or engaged in forward contracting, depending on their assessment and expectations of regional market prices (Steve Gwynne-Vaughn, personal communication).

Currently, the use of trade policy tools has gained prominence because of high food prices; however, such policies can be problematic because they can discourage trade and production and could have negative effects on other countries.

Augmenting complementary markets and market access

Direct interventions in food markets risk failure if the complementary markets to which they are linked are underdeveloped. When this is the case, market interventions may have little impact on income redistribution and will support producer prices only modestly (Coxhead, 2000). Food availability and access are enhanced by low transaction costs, improved income, and interventions in public goods, market performance and credit markets. Making complementary markets work in relation to the staple

market may support, or replace, direct interventions. In several cases, interventions in complementary markets are more effective than those made directly in food markets.

Labour markets and employment

Minimum wage legislation can boost incomes for those formal sector workers whose wages are increased up to the minimum. However, minimum wage legislation may also drive employment out of the formal economy and into the informal sector, particularly in countries with weak institutional infrastructure for monitoring employment regulations. In addition, many workers are employed outside the formal wage sector, and it is difficult to encompass small producers in minimum wage legislation. The introduction of minimum wages in Brazil has so far had no adverse impacts on the formal or informal employment sectors, and several positive spill-over effects have been observed, but the poorest Brazilian workers are employed in the informal sector and do not reap the benefits of a minimum wage (Lemos, 2006).

Food- or cash-for-work programmes can play an important role in offering employment, providing social protection and creating assets, such as roads, irrigation systems and health and education facilities (Hoddinott, 2008). Examples include Ethiopia's Productive Safety Net Programme (PSNP) and India's employment guarantee scheme. Communities are increasingly involved in decision-making about the construction and maintenance of the assets. By setting wages below the market rate, beneficiaries are often self-targeted.

Table 9.4 – Actions in complementary markets

	Effect on food security			Time frame between intervention and effect	
	Availability	Access	Utilization	Within 1 season	Longer than 1 season
Improving labour markets		✗			✗
Protecting productive assets	✗	✗		✗	✗
Delivering credit	✗	✗		✗	
Insuring against weather	✗	✗			✗

Protecting productive assets

Protecting productive assets may enhance longer-term food security. Such measures can be established either through the market, such as insurance or credit interventions, or through safety net interventions. Pastoralists can be protected from food insecurity by livestock support programmes, such as subsidized transportation to markets and offtake programmes (Alderman and Haque, 2006), but this type of programming is best done on a small scale (Jaspars, 2006). Land is generally a household's most valuable productive asset, and securing land tenure may encourage landholders to invest in their land. However, simply securing land titles or making land ineligible for redistribution has not improved productivity or conservation (Hagos and Holden, 2006).

Financial services

Obtaining credit through traditional banking channels is seldom an option for poor people. Rather than employing price stabilization policies, it may be more worthwhile to intervene in credit-constrained or uninsured markets and to encourage innovation (Myers, 2006). Actions to improve access to credit can occur at any point of the food value chain – from input traders to producers, wholesalers, importers and households – and include a variety of programmes, from microcredit to granting larger loans to producers' associations. These may help processors and producers to purchase inputs and encourage additional traders to enter the local or import market, improving local market competition and availability.

A common intervention is the extension of credit to households. Households that use credit for consumption may be able to avoid distress sales of productive assets – loss of assets during periods of food insecurity leaves households vulnerable to future food insecurity. However, when credit is used for consumption rather than investment in productive assets, repayment may be difficult.

There is mounting evidence that many government-run credit programmes are not cost-efficient mechanisms for developing input markets (Kelly, Adesina and Gordon, 2003). In sub-Saharan Africa, such programmes often provide credit below market rates, but have tended to

be plagued by low repayment rates and windfall profit-seeking activity (Kelly, Adesina and Gordon, 2003). Part of the success of Ethiopia's Participatory Agricultural Development and Extension Training Service (PADETS), which includes government-guaranteed credit, is due to its strong efforts to encourage repayment (Kelly, Adesina and Gordon, 2003).

Other financial services, such as savings and insurance, are often even more important for the hungry poor than credit, which inevitably creates debt. During a shock, access to financial services can be very important for the hungry poor. Having savings or a micro-insurance policy can make a valuable difference when drought or flood reduces the crop, a cow dies or a child becomes sick and needs medical attention. For example, customers with a *Jijenge* savings account at Kenya's Equity Bank define the timing for deposits and withdrawals, and have access to an emergency loan of up to 90 percent of the value saved (Mendoza and Thelen, 2008).

Microfinance has expanded considerably over recent decades, and new and innovative schemes are emerging, some linking microfinance initiatives to the formal finance sector. Among the most promising are schemes using mobile telephones to transfer money. Nevertheless, microfinance remains largely dependent on subsidies and hundreds of millions of hungry poor still lack access to a safe place to put money away for emergencies.

Subsidized agricultural inputs

Subsidizing such inputs as fuel, fertilizer and seed may encourage producers to adopt productivity-enhancing technologies. Government policies to subsidize inputs and credit in sub-Saharan Africa have tended to encourage production, but have often failed to address underlying dysfunctions of local input markets, resulting in financially unsustainable programming (Kelly, Adesina and Gordon, 2003). Input interventions are most successful when they are incorporated into strategies addressing structural causes of market failure, such as lack of public goods and failing institutional mechanisms. During the Asian green revolution, subsidized inputs were often combined with other interventions, such as food aid distribution,

Input subsidies in Malawi: a success against all odds?

After the 2005 harvest in Malawi – the worst in a decade – the government reinstated its fertilizer subsidies, despite the scepticism of major donors.

The land of many smallholders has severely depleted soil because the smallholders are too poor to buy fertilizers. "For more than half of the smallholder population, commercial fertilizer purchases in adequate quantities are unaffordable, leaving many farmers locked into impoverished livelihoods based on low-productivity maize cultivation and casual labouring" (SOAS, 2008).

The Agricultural Input Subsidy Programme (AISP) aimed to improve smallholder productivity and cash crop production, and reduce vulnerability to food insecurity and hunger. About 2 million households were able to buy fertilizer at the subsidized price of US$7 per 50 kg bag – less than a third of the market price (DFID, 2007).

Subsidies for fertilizers and seeds helped farmers to increase yields. Maize production increased from 1.2 million MT in 2005 to 1.6 million MT in 2006. As a result, Malawi was able to donate food to Lesotho and export to neighbouring countries, including Zimbabwe (Masine, 2008).

Regarding the programme's cost-efficiency, the School of Oriental and African Studies (SOAS, 2008) estimated the cost–benefit ratio at between 0.76 and 1.36, demonstrating that with good management the programme can yield favourable economic returns. Moreover, "implementation of the programme does not appear to have had adverse effects on macroeconomic stability or on budgetary allocations to other sectors" (SOAS, 2008). However, the subsidies reduced commercial purchases by 30–40 percent. Special attention should be given to improving the effectiveness and costs of the programme, which risks developing into an unsustainable drain on resources, with negative effects on growth, food security and poverty (SOAS, 2008). The World Bank points out that controlling the efficiency of the subsidies is crucial given the trade-offs involved. For example, "money allocated to an extra bag of fertilizer may be money taken away from the vaccination of chickens. Or this may reduce the funds available for developing a new, disease-resistant, bean variety. Or the subsidies may reduce the resources necessary to build rural roads in order to lower the costs of future agricultural inputs" (World Bank, 2007b). Subsidies can be difficult to retarget or eliminate because they create politically significant constituencies which demand continuing payouts.

Higher productivity had positive effects on the poor, resulting in enhanced access to food due to greater availability and lower prices (DFID, 2007). The successful Malawian experience emphasizes agriculture's crucial role in alleviating poverty in Africa, and the importance of public investments in the basics of a farm economy: fertilizers, improved seed, farmer education, credit and agricultural research.

infrastructure investments and research and development to increase production (Crawford et al., 2003).

Producers' marketing associations and cooperatives

Producers' marketing associations encourage their members to demand better prices from traders and processors, and strive to decrease the costs of credit and input purchases. They can also engage in collective forward contracting. Members of marketing associations generally share not only marketing information, but also data on weather changes and extension services. These benefits improve market functioning and producer incentives, potentially leading to enhanced productivity. Marketing associations tend to be more effective when they facilitate marketing, rather than establishing parallel market channels (Jayne and Jones, 1997). Producers' marketing associations can be effective in increasing the bargaining power of small producers, who often face collusive behaviour along the supply chain and information asymmetries. WFP's P4P initiative seeks to address some of these problems, especially in areas where smallholder farmers are isolated from main marketing channels and thus face greater risks of facing collusive behaviour (Intermezzo 5.1). However, establishing and maintaining marketing associations can be resource intensive, for example, because of capacity development needs (World Bank, 2007c).

In many situations, interventions in complementary markets are more effective than those in food markets, and are essential to improving the effectiveness of intervention in food markets.

Seed fairs

Seed fairs bring beneficiaries and sellers together so that beneficiaries can choose from different seed varieties and other inputs (Jaspars, 2006). During emergencies, seeds and tools are common input interventions; donors tend to assume that producers need inputs after an emergency, but this is not always correct (Kelly, Adesina and Gordon, 2003; Levine and Chastre, 2004). A thorough needs assessment must be carried out before a seed fair is established (The Sphere Project, 2004). Providing inputs at subsidized rates, or for free, can harm local input traders and longer-run market recovery, when delivery-flooded markets cease to face input shortages and remain weak or non-functioning. When inputs are necessary, seed fairs can be particularly successful in encouraging traders to operate in locations with thin or non-existent markets, potentially developing market linkages (Jaspars, 2006). Providing choice is generally preferable to distributing seed baskets that may not reflect producers' preferences or capabilities. Voucher distribution, sometimes in conjunction with seed fairs, can also support local market recovery by providing flexibility.

Social protection and safety net interventions

Social protection is becoming a central pillar of poverty reduction strategies, and offers a framework for better bridging among development and humanitarian policies and interventions. As mentioned in Chapter 7, however, countries' capacity to institutionalize, sustain and implement social protection programmes varies considerably (WFP, 2004; Gentilini, 2009).

In general, social protection is a broader concept than safety nets, and includes national measures to manage vulnerability, reduce poverty and food insecurity and enhance social inclusion (Devereux and Sabates-Wheeler, 2004). Such measures include transfers of cash, food or vouchers (safety net transfers); risk management options for the poor, such as index-based weather or price insurance; and access to basic social services (World Bank, 2001; DFID, 2005b).

The appropriateness of each social protection intervention depends on context-specific factors, such as programme objectives, market functioning, implementation capacities, cost efficiency and beneficiaries' preferences (Intermezzo 9.2).

Subsidies and ration shops

Ration shops, also called fair-price shops, sell food at fixed or subsidized prices. They were particularly popular in several developing countries during the 1980s (Pinstrup-Andersen, 1988). Subsidies can be either universal or targeted. In the former, higher-income households tend to benefit relatively more, so subsidies should be targeted when possible and

feasible (Alderman, 2002). By using a ration card system, these shops generally impose limits on the amount a household or individual can purchase, so tend to affect prices less than untargeted subsidies do.

Food transfers

Food transfers provide people with internationally or locally procured food commodities, which often include fortified nutritious foods. As with vouchers and cash transfers, food transfers can be distributed to beneficiaries either unconditionally or conditionally. In unconditional transfers, food is provided as a hand-out without any reciprocal behaviour or activity on the part of beneficiaries. The provision of conditional transfers is linked to a specific activity, such as attending schools or health clinics, or undertaking work. Although the comparative impacts of conditional and unconditional transfers are debated (de Brauw and Hoddinott, 2008), their effectiveness depends on programme objectives and administrative capacities on the ground, such as delivery and monitoring capacity (Schubert and Slater, 2006; Britto, 2008).

The market impact of food, cash and voucher transfers hinges on targeting and timing. Poorly targeted transfers are more likely to distort markets. The timing, location, volume and frequency of distributions all affect the extent of transfers' impact on markets (Barrett, 2002).

Recent reviews of food transfers' possible distortion of market prices, food production and labour supply revealed that the supposed disincentive effects tend to vanish when controlling for household characteristics, such as age, sex and education of head, landholdings, size and location (Abdulai, Barrett and Hoddinott, 2005; Barrett and Maxwell, 2005; Barrett, 2006). This does not mean that food transfers cannot have negative effects, but rather that the effects have to be systematically verified and not based on anecdotes (Levinsohn and McMillan, 2005; Maunder, 2006).

Cash transfers

Cash transfers are used increasingly to respond to acute needs during emergencies and to address chronic and structural food insecurity (Harvey, 2007). Cash enables recipients to choose the food they prefer or need the most. Most cash programmes in emergencies, for example those following the 2004 tsunami, have been implemented on a relatively small scale and for short durations (Harvey and Adams, 2007). In transition or more stable situations, cash transfers have been implemented on a wider scale, especially as part of social protection systems in contexts where implementation capacities were adequate, such as in Brazil, Mexico, South Africa and Turkey.

Cash transfers are increasingly used to link food-insecure beneficiaries more directly to markets. For example, in Ethiopia cash transfers are a core component of the PSNP, and reach about half of the programme's 8.3 million beneficiaries in four regions. After initial administrative and market-related difficulties, cash transfers have enhanced people's own consumption and improved local economic conditions through spill-over effects (Devereux, 2007a).

Vouchers

Vouchers can be used to purchase items for a certain value or from a set of goods at local shops. Participating shopkeepers redeem the vouchers for cash from the organizing agency or selected banks. As with cash, vouchers can stimulate local markets and may support local traders and producers (Jaspars, 2006). Vouchers may be better suited to pursuing nutrition-related objectives than cash transfers are, and may also be less susceptible to leakages and security issues (Harvey, 2005). However, vouchers require more resources and control mechanisms than do cash and food transfers (Brinkman and Gentilini, 2008).

Weather insurance

In most countries, weather insurance is a relatively new product (Intermezzo 9.1) that may mitigate the effects of weather-related price instability and constitute an important component of social protection programmes for food producers. When bundled with credit, insurance for producers may decrease the likelihood of default by covering losses due to adverse weather. To develop weather insurance effectively, public investment and institutional support are necessary (Byerlee, Jayne and Myers, 2006). In 2005, the pilot phase of a weather insurance programme was initiated in Mali. Credit agencies, previously unwilling to lend to smallholders owing to the high correlation between drought and defaults, made credit available to the producers who purchased weather insurance. The index-based weather insurance pays out when rain is insufficient, mitigating the risks faced by both producers and credit providers (USAID, 2006a).

The introduction and expansion of social protection systems are key to addressing food insecurity in both emergency and development situations. However, countries' capacities to set up, scale up and sustain these systems vary considerably, and have implications on the type of social protection instruments provided. Depending on local contexts, these can include food, voucher and cash transfers and insurance mechanisms.

Interventions to improve nutrition

When food availability or access is hampered, food utilization is almost certain to suffer. Incorporating nutrition interventions into safety net programmes is usually very cost-effective, as nutrition interventions have among the highest benefit–cost ratios of any development intervention (Behrman, Alderman and Hoddinott, 2004). Food can be fortified with added micronutrients or special blends of amino acids, vitamins, grains and pulses. Food quality may also be improved through better storage or processing and the introduction of new consumption and preparation patterns. Protecting and improving non-food factors that have an impact on the body's ability to utilize

Micronutrient powders

Micronutrient powders, also known as sprinkles, are sachets of vitamins and trace minerals, which generally include iron, vitamin A and iodine, and other elements depending on local needs. Sprinkles can be designed to meet the needs of children or other populations who may have needs beyond what is available locally or through fortified foods. Sprinkles are a home fortification product; households sprinkle or mix the contents of a sachet with food after cooking. "Cost depends on the quantity of sachets ordered, the composition of the mixture, and the site of production, but generally runs between 1.5 and 3.5 cents per sachet. In addition to their beneficial effects and high impact on health and nutritional status, the sachets are lightweight for easy commodity transportation and distribution and thus offer a cost-effective and operationally feasible approach to deliver micronutrient to vulnerable children" (Zlotkin, 2007). In addition to children and mothers, households with people living with HIV/AIDS are potential beneficiaries of fortified foods. Providing a sprinkle-type fortificant as part of HIV/AIDS "cocktails" of medications could improve long-term health. Sprinkles are potentially easier and more cost-effective to transport and distribute than fortified food and could be bundled with cash, vouchers, medicine or food transfers. They have been successful in non-market interventions, such as a school feeding programme in post-tsunami Indonesia and integrated health programmes in Mongolia (de Pee, 2005; Zlotkin and Tondeur, 2006). A Bangladeshi NGO piloted sprinkles through its ongoing Female Community Health Worker Programme. Most care givers preferred purchasing sprinkles at their own pharmacies to having them delivered by the NGO (Zlotkin et al., 2005), which suggests that sprinkles could make a successful transition to market-based delivery.

food, such as water, sanitation and health, may also enhance food utility. Long-term investments in basic services, including access to health care, also improve the effectiveness of food intake (Barrett, 2002).

Utilization efforts are increasingly incorporated into access programming, and are delivered through non-market public programming, rather than as services or products provided by market forces. The public goods nature of some utilization interventions, such as providing clean water and sanitation, means that government and private organizations may be more effective than market mechanisms. Other non-food factors with impacts on food utilization – nutrition education, school feeding programmes, labelling the nutrient content of foods, and mandatory food fortification, including fortifying salt with iodine – are also generally implemented by government agencies, NGOs or through partnerships.

Fortification, supplementation and micronutrient powders

Micronutrient deficiencies are due to inadequate intake of minerals and vitamins, such as iron, iodine and vitamins A, C and D, and may differ depending on local needs (Barrett, 2002). Micronutrient deficiencies can be reduced through fortification, supplementary feeding (food transfers), supplements of specific nutrients such as vitamin A capsules or micronutrient powders, and own production of nutritious food such as vegetables. Mandating fortification, combined with technical support to processors, is a relatively cost-effective response to micronutrient deficiencies (Barrett, 2002). For example, in 1990, only 20 percent of the world's population had access to iodized salt (UNICEF, 2003), compared with approximately 70 percent today. In nations with mandatory iodization of salt, endemic goitre has been controlled and the incidence of iodine deficiency-related mental retardation and cretinism has decreased globally. When a sub-population is at risk of anaemia – particularly pregnant and lactating women – governments may combine targeted social marketing or nutrition education with support to the production of fortified foods.

Market interventions to improve nutrition

Currently, fortificants and fortified foods are rarely available in developing country markets. Governments and NGOs coordinate most nutrition efforts, partly because consumers do not demand information about nutrition and micronutrients, but opportunities are opening up for market-based interventions. For example, Danone, a French food producer, and Grameen, a Bangladeshi NGO, are collaborating to make a micronutrient-fortified dairy product available at rural shops and markets throughout Bangladesh.

The product is currently marketed towards Bangladeshi children. Grameen Danone Foods provides financing and technical expertise to producers, processors, sellers and distributors.

Education

Education may improve household nutrition, and can either substitute or complement other utilization interventions. Improvements to women's education levels have been associated with a 43 percent decline in child malnutrition (Smith and Haddad, 2000). Nutrition education has been linked to increased caloric and micronutrient consumption (Barrett, 2002), and mothers' nutrition education appears to be more strongly linked to improved child micronutrient outcomes than their general education is (Block et al., 2004). Nevertheless, findings from Honduras and Nicaragua suggest that direct nutrition/health interventions may have less impact than income in determining stunting levels among children (Block et al., 2004).

Labelling and quality assurance

Labelling may alert local populations about key ingredients and nutrients. Labelling interventions are usually combined with the posting of maximum retail prices, food fortification and quality assurances. Such interventions require institutional capacity to guarantee the validity of nutrition information. Labelling requirements may create additional costs to consumers and may not be particularly effective in low-literacy countries.

Labelling may be helpful in creating incentives for market agents to market safe foods. In Bangladesh, the Dhaka City Corporation has created a system of mobile courts run by food and sanitation officers. The courts arrive unannounced at markets, and test products for illegal chemicals, adulterations and unhygienic conditions. They impound any tainted products and hand down fines or sentences (Khan and Khandker, 2006). Media coverage of such raids is encouraging consumer safety by alerting consumers to various signs of adulteration.

Utilization of and access to proper nutrients go beyond the market mechanism. Public action is often needed to supplement the market and ensure access to nutritious food. Public–private partnerships are very prominent in this area.

Conclusion

Social protection and market support policies to shore up food security

Markets provide opportunities to increase well-being. Historically, markets and trade are often the engine of wealth creation, but this process is neither automatic, nor quick, nor necessarily inclusive. Public interventions to support markets and provide social protection are not mutually exclusive. On the contrary, they can represent complementary components of food security strategies designed to make markets work better for the poor.

Policy-makers can strengthen or correct markets in a number of ways. They can use solid institutions and price and non-price interventions to make markets more effective, and can supplement markets with social protection systems. The appropriateness of such social protection interventions as food, cash transfers or insurance options hinges on context-specific factors.

Intermezzo 9.1: WFP and Ethiopia's drought insurance

In 2005, the Government of Ethiopia initiated the Productive Safety Net Programme (PSNP) as its primary instrument for addressing food insecurity, with a focus on building productive community assets and protecting assets during shocks. PSNP has shifted the emphasis from emergency humanitarian aid to long-term initiatives that address major underlying causes of food insecurity.

In this context, in 2006, WFP entered into a humanitarian aid weather insurance contract with a leading European reinsurer, Paris Re. The contract provided contingency funding for up to 62,000 vulnerable households in case of extreme drought during Ethiopia's 2006 agricultural season. Although there was no payout because rainfall was adequate, the pilot demonstrated the feasibility of using market mechanisms to finance drought risk in a least developed country; developed objective, timely and accurate indicators for triggering drought assistance; and put government contingency plans in place for earlier response to shocks.

In 2007, WFP, the World Bank and the Government of Ethiopia began to develop a broader risk management framework for droughts and floods in the context of PSNP. Although PSNP delivers timely livelihood protection to the chronically food-insecure, the transiently food-insecure remain subject to the vagaries of the emergency relief system. The second phase of PSNP (2008–2010) includes a drought risk financing component, clearer contingency planning, capacity building and more robust early-warning systems. It will facilitate early and predictable disbursements of resources for less predictable shocks. Donors are interested in scaling up this facility beyond the PSNP areas.

Index-based financing instruments – be they contingent grants, loans or risk transfer tools – are designed to relate an index, based on objective indicators that capture a systemic risk such as drought, to financing needs. Indices are monitored during a given period, and if certain index trigger levels are reached, payouts are made. Because payouts are settled on an objective index representing a geographic area affected by the risk, these mechanisms have fewer transaction costs and avoid some of the operational problems associated with traditional insurance approaches based on loss assessment of individuals.

Index-based risk financing tools are an innovative and potentially effective way of assisting poor people – and those who support them – whose livelihoods are threatened by extreme weather conditions and natural disasters. Experience of index-based risk transfer products in developing countries is increasing, and interest in these risk management solutions growing.

It is expected that climate change will lead to a rise in weather-related disasters, meaning that premiums for index-based risk transfer tools will go up, assuming all other factors remain constant. However, the increase in cost may be offset by climate adaptation measures and strategies.

Intermezzo 9.2: Unbundling the cash versus food debate

The cash versus food debate revolves around the identification and implementation of instruments such as cash, vouchers and in-kind food transfers to support households affected by food insecurity.

Cash transfer programmes provide people with money; vouchers provide coupons for purchasing a fixed quantity or value of food in selected stores. Food transfer programmes provide people with imported or locally purchased food commodities.

The comparative advantages and limitations of each option – and therefore their appropriateness and feasibility – are determined by five context-specific factors: (1) programme objectives; (2) market conditions; (3) implementation capacities; (4) cost efficiency; and (5) beneficiaries' preferences (Gentilini, 2007).

When the objective is to increase people's purchasing power, economic theory suggests that cash is more appropriate because consumers' utility increases as a result of more choice and fungibility. When the objective is to increase food consumption, microeconomic theory suggests that effectiveness depends on the size of the transfer. If an in-kind food transfer is infra-marginal, i.e. less than a household would have consumed without the transfer, cash and in-kind food transfers are economically equivalent. If the in-kind food transfer is extra-marginal, i.e. more than a household would have consumed without the transfer, food is more effective than cash.

A crucial factor in deciding the appropriateness of transfers is an understanding of whether the market functions or not. When markets work poorly, because of structural constraints or temporary disruptions in the food supply system, food transfers may be the appropriate response. In such situations, vouchers and cash transfers are likely to make beneficiaries bear the risk of supply failures, and might generate inflationary effects. When markets are functioning properly, cash and vouchers may be more appropriate than food transfers.

Even when food is available and markets are functioning, traders may adopt speculative practices to gain extra profits, for example through strategic storage or delay in food delivery. Perfect markets do not exist, and a pragmatic, localized approach has to be applied to identify market imperfections. There is a need to understand the extent to which markets work for the poor, particularly when effective demand is lacking (Donovan et al., 2006).

In general, evaluations of market performance revolve more around targeting issues, such as the timing, place and recipients of assistance, than around the type of transfer provided (Barrett, 2002, 2006). Emerging evidence shows that multipliers could be created with both cash and food transfers, even in emergencies or ultra-poor contexts if well targeted (Ahmed et al., 2007; Davies and Davey, 2008).

To maximize impact, it is important to consider how transfers are provided, especially their size, frequency and predictability (Devereux and Sabates-Wheeler, 2007).

Adequate and accessible financial partner institutions and appropriate monitoring, reporting and control systems are essential for effective and efficient voucher and cash transfer programming. Such conditions are not always present in the most food-insecure, unstable or marginalized contexts.

When markets work well and implementation capacities are adequate, vouchers and cash are generally more cost-efficient than food aid. When these conditions are not in place, however, voucher and cash transfers may be less effective and efficient than food transfers (Harvey and Savage, 2006). All the costs – including those for set up, monitoring and administration, which can be larger for voucher and cash programmes – have to be taken into account.

Although it is difficult to generalize about which transfers people prefer, some general patterns can be discerned. Preferences for cash, vouchers or food aid tend to vary by location, season and gender. Households living far from markets often prefer food transfers, while those living close to markets prefer vouchers and cash transfers. There are indications that people prefer food transfers during the lean season, owing to higher food prices, while cash is often preferred around the harvest period. Gender also matters, as women tend to prefer food, which they are more likely to control, while men may prefer cash transfers (WFP, 2006d).

Many hungry households are stuck in a hunger–poverty trap. Poor people do not eat well. They do not get enough nutrients, so their health, education and productivity suffer. Consequently, they remain poor and hungry.

Markets create remarkable opportunities, but many of the hungry poor cannot benefit from them. First, stuck in the hunger–poverty trap, their productivity is too low, their skills too few, their health too precarious and their access to assets, inputs and finance too limited. Second, they are too far from markets and do not have enough information about them; participation in markets is often too costly for the hungry poor. Third, they live on the edge, and are risk-averse, to avoid falling deeper into hunger and poverty. They stick to proven but low-income activities and do not adopt new, but risky, technologies; participation in markets is often too risky for the hungry poor.

In spite of their limited capabilities to benefit from market opportunities, the hungry poor depend on markets – to buy food, sell their produce or earn extra income. Whether the hungry poor can buy enough nutritious food to live healthy and productive lives depends partly on markets.

Markets are essential in the fight against hunger. Alone, they are unlikely to be able to pull people out of the hunger–poverty trap, but they can assist and facilitate through incentives. Markets enable the hungry poor to get higher prices for their products and better wages for their labour, but complementary actions are required, for example, in nutrition, technology, training and social protection. Markets can also exacerbate hunger and worsen the nutrition status, as the current situation of high food prices makes evident.

Markets can help or hurt the hungry poor. To find the right balance between strengthened markets and government actions, three principles could be followed:

1 Do no harm; avoid measures that may increase market volatility, barriers to trade or excessive market power for a few traders.

2 Enhance the positive aspects; improve market functioning to increase the hungry poor's access to markets, inputs, finance and market information, for example through policies, institutions and infrastructure.

3 Reduce, protect from or compensate for the negative aspects; markets can fail, they can be volatile and they can produce socially unacceptable outcomes.

The global food and financial crises have created a sense of urgency, which should be translated into commitments and actions at the national, regional and international levels. Vicious circles should be transformed into virtuous ones. The box below highlights ten important market-based actions.

Market-based priority actions

Action 1: Take market dynamics into consideration for sound hunger alleviation initiatives.
Action 2: Support markets through investments in institutions and infrastructure.
Action 3: Improve access to complementary markets.
Action 4: Use the power of markets to transform market dependency into opportunities.
Action 5: Reduce market-based risks and vulnerabilities, and safeguard markets.
Action 6: Invest in social protection.
Action 7: Invest more in nutrition, and differently in agriculture.
Action 8: Ensure that trade supports food security.
Action 9: Engage domestic and international actors in the fight against hunger.
Action 10: Create and leverage knowledge.

Action 1: Take market dynamics into consideration for sound hunger alleviation initiatives

Initiatives to fight hunger can support or deter markets. An understanding of markets is crucial for identifying the reasons for hunger and vulnerability and for designing responses, including food assistance interventions and food security policies:

- Base all interventions and policies to fight hunger on a needs assessment that includes a solid market component.

- Consider using market-based interventions, such as cash and vouchers in food assistance programmes, where appropriate and feasible. This would strengthen markets, but cannot substitute market development where markets are rudimentary.

- Use local procurement programmes for food commodities, to strengthen markets.

- Food security policies should account for the market-related context and the reactions – positive or negative – of markets.

Action 2: Support markets through investments in institutions and infrastructure

Markets do not function in a vacuum. They need supportive infrastructure and institutions. Without these, markets are more likely to harm than benefit the poor:

- Enhance the legal and regulatory support system, including property rights and contract law enforcement, building on existing institutions.

- Encourage competition and avoid the concentration of market power among a few participants, by implementing policies, regulation and reductions in the cost of business formation.

- Strengthen or develop a system and the enforcement of standards, for example on measurements and quality.

No single set of institutions suits all situations. For institutional reform, the priority, speed, comprehensiveness and sequencing of policy reforms and growth depend on the context, including existing formal and informal institutions and socio-economic and political circumstances.

Action 3: Improve access to complementary markets

Hundreds of millions of hungry poor people do not have access to financial services. Many also lack access to input and labour markets:

- Improve the hungry poor's access to financial services, guaranteeing them a safe place to put their money – and even earn some interest – a source of loans for investing in sustainable livelihoods, and insurance cover against harvest failures, illness and death.

- Enhance the hungry poor's access to labour markets by:

  - offering food- or cash-for-work programmes, where appropriate;

  - providing education and skills formation, which improve their possibilities for supplementing incomes with new opportunities; and

  - developing information systems on wages, improving regulations on safety in the workplace and enhancing labour organizations, which could strengthen their position.

- Improve and secure access to land for the hungry poor. In many instances, the exclusion of women from owning and inheriting land needs special attention.

Action 4: Use the power of markets to transform market dependency into opportunities

Markets can be a powerful means of transformation and income generation, but the hungry poor have a weak starting position. Various innovations address the constraints faced by the hungry poor, and may provide possibilities for low-income farmers to improve their connections to markets, giving them incentives and bargaining power to sell food at higher prices:

- Encourage innovations along the market value chain, for example, through contract farming, farmers' associations, warehouse receipt systems and market-information systems. Such initiatives can reduce risk and transaction costs, while increasing access to inputs, finance and market outlets. WFP's Purchase for Progress is one example of such an innovation.

- Provide training and capacity development so that the hungry poor can benefit from opportunities.

- Ensure that the hungry poor can benefit from rapidly changing food systems, including the supermarkets that are being established across the developing world. Supermarkets could increase market access for the hungry poor, as both sellers and buyers. However, there are also risks that the hungry poor change their diets towards cheaper but less nutritious processed foods, and that smallholder farmers will not be able to meet the quality and quantity standards of supermarket and supply chains. Public–private partnerships and corporate social responsibility could be crucial in addressing these risks.

Action 5: Reduce market-based risks and vulnerabilities, and safeguard markets

Participation in markets exposes the hungry poor to market volatility, market risks and market failures. These risks should be taken into account and addressed when assisting vulnerable households in pro-growth behaviour that might reduce hunger. Markets can transfer, increase or reduce risks, making market dynamics either an ally or an adversary in the fight against hunger. There are several opportunities for making markets valuable in more ways than just their redistributive capacity:

- Monitor market-based risks, including those related to food prices, (informal) cross-border trade and trade and market policies.

- Reduce market-based risk, improve resilience and strengthen markets. As natural and human-made disasters become more frequent, markets become more likely to fail, with potentially disastrous impacts on vulnerable households. This risk is lower when markets function well before disaster strikes.

- Establish or strengthen the disaster-risk management frameworks that integrate markets, to ensure

preventive, adaptive and mitigating efforts, which could include weather-based insurance and national strategic reserves.

- Assist markets and do no harm during relief and recovery operations. Care should be taken that assistance programmes do not discourage markets, and specific programmes to assist market recovery should be initiated early on, for example through local procurement of food commodities, where appropriate and feasible.

Action 6: Invest in social protection

The hungry poor are subject to many risks, some of which are market-based. Market forces can be detrimental to the most vulnerable, and markets can fail. Markets respond to demand and not to needs; they are not intended to reach social objectives, such as fighting hunger:

- Invest in and strengthen social protection, to reduce risk and vulnerabilities and complement markets, including through transfers of food, cash, vouchers, nutritious food products and supplements, school feeding and cash- or food-for-work programmes.

- Focus on the most vulnerable, such as ethnic minorities, women, children, disabled people and people living with chronic illnesses.

- Consider market-based social protection measures, such as insurance, vouchers and cash transfers, where appropriate and feasible.

Social protection can play an important role in transforming a vicious cycle into a virtuous one, through its positive impact on growth, markets, risk reduction and human capital.

Action 7: Invest more in nutrition, and differently in agriculture

Support for agriculture has declined for more than two decades, and smallholders have been neglected for much longer. Nutrition interventions are among the most cost-effective development interventions, but do not receive commensurate funding:

- Invest in research and development for crops grown by smallholders. The focus should be on developing crops that can withstand weather-related shocks, are less dependent on water, are more nutritious, maintain biodiversity, and use fewer chemical fertilizers, which have become expensive because of high energy prices.

- Invest in nutrition, for example, through fortification, food supplements, the development of nutritious food products, production for own consumption of nutritious foods, and development of markets for nutritious foods at affordable prices. Higher productivity for staple food crops, driven by new technologies, is not always accompanied by improved nutritional status. Investments in agriculture should be complemented by investments in nutrition, to ensure that the hungry poor have access to nutritious food and to address micronutrient deficiencies.

- Invest in infrastructure, including through food- or cash-for-work programmes, particularly for roads and irrigation systems, focusing on smallholders.

- Invest in storage systems, including those adapted to household needs, and in methods of reducing post-harvest losses.

Governments have a crucial role to play in most of these investments. Charging users is difficult and the private sector is likely to supply fewer services than needed. Public–private partnerships are important in several areas. Official development assistance (ODA) can also be instrumental.

Action 8: Ensure that trade supports food security

International trade plays an important role in food security. Trade barriers distort and inhibit the smooth working of international markets. Complementary trade and food security policies are necessary, to reduce liberalization's adverse effects on the hungry poor:

- Enhance consistency between trade and food security policies.

- Ensure that existing international and regional platforms include discussion of this consistency.

- Reduce export restrictions, and strengthen disciplines to avoid them.

- Ensure humanitarian access to food commodities, including through exemptions from export restrictions.

- Facilitate food trade and systematically reduce food trade restrictions, while minimizing and mitigating the possible negative effects on vulnerable people and countries.

- Improve the predictability of governments' market interventions to support food security. Unpredictable and sporadic measures discourage the private sector. Governments should consult the private sector regularly, including about the establishment of decision rules on trade barriers. For example, such rules could set thresholds for when and how the government intervenes.

Action 9: Engage domestic and international actors in the fight against hunger

Rising incomes and markets will not lead automatically and promptly to improvements in nutrition status, especially not among poorer households. Complementary measures that increase access to nutritious foods are indispensable, and the private sector has an important role. This is particularly relevant in the current environment of high food prices and global financial crisis:

- Support emergency interventions to prevent the deterioration of nutrition status resulting from high food prices and financial crisis.

- Support the strengthening of social protection systems.

- Use ODA to strengthen markets, to bridge relief and development while enhancing food security. Emergency humanitarian assistance should include a component focusing on market recovery.

- Support innovations and experimentation in measures that increase the hungry poor's access to markets and nutritious foods, including through public–private partnerships.

- Develop public–private partnerships involving governments, the private sector and civil society, including in finance, nutrition, value chains and market information systems.

Action 10: Create and leverage knowledge

There is insufficient research on the complex interrelations between markets and hunger, in spite of the large communities of experts in food security, nutrition, health, trade and development economics. Not enough knowledge is used for decision-making:

- More research is needed to answer such questions as:

  - What is the nutrition impact of high food prices?

  - How is the global financial crisis affecting food security?

  - How can households' access to nutritious foods through markets be enhanced?

  - What impact does speculation have on the prices of food commodities?

  - How can the potential negative effects of speculation in food markets be minimized?

  - What is the link between financial and food commodity markets?

  - How can volatility in grain markets be reduced?

  - Is there need for a global grain reserve?

  - What effective instruments can be developed for avoiding export restrictions?

  - How should the world ensure that adequate amounts of nutritious food are available and accessible, even during times of market turbulence?

- Encourage South–South collaboration on experiences and lessons learned. Such cross-fertilization could also help improve the use of knowledge for policy- and decision-making.

Part IV Resource Compendium

This compendium provides data relevant to the topic discussed in this publication. Each table shows a number of indicators concerning the same issue. The first table covers indicators related to hunger and malnutrition. The second provides indicators related to food availability and access. The last table shows indicators pertaining to international assistance.

Data sources

The data in the compendium are from several sources, most of which are entities of the United Nations system or other international organizations. Most data are available online. Whenever possible, data are presented from original sources or from the institution mandated to collate them.

Country classifications

The tables present data for 168 countries and territories grouped into five geographical areas. In some cases, aggregate data are provided. No judgement on the development of a particular country is intended. The term "country" does not imply political independence, but may refer to any territory for which authorities provide separate statistics.

Notes

Because data come from a number of sources, year spans are not the same for every indicator. Data for a year span refer to either an average for the period, or the most recent year available for that period. This information is provided in footnotes.

A dash (–) indicates missing values (not available or not computable).

Zero (0) means that the value is zero.

'ns' means not statistically significant.

At the bottom of each table, footnotes explain indicator definitions, computations and data sources.

Table 1 – Hunger

| | Undernourishment | | | | | | Malnutrition | | | | | | | Hidden hunger | | |
| | Number of people undernourished (millions) | | | Proportion of undernourished in total population (%) | | | Prevalence of under-5 children stunting (%) | | | Prevalence of under-5 children underweight (%) | | | Prevalence of under-5 children wasting (%) | Iron-deficiency anaemia in women aged 15–49 (%) | Iodine deficiency (% of population with goitre) | Vitamin A deficiency |
	1990–1992	1995–1997	2003–2005	1990–1992	1995–1997	2003–2005	1990–1992	1995–1997	2003–2005	1990–1992	1995–1997	2003–2005	2000–2006			
SUB-SAHARAN AFRICA	**168.8**	**194.0**	**212.1**	**34**	**34**	**30**										
Angola	7.2	7.3	7.1	66	58	46	–	61.7	50.8	–	–	30.5	6	59	33	55
Benin	1.5	1.7	1.6	28	26	19	–	–	43.1	–	–	22.9	7	65	<5	70
Botswana	0.3	0.4	0.5	20	24	26	–	–	29.1	–	–	12.5	5	31	17	30
Burkina Faso	1.3	1.3	1.3	14	12	10	–	–	43.1	32.7	34.3	37.7	23	48	29	46
Burundi	2.6	3.6	4.8	44	57	63	–	–	63.1	–	–	45.1	7	60	42	44
Cameroon	4.3	5.1	4.0	34	35	23	–	36.7	35.4	13.6	21	18.1	6	32	12	36
Cape Verde	–	–	–	–	–	–	–	–	–	13.5	–	–	–	–	–	–
Central African Republic	1.4	1.8	1.8	47	50	43	–	40.2	44.6	–	–	24.3	10	49	11	68
Chad	3.7	3.8	3.8	59	51	39	–	45	44.8	–	–	36.7	14	56	24	45
Comoros	–	–	–	–	–	–	–	41.4	46.9	18.9	–	24.9	8	–	–	–
Congo, Republic of	1.0	1.2	0.8	40	43	22	–	–	31.2	–	13.9	14.4	7	48	36	32
Congo, Dem. Rep. of	11.4	26.5	43.0	29	57	76	–	–	44.4	–	–	31.1	13	54	–	58
Côte d'Ivoire	2.0	2.4	2.6	15	16	14	–	31.5	34	23.6	21.2	17.2	7	–	–	–
Djibouti	–	–	–	–	–	–	–	–	38.8	22.9	18.2	26.8	21	–	–	–
Equatorial Guinea	–	–	–	–	–	–	–	–	42.6	–	–	18.6	7	–	–	–
Eritrea	2.1	2.1	3.0	67	64	68	–	44.4	43.7	41	–	39.6	13	53	10	30
Ethiopia	37.4	39.3	35.2	71	63	46	–	–	50.7	47.6	–	38.4	11	58	23	30
Gabon	–	–	–	–	–	–	–	–	26.3	–	–	11.9	3	32	27	41
Gambia	0.2	0.4	0.5	20	31	30	–	–	24.1	–	–	17.1	6	53	20	64
Ghana	5.4	3.0	1.9	34	16	9	–	31.3	35.6	–	24.9	22.1	5	40	18	60
Guinea	1.2	1.3	1.5	19	18	17	–	34.3	39.3	26.3	23.2	25.8	9	43	23	40
Guinea Bissau	–	–	–	–	–	–	–	–	36.1	–	–	25	7	53	17	31
Kenya	8.0	8.4	11.0	33	30	32	–	37	35.8	22.3	–	19.9	6	43	10	70
Lesotho	0.2	0.2	0.3	15	13	15	–	–	45.2	15.8	–	19.8	4	43	19	54
Liberia	0.6	0.9	1.3	30	39	40	–	–	45.3	–	–	26.4	6	44	18	38
Madagascar	3.9	5.4	6.6	32	37	37	–	55.5	52.8	39.1	–	41.9	13	42	6	42
Malawi	4.3	3.7	3.8	45	36	29	55.8	–	52.5	27.2	–	22	3	27	22	59
Mali	1.1	1.3	1.2	14	15	11	–	36.2	42.7	–	–	33.2	11	47	42	47
Mauritania	0.2	0.2	0.2	10	8	8	–	–	39.5	47.6	–	31.8	13	42	21	17
Mauritius	0.1	0.1	0.1	7	6	6	–	–	–	–	14.9	–	–	–	–	–
Mozambique	8.2	8.6	7.5	59	52	38	–	45.3	47	–	–	23.7	4	54	17	26
Namibia	0.4	0.5	0.4	29	29	19	35.7	–	29.5	26.2	–	24	9	35	18	59
Niger	3.1	3.8	3.7	38	40	29	–	47	54.8	42.6	–	39.6	10	47	20	41
Nigeria	14.7	10.8	12.5	15	10	9	50.5	–	43	35.7	–	28.7	9	47	8	25
Rwanda	3.2	3.3	3.6	45	56	40	56.8	–	51.7	29.2	–	22.5	5	43	13	39
Sao Tome and Principe	–	–	–	–	–	–	–	–	35.2	–	–	12.9	8	–	–	–
Senegal	2.3	3.0	3.0	28	32	26	33.7	–	20.1	21.6	–	17.3	8	43	23	61
Seychelles	–	–	–	–	–	–	–	–	–	–	–	–	–	–	–	–
Sierra Leone	1.9	1.8	2.5	45	43	47	–	–	38.4	28.7	–	27.2	9	68	16	47
Somalia	–	–	–	–	–	–	–	–	42.1	–	25.8	–	11	–	–	–
South Africa	–	–	–	–	–	–	–	–	–	–	11.5	–	–	26	16	33
Sudan	8.3	7.2	7.4	31	24	21	–	–	47.6	34.4	–	40.7	16	–	–	–
Swaziland	0.1	0.2	0.2	12	20	18	–	–	36.6	–	–	10.3	1	32	12	38
Tanzania, United Rep of	7.5	12.7	13.0	28	41	35	–	48.3	44.4	28.8	29.4	21.8	3	45	16	37
Togo	1.8	1.8	2.3	45	39	37	–	29.8	–	–	25.1	–	14	45	14	35
Uganda	3.6	5.1	4.1	19	23	15	–	45	44.8	–	–	22.8	5	30	9	66
Zambia	3.3	3.9	5.1	40	41	45	–	48.6	52.5	25.1	–	20	6	46	25	66
Zimbabwe	4.3	5.5	5.2	40	46	40	–	33.7	35.8	–	13	17.2	6	44	9	28

	Undernourishment						Malnutrition							Hidden hunger		
	Number of people undernourished (millions)			Proportion of undernourished in total population (%)			Prevalence of under-5 children stunting (%)			Prevalence of under-5 children underweight (%)			Prevalence of under-5 children wasting (%)	Iron-deficiency anaemia in women aged 15–49 (%)	Iodine deficiency (% of population with goitre)	Vitamin A deficiency
	1990–1992	1995–1997	2003–2005	1990–1992	1995–1997	2003–2005	1990–1992	1995–1997	2003–2005	1990–1992	1995–1997	2003–2005	2000–2006			
ASIA AND OCEANIA	**582.4**	**535.0**	**541.9**	**20**	**17**	**16**										
Afghanistan	–	–	–	–	–	–	–	–	59.3	–	48	39.3	7	61	48	53
Bangladesh	41.6	51.4	40.1	36	40	27	–	–	47.8	65.8	–	47.5	13	36	18	28
Bhutan	–	–	–	–	–	–	–	47.7	–	–	18.7	–	–	55	–	32
Brunei Darussalam	–	–	–	–	–	–	–	–	–	–	–	–	–	–	–	–
Cambodia	3.8	4.8	3.6	38	41	26	–	58.6	43.7	39.8	–	45.2	7	58	18	42
China	178.0	143.7	122.7	15	12	9	–	–	21.8	19.1	–	7.8	–	21	5	12
Cook Islands	–	–	–	–	–	–	–	–	–	–	–	–	–	–	–	–
Fiji	–	–	–	–	–	–	–	–	7.9	–	–	–	–	–	–	–
Hong Kong SAR	–	–	–	–	–	–	–	–	–	–	–	–	–	–	–	–
India	206.6	199.9	230.5	24	21	21	–	51	47.9	53.4	48.5	–	20	51	26	57
Indonesia	34.5	26.7	37.1	19	13	17	–	–	28.6	–	26.4	28.2	–	26	10	26
Kiribati	–	–	–	–	–	–	–	–	–	–	–	–	–	–	–	–
Korea, Dem. People's Rep. of	4.2	6.7	7.6	21	31	32	–	–	44.7	–	–	23.9	7	–	–	–
Korea, Republic of	ns	ns	ns	–	–	–	–	–	–	–	–	–	–	–	–	–
Lao People's Dem. Rep.	1.1	1.3	1.1	27	26	19	–	–	48.2	44	–	40	15	48	14	42
Malaysia	ns	ns	ns	–	–	–	–	–	–	23.3	–	10.6	–	–	–	–
Maldives	–	–	–	–	–	–	–	46.7	31.9	38.9	–	30.4	13	–	–	–
Marshall Islands	–	–	–	–	–	–	–	–	–	–	–	–	–	–	–	–
Micronesia	–	–	–	–	–	–	–	–	–	–	–	–	–	–	–	–
Mongolia	0.7	1.0	0.8	30	40	29	–	30.1	23.5	12.3	–	6.7	2	18	15	29
Myanmar	18.1	14.8	8.8	44	34	19	–	–	40.6	32.4	–	31.8	9	45	17	35
Nauru	–	–	–	–	–	–	–	–	–	–	–	–	–	–	–	–
Niue	–	–	–	–	–	–	–	–	–	–	–	–	–	–	–	–
Nepal	4.0	5.3	4.0	21	24	15	–	61.1	49.3	–	–	48.3	13	62	24	33
Pakistan	25.7	23.7	35.0	22	18	23	54.5	–	41.5	40.4	–	37.8	13	59	38	35
Palau	–	–	–	–	–	–	–	–	–	–	–	–	–	–	–	–
Papua New Guinea	–	–	–	–	–	–	–	–	–	–	–	–	–	43	–	37
Philippines	13.3	12.8	13.3	21	18	16	–	–	33.8	33.5	28.2	27.6	6	35	15	23
Samoa	–	–	–	–	–	–	–	–	–	–	–	–	–	–	–	–
Singapore	–	–	–	–	–	–	–	–	4.4	–	–	3.4	2	–	–	–
Solomon Islands	–	–	–	–	–	–	–	–	–	–	–	–	–	–	–	–
Sri Lanka	4.6	4.4	4.0	27	24	21	–	–	18.4	–	–	29.4	14	–	–	–
Thailand	15.7	12.3	10.9	29	21	17	–	–	15.7	18.6	17.6	–	4	27	13	22
Timor-Leste	–	–	–	–	–	–	–	–	55.7	–	–	45.8	12	–	–	–
Tonga	–	–	–	–	–	–	–	–	–	–	–	–	–	–	–	–
Tuvalu	–	–	–	–	–	–	–	–	–	–	–	–	–	–	–	–
Vanuatu	–	–	–	–	–	–	–	–	–	–	–	–	–	–	–	–
Viet Nam	18.7	15.6	11.5	28	21	14	61.4	–	35.8	–	–	26.6	12	33	11	12
LATIN AMERICA AND CARIBBEAN	**52.6**	**51.8**	**45.2**	**12**	**11**	**8**										
Antigua and Barbuda	–	–	–	–	–	–	–	–	–	–	–	–	–	–	–	–
Argentina	ns	ns	ns	–	–	–	–	–	8.2	–	5.4	3.8	1	–	–	–
Bahamas	–	–	–	–	–	–	–	–	–	–	–	–	–	–	–	–
Barbados	–	–	–	–	–	–	–	–	–	–	–	–	–	–	–	–
Belize	–	–	–	–	–	–	–	–	–	6.2	–	–	1	–	–	–
Bolivia	1.6	1.5	2.0	24	20	22	–	33.1	32.5	–	9.5	7.5	1	30	<5	23
Brazil	15.8	15.6	11.7	10	10	6	–	13.5	–	–	5.7	–	–	21	<5	15

	Undernourishment						Malnutrition							Hidden hunger		
	Number of people undernourished (millions)			Proportion of undernourished in total population (%)			Prevalence of under-5 children stunting (%)			Prevalence of under-5 children underweight (%)			Prevalence of under-5 children wasting (%)	Iron-deficiency anaemia in women aged 15–49 (%)	Iodine deficiency (% of population with goitre)	Vitamin A deficiency
	1990–1992	1995–1997	2003–2005	1990–1992	1995–1997	2003–2005	1990–1992	1995–1997	2003–2005	1990–1992	1995–1997	2003–2005	2000–2006			
Chile	0.9	ns	ns	7	–	–	–	–	–	0.9	–	0.7	0	–	–	–
Colombia	5.2	4.2	4.3	15	11	10	–	19.7	16.2	–	–	7	1	–	–	–
Costa Rica	ns	ns	ns	–	–	–	–	–	–	2.8	5.1	–	–	–	–	–
Cuba	0.6	1.5	ns	5	14	–	–	–	–	–	–	3.9	2	–	–	–
Dominica	–	–	–	–	–	–	–	–	–	–	–	–	–	–	–	–
Dominican Republic	2.0	2.0	2.0	27	24	21	–	13.9	11.7	10.4	–	5.3	1	31	11	18
Ecuador	2.5	2.0	1.9	24	17	15	–	–	29	–	14.8	11.6	2	–	–	–
El Salvador	0.5	0.6	0.6	9	11	10	29.5	–	24.6	–	11.8	10.3	1	34	11	17
Grenada	–	–	–	–	–	–	–	–	–	–	–	–	–	–	–	–
Guatemala	1.3	1.7	2.0	14	17	16	–	53.1	54.3	–	24.2	22.7	2	20	16	21
Guyana	–	–	–	–	–	–	–	–	13.8	18.3	–	13.6	11	–	–	–
Haiti	4.5	4.8	5.3	63	60	58	–	37.2	29.7	26.8	–	17.3	9	54	12	32
Honduras	1.0	0.9	0.8	19	16	12	–	43.3	29.9	–	–	16.6	1	31	12	15
Jamaica	0.3	0.2	0.1	11	7	5	–	6.3	4.5	–	–	4	4	–	–	–
Mexico	ns	4.3	ns	–	5	–	–	21.7	15.5	–	7.5	–	2	–	–	–
Nicaragua	2.2	1.9	1.2	52	40	22	–	23.4	25.2	11.9	–	9.6	2	40	4	9
Panama	0.4	0.6	0.5	18	20	17	–	21.5	–	7	6.8	–	–	–	–	–
Paraguay	0.7	0.5	0.7	16	11	11	18.3	–	–	3.7	5	4.6	1	25	13	13
Peru	6.1	4.9	3.9	28	20	15	–	31.6	31.3	10.8	–	7.6	1	32	10	17
Saint Kitts and Nevis	–	–	–	–	–	–	–	–	–	–	–	–	–	–	–	–
Saint Lucia	–	–	–	–	–	–	–	–	–	–	–	–	–	–	–	–
Saint Vincent & Grenadines	–	–	–	–	–	–	–	–	–	–	–	–	–	–	–	–
Suriname	0.0	0.0	0.0	11	8	7	–	–	14.5	–	–	13.3	7	–	–	–
Trinidad and Tobago	0.1	0.2	0.1	11	13	10	–	–	5.3	–	–	5.9	4	–	–	–
Uruguay	0.2	ns	ns	5	–	–	–	–	13.9	–	4.5	–	2	–	–	–
Venezuela	2.1	3.1	3.2	10	14	12	–	–	–	4.5	–	5.2	4	38	10	5
MIDDLE EAST AND NORTH AFRICA	**19.1**	**29.6**	**33.0**	**6**	**8**	**8**										
Algeria	ns	1.5	ns	–	5	–	–	22.5	21.6	9.2	–	10.4	3	–	–	–
Bahrain	–	–	–	–	–	–	–	–	–	–	8.7	–	–	–	–	–
Egypt	ns	ns	ns	–	–	–	–	–	23.8	10.4	10.7	6.2	4	28	12	7
Iran, Islamic Rep. of	ns	ns	ns	–	–	–	–	–	–	–	10.9	–	–	29	9	23
Iraq	–	–	–	–	–	–	–	–	27.5	11.9	–	11.7	5	–	–	–
Israel	–	–	–	–	–	–	–	–	–	–	–	–	–	–	–	–
Jordan	ns	0.2	ns	–	5	–	–	11.1	12	6.4	–	4.4	2	–	–	–
Kuwait	0.4	0.1	ns	20	5	–	–	–	–	–	9.8	–	–	–	–	–
Lebanon	ns	ns	ns	–	–	–	–	–	15.2	–	3	3.9	5	24	11	20
Libyan Arab Jamahiriya	ns	ns	ns	–	–	–	–	20.7	–	–	4.7	–	–	–	–	–
Morocco	1.2	1.4	ns	5	5	–	29.9	–	23.1	9	8.9	10.2	9	34	–	29
Occupied Palestinian Terr.	–	–	–	–	–	–	–	–	–	–	–	4.9	1	–	–	–
Oman	–	–	–	–	–	–	–	15.9	–	–	17.8	–	–	–	–	–
Qatar	–	–	–	–	–	–	–	–	–	–	5.5	–	–	–	–	–
Saudi Arabia	ns	ns	ns	–	–	–	–	–	–	–	14.3	–	–	–	–	–
Syria	ns	ns	ns	–	–	–	–	–	28.2	12.1	–	6.9	9	30	8	8
Tunisia	ns	ns	ns	–	–	–	–	–	–	–	–	4	2	–	–	–
United Arab Emirates	ns	ns	ns	–	–	–	–	–	–	–	14.4	–	–	–	–	–
Yemen	3.8	5.0	6.5	30	31	32	–	59.3	58.2	–	46.1	45.6	12	49	16	40

| | Undernourishment | | | | | | Malnutrition | | | | | | | Hidden hunger | | |
| | Number of people undernourished (millions) | | | Proportion of undernourished in total population (%) | | | Prevalence of under-5 children stunting (%) | | | Prevalence of under-5 children underweight (%) | | | Prevalence of under-5 children wasting (%) | Iron-deficiency anaemia in women aged 15–49 (%) | Iodine deficiency (% of population with goitre) | Vitamin A deficiency |
	1990–1992	1995–1997	2003–2005	1990–1992	1995–1997	2003–2005	1990–1992	1995–1997	2003–2005	1990–1992	1995–1997	2003–2005	2000–2006			
EASTERN AND SOUTHERN EUROPE AND CIS																
Albania	–	–	–	–	–	–	–	–	39.2	–	–	14	7	–	–	–
Armenia	–	–	–	–	–	–	–	15.1	18.2	–	–	4	5	12	12	12
Azerbaijan	–	–	–	–	–	–	–	–	24.1	–	–	6.8	2	35	15	23
Belarus	–	–	–	–	–	–	–	–	4.5	–	–	–	1	–	–	–
Bosnia and Herzegovina	–	–	–	–	–	–	–	–	11.8	–	–	4.1	3	–	–	–
Bulgaria	–	–	–	–	–	–	–	–	8.8	–	–	–	–	–	–	–
Croatia	–	–	–	–	–	–	–	–	–	–	0.6	–	–	–	–	–
Cyprus	–	–	–	–	–	–	–	–	–	–	–	–	–	–	–	–
Czech Republic	–	–	–	–	–	–	–	–	2.6	1	–	–	–	–	–	–
Estonia	–	–	–	–	–	–	–	–	–	–	–	–	–	–	–	–
Georgia	–	–	–	–	–	–	–	–	–	–	3.1	–	–	31	21	11
Hungary	–	–	–	–	–	–	–	–	–	–	–	–	–	–	–	–
Kazakhstan	–	–	–	–	–	–	–	13.9	17.4	–	4.2	–	6	36	21	19
Kyrgyzstan	–	–	–	–	–	–	–	32.6	18.1	–	11	–	15	31	21	18
Latvia	–	–	–	–	–	–	–	–	–	–	–	–	–	–	–	–
Lithuania	–	–	–	–	–	–	–	–	–	–	–	–	–	–	–	–
Macedonia, FYR	–	–	–	–	–	–	–	8	1.2	–	6	–	–	–	–	–
Malta	–	–	–	–	–	–	–	–	–	–	–	–	–	–	–	–
Moldova, Rep of	–	–	–	–	–	–	–	–	11.3	–	3.2	4.3	–	–	–	–
Poland	–	–	–	–	–	–	–	–	–	–	–	–	–	–	–	–
Romania	–	–	–	–	–	–	–	15.3	12.8	5.7	3.1	3.2	2	–	–	–
Russian Federation	–	–	–	–	–	–	–	–	–	–	3	–	–	–	–	–
Serbia and Montenegro	–	–	–	–	–	–	–	–	8.1	–	–	1.9	3	–	–	–
Slovakia	–	–	–	–	–	–	–	–	–	–	–	–	–	–	–	–
Slovenia	–	–	–	–	–	–	–	–	–	–	–	–	–	–	–	–
Tajikistan	–	–	–	–	–	–	–	–	–	–	–	–	7	42	28	18
Turkey	–	–	–	–	–	–	–	19.1	15.6	10.4	8.3	3.9	1	33	23	18
Turkmenistan	–	–	–	–	–	–	–	–	–	–	–	12	6	46	11	18
Ukraine	–	–	–	–	–	–	–	–	22.9	–	–	1	0	–	–	–
Uzbekistan	–	–	–	–	–	–	–	39	19.6	–	–	7.9	3	63	24	40

Indicator definitions and sources

Number of people undernourished: Number of people consuming (on average for each period) less than the estimated sex-/age-specific minimum dietary energy requirements.
Source: FAO, 2008c.

Proportion of undernourished in total population: Percentage of total population consuming (on average for each period) less than the estimated sex-/age-specific minimum dietary energy requirements.
Source: FAO, 2008c.

Prevalence of under-5 children stunting (moderate and severe): Proportion of children under 5 years of age falling below minus 2 standard deviations from the median height for age of the reference population. Data shown are the latest available for the considered period.
Source: WHO Statistical Information System (WHOSIS). Available at: www.who.int/whosis/.

Prevalence of under-5 children underweight (moderate and severe): Proportion of children under 5 years of age falling below minus 2 standard deviations from the median weight for age of the reference population. Data shown are the latest available for the considered period.

Source: WHO Statistical Information System (WHOSIS). Available at: www.who.int/whosis/.

Prevalence of under-5 children wasting (moderate and severe): Proportion of children under 5 years of age falling below minus 2 standard deviations from the median weight for height of the reference population. Data shown are the latest available for the considered period.
Source: UNICEF, 2008. Data posted at: www.unicef.org/sowc08/docs/sowc08_table_2.xls.

Iron-deficiency anaemia in women aged 15–49: Percentage of women affected by anaemia caused by iron deficiency (haemoglobina < 120 g/litre in non-pregnant women > 15 years of age, Hb < 110g/litre in pregnant women of any age).
Source: Micronutrient Initiative and UNICEF, 2004.

Iodine deficiency (goitre): Percentage of population affected by a swelling of thyroid gland.
Source: Micronutrient Initiative and UNICEF, 2004.

Vitamin A deficiency: Percentage of children under 6 years of age with sub-clinical levels of vitamin A deficiency.
Source: Micronutrient Initiative and UNICEF, 2004.

Table 2 – Food availability and access

	Dietary energy consumption (kcal/person/day)				Food production per capita (1999–2001 = 100)				Food imports as a percentage of food production		
	1969–1971	1979–1981	1990–1992	2002–2004	1969–1971	1979–1981	1990–1992	2002–2004	1990–1994	1995–1999	2000–2005
SUB-SAHARAN AFRICA									9	9	12
Angola	2,110	2,110	1,780	2,120	136	99	84	116	31	30	43
Benin	1,990	2,040	2,330	2,590	71	70	81	107	24	12	15
Botswana	2,010	2,030	2,260	2,150	230	169	142	101	92	120	101
Burkina Faso	1,770	1,720	2,350	2,500	80	71	95	106	7	9	7
Burundi	2,110	2,030	1,900	1,660	140	128	123	98	2	1	3
Cameroon	2,230	2,280	2,120	2,260	111	104	93	101	8	6	11
Cape Verde	–	–	–	–	60	57	78	87	191	175	159
Central African Republic	2,260	2,300	1,860	1,960	80	89	86	103	5	4	4
Chad	2,080	1,640	1,780	2,130	110	96	95	101	3	2	3
Comoros	1,920	1,800	1,910	1,770	143	115	107	95	35	29	31
Congo, Republic of	1,960	2,040	1,860	2,160	160	128	106	99	41	46	64
Congo, Democratic Rep. of the	2,220	2,110	2,170	1,590	168	151	152	90	5	8	10
Côte d'Ivoire	2,500	2,830	2,470	2,640	88	96	89	96	15	15	20
Djibouti	1,700	1,700	1,800	2,270	97	107	118	118	208	228	343
Equatorial Guinea	–	–	–	–	–	–	–	–	24	20	37
Eritrea	–	–	–	1,500	–	–	–	73	61	59	126
Ethiopia	–	–	–	1,850	–	–	–	103	4	5	10
Gabon	2,180	2,420	2,450	2,680	123	125	114	96	30	38	42
Gambia	2,160	1,770	2,370	2,240	230	117	82	77	57	62	58
Ghana	2,280	1,700	2,080	2,690	99	69	76	109	12	6	13
Guinea	2,220	2,230	2,110	2,430	115	107	93	106	11	11	11
Guinea Bissau	1,870	2,010	2,300	2,030	88	83	95	94	–	–	–
Kenya	2,290	2,250	1,980	2,150	104	101	107	102	8	11	13
Lesotho	2,070	2,360	2,440	2,580	138	123	96	99	156	122	50
Liberia	2,380	2,550	2,210	1,930	146	145	112	85	41	47	50
Madagascar	2,430	2,370	2,080	2,050	149	131	117	93	3	4	6
Malawi	2,360	2,270	1,880	2,120	89	89	58	84	17	8	6
Mali	1,960	1,700	2,220	2,200	108	102	101	97	3	4	5
Mauritania	1,870	2,050	2,560	2,740	149	123	110	98	56	69	66
Mauritius	2,330	2,670	2,890	2,980	126	109	112	102	274	254	261
Mozambique	1,870	1,860	1,730	2,080	151	113	91	99	47	20	28
Namibia	2,150	2,230	2,070	2,240	257	214	139	118	85	117	70
Niger	2,040	2,140	2,020	2,150	140	124	98	97	3	4	8
Nigeria	2,220	2,050	2,540	2,720	96	64	89	96	–	–	–
Rwanda	2,180	2,270	1,950	2,110	120	124	129	108	4	3	3
Sao Tome and Principe	2,110	2,090	2,270	2,490	183	114	78	99	38	26	28
Senegal	2,280	2,280	2,280	2,360	135	94	90	70	36	41	54
Seychelles	2,020	2,260	2,310	2,460	163	119	81	94	179	188	219
Sierra Leone	2,230	2,110	1,990	1,910	160	142	131	101	17	25	20
Somalia	–	–	–	–	–	–	–	–	10	7	8
South Africa	2,740	2,780	2,830	2,980	115	121	98	104	13	12	12
Sudan	2,050	2,180	2,170	2,270	91	100	82	100	8	5	10
Swaziland	2,280	2,400	2,450	2,300	139	151	131	102	40	40	69
Tanzania, United Rep of	1,680	2,190	2,050	1,960	122	129	115	99	3	5	9
Togo	2,220	2,190	2,150	2,350	127	112	96	97	13	12	20
Uganda	2,390	2,110	2,270	2,370	154	105	104	98	1	2	3
Zambia	2,250	2,220	1,930	1,950	129	117	104	100	18	15	14
Zimbabwe	2,260	2,260	1,980	1,980	149	128	91	84	25	12	18

GDP per capita (US$)	Poverty rate (%)			Inequality of income				Proportion of consumption spent on food			Road density
				Income share of lowest 20%		Gini coeficient					
2008	1990–1994	1995–1999	2000–2006	1990–1999	2000–2005	Year of survey	Gini coeficient	1990–1994	1995–1999	2000–2004	1993–2004
6,443	–	–	–	–	–	–	–	–	–	–	–
1,610	–	29.0	–	–	7.4	–	–	–	–	–	32
17,947	–	–	–	3.2	–	1993	63.0	71.0	–	–	–
1,259	–	54.6	46.4	5.9	6.9	1998	48.2	–	–	–	25
389	36.4	68.0	–	5.1	–	1998	33.3	–	–	–	19
2,161	–	53.3	40.2	5.7	5.6	2001	44.6	–	–	–	20
3,475	–	–	–	–	4.4	–	–	–	–	–	–
754	–	–	–	2.0	–	1993	61.3	57.7	–	–	–
1,670	–	64.0	–	–	–	–	–	–	57.8	–	5
1,150	–	–	–	–	–	–	–	–	–	–	–
4,044	–	–	–	–	–	–	–	–	–	–	–
340	–	–	–	–	–	–	–	–	–	–	26
1,800	–	–	–	5.8	5.2	2002	44.6	–	–	–	–
2,400	–	–	–	–	–	–	–	–	–	–	–
17,407	–	–	–	–	–	–	–	–	–	–	–
748	53.0	–	–	–	–	–	–	–	–	–	–
871	–	45.5	44.2	9.1	–	1999	30.0	–	52.8	–	32
14,747	–	–	–	–	–	–	–	–	–	–	–
1,385	64.0	57.6	61.3	4.0	4.8	1998	47.5	–	–	–	–
1,513	50.0	39.5	28.5	5.6	–	1998	40.8	58.0	–	–	61
1,008	40.0	–	–	–	7.0	1994	40.3	–	–	–	22
497	–	–	65.7	5.2	–	1993	47.0	–	–	–	–
1,735	40.0	52.0	–	6.0	–	1997	42.5	–	–	–	44
1,358	49.2	68.0	–	1.5	–	1995	63.2	–	–	–	–
378	–	–	–	–	–	–	–	–	–	–	–
995	–	71.3	–	5.9	4.9	2001	47.5	71.8	–	–	25
850	54.0	65.3	–	–	7.0	1997	50.3	28.3	–	–	38
1,088	–	63.8	–	4.6	6.1	1994	50.5	–	–	–	–
2,108	–	50.0	46.3	6.3	6.2	2000	39.0	–	–	–	–
12,017	–	–	–	–	–	–	–	44.0	43.0	40.0	–
900	–	69.4	54.1	5.6	5.4	1996	39.6	–	72.3	50.0	–
5,526	–	–	–	1.4	–	1993	70.7	–	–	–	57
691	63.0	–	–	2.6	–	1995	50.5	–	–	–	37
2,142	34.1	–	–	5.0	5.0	1996	50.6	–	–	–	47
954	51.2	–	60.3	–	5.3	1983	28.9	–	–	71.7	44
1,749	–	–	–	–	–	–	–	–	–	–	–
1,762	33.4	–	–	6.5	6.6	1995	41.3	53.0	–	–	–
17,560	–	–	–	–	–	–	–	46.6	36.7	–	–
728	–	–	70.2	1.1	6.5	1989	62.9	–	–	49.3	–
–	–	–	–	–	–	–	–	–	–	–	–
10,187	–	–	–	3.6	3.5	2000	57.8	–	23.0	25.0	21
2,335	–	–	–	–	–	–	–	–	–	–	–
5,645	–	–	69.2	2.7	4.3	1994	60.9	28.0	–	–	–
1,352	38.6	–	35.7	7.4	7.3	1993	38.2	71.3	–	65.4	38
824	–	–	–	–	–	–	–	–	–	–	–
1,148	–	–	37.7	6.0	5.7	1999	43.0	64.0	52.0	44.0	–
1,397	–	72.9	68.0	3.4	3.6	1998	52.6	–	63 3	64.0	–
–	25.8	34.9	–	4.6	–	1995	56.8	37.3	–	–	–

Resource compendium

	Dietary energy consumption (kcal/person/day)				Food production per capita (1999–2001 = 100)				Food imports as a percentage of food production		
	1969–1971	1979–1981	1990–1992	2002–2004	1969–1971	1979–1981	1990–1992	2002–2004	1990–1994	1995–1999	2000–2005
ASIA AND OCEANIA									**5**	**5**	**5**
Afghanistan	–	–	–	–	–	–	–	–	4	4	19
Bangladesh	2,120	1,980	2,070	2,200	103	93	91	100	6	10	11
Bhutan	–	–	–	–	–	–	–	–	17	16	15
Brunei Darussalam	2,410	2,590	2,800	2,800	72	68	50	109	458	422	259
Cambodia	2,090	1,710	1,860	2,070	133	66	85	101	2	2	2
China	1,990	2,330	2,710	2,930	40	46	65	111	4	3	3
Cook Islands	–	–	–	–	–	–	–	–	48	54	86
Fiji	2,440	2,500	2,640	2,940	116	116	114	93	92	112	122
Hong Kong SAR	–	–	–	–	–	–	–	–	–	–	–
India	2,040	2,080	2,370	2,470	73	74	89	98	0	1	2
Indonesia	1,860	2,220	2,700	2,890	60	71	96	111	5	9	8
Kiribati	2,420	2,730	2,650	2,800	110	109	89	98	34	36	35
Korea, Dem. People's Rep. of	2,090	2,300	2,470	2,180	85	111	132	108	8	14	20
Korea, Republic of	2,770	2,990	3,000	3,030	58	77	86	93	53	59	64
Lao People's Democratic Rep.	2,080	2,070	2,110	2,370	65	67	73	108	1	2	2
Malaysia	2,570	2,760	2,830	2,880	42	61	89	106	23	24	24
Maldives	–	–	–	–	104	99	95	109	100	133	168
Marshall Islands	–	–	–	–	–	–	–	–	–	–	–
Micronesia	–	–	–	–	–	–	–	–	–	–	–
Mongolia	2,230	2,380	2,060	2,250	143	133	109	70	–	–	–
Myanmar	2,040	2,330	2,630	2,940	64	75	72	113	1	1	1
Nauru	–	–	–	–	–	–	–	–	86	78	70
Niue	–	–	–	–	–	–	–	–	17	18	16
Nepal	1,800	1,850	2,340	2,430	79	78	93	103	1	2	4
Pakistan	2,250	2,210	2,300	2,320	77	80	89	98	7	7	4
Palau	–	–	–	–	–	–	–	–	–	–	–
Papua New Guinea	–	–	–	–	106	104	101	99	13	14	12
Philippines	–	–	–	–	89	105	94	107	10	14	14
Samoa	2,220	2,460	2,570	2,930	120	129	92	100	32	28	33
Singapore	–	–	–	–	1,340	1,621	453	96	699	582	618
Solomon Islands	2,250	2,220	2,020	2,230	137	147	113	97	16	21	17
Sri Lanka	2,290	2,360	2,230	2,390	91	120	98	98	25	36	37
Thailand	2,110	2,280	2,200	2,400	71	87	93	103	5	6	7
Timor-Leste	2,240	2,410	2,560	2,750	95	90	94	101	28	45	43
Tonga	–	–	–	–	137	139	102	100	26	33	26
Tuvalu	–	–	–	–	–	–	–	–	71	111	142
Vanuatu	2,550	2,560	2,530	2,600	169	160	130	91	13	17	19
Viet Nam	2,100	2,030	2,180	2,630	53	57	73	113	1	2	5
LATIN AMERICA AND CARIBBEAN									**10**	**11**	**11**
Antigua and Barbuda	–	–	–	–	91	99	114	104	82	86	99
Argentina	3,270	3,210	3,000	2,920	79	85	83	99	1	1	1
Bahamas	2,590	2,470	2,620	2,660	84	91	80	95	189	146	158
Barbados	2,850	3,040	3,060	3,070	139	134	105	94	253	234	247
Belize	2,290	2,770	2,650	2,850	51	69	76	101	9	7	7
Bolivia	2,000	2,130	2,110	2,220	65	77	85	107	10	6	8
Brazil	2,430	2,680	2,810	3,110	52	66	80	114	5	6	5
Chile	2,660	2,670	2,610	2,870	66	69	84	105	11	18	18
Colombia	1,950	2,290	2,440	2,580	80	93	98	104	10	20	18
Costa Rica	2,250	2,510	2,720	2,810	68	76	90	94	11	15	16

154

GDP per capita (US$)	Poverty rate (%)			Inequality of income				Proportion of consumption spent on food			Road density
				Income share of lowest 20%		Gini coeficient					
2008	1990–1994	1995–1999	2000–2006	1990–1999	2000–2005	Year of survey	Gini coeficient	1990–1994	1995–1999	2000–2004	1993–2004
783	–	–	–	–	–	–	–	–	–	–	–
1,408	–	51.0	49.8	8.7	8.8	2000	31.8	66.6	58.0	54.6	37
5,240	–	–	–	–	–	–	–	–	–	–	–
50,596	–	–	–	–	–	–	–	–	–	–	–
1,955	47.0	36.1	35.0	8.0	6.8	1997	40.4	53.0	59.0	–	81
5,943	–	4.6	–	–	4.3	2001	44.7	–	–	–	97
–	–	–	–	–	–	–	–	–	–	–	–
4,443	–	–	–	–	–	–	–	–	–	–	–
44,413	–	–	–	–	–	–	–	–	–	–	–
2,787	36.0	–	28.6	–	8.1	1999	32.5	–	–	49.5	61
3,990	–	27.1	16.7	8.9	7.1	2002	34.3	52.0	58.0	51.7	94
3,707	–	–	–	–	–	–	–	–	–	–	–
–	–	–	–	–	–	–	–	–	–	–	–
26,341	–	–	–	7.9	–	1998	31.6	–	–	–	–
2,216	45.0	38.6	33.0	7.6	8.1	1997	37.0	64.3	60.9	–	64
14,225	–	–	–	4.4	–	1997	49.2	–	37.1	–	–
5,011	–	–	–	–	–	–	–	–	–	–	–
–	–	–	–	–	–	–	–	–	–	–	–
3,537	–	35.6	36.1	7.7	7.5	1998	30.3	–	–	–	36
1,063	–	–	–	–	–	–	–	–	–	–	–
–	–	–	–	–	–	–	–	–	–	–	–
–	–	–	–	–	–	–	–	–	–	–	–
1,143	–	41.8	30.9	7.5	6.0	1995	36.7	–	–	–	17
2,757	28.6	32.6	–	8.7	9.1	1998	33.0	47.0	47.5	48.3	61
–	–	–	–	–	–	–	–	–	–	–	–
2,085	–	37.5	–	4.5	–	1996	50.9	–	–	–	68
3,539	32.1	25.1	–	5.2	5.4	2000	46.1	48.7	45.1	43.5	–
5,735	–	–	–	–	–	–	–	–	49.2	–	–
51,649	–	–	–	5.0	–	1998	42.5	27.0	–	–	–
2,049	–	–	–	–	–	–	–	–	–	–	–
4,589	20.0	25.0	22.7	8.0	7.0	1999	33.2	64.6	55.0	44.5	–
8,380	9.8	13.6	–	6.0	6.3	2000	43.2	–	40.0	39.0	–
2,560	–	–	–	–	–	–	–	–	–	–	–
5,375	–	–	–	–	–	–	–	–	–	43.7	–
–	–	–	–	–	–	–	–	–	–	–	–
4,202	–	–	–	–	–	–	–	–	–	–	–
2,774	–	37.4	28.9	7.8	7.1	2002	37.0	–	–	–	84
18,942	–	–	–	–	–	–	–	–	–	–	–
14,354	–	–	–	3.7	3.1	2001	52.2	–	–	–	–
25,466	–	–	–	–	–	1993	45.3	–	–	–	–
19,233	–	–	–	–	–	–	–	–	–	–	–
7,960	–	–	–	–	–	–	–	–	–	–	–
4,333	–	62.7	65.2	1.3	1.5	1999	44.7	–	–	–	–
10,298	–	22.0	21.5	2.5	2.9	2001	59.3	–	–	–	53
14,688	–	17.0	–	3.3	3.8	2000	57.1	–	–	–	–
8,337	–	64.0	–	2.8	2.9	1999	57.6	–	–	–	–
10,833	22.0	–	23.9	3.9	4.1	2000	46.5	–	–	–	–

	Dietary energy consumption (kcal/person/day)				Food production per capita (1999–2001 = 100)				Food imports as a percentage of food production			
	1969–1971	1979–1981	1990–1992	2002–2004	1969–1971	1979–1981	1990–1992	2002–2004	1990–1994	1995–1999	2000–2005	
Cuba	2,660	2,880	2,720	3,320	119	122	117	109	51	42	27	
Dominica	2,020	2,240	2,940	2,760	87	77	130	93	35	47	49	
Dominican Republic	2,020	2,270	2,260	2,270	143	135	121	105	–	–	–	
Ecuador	2,160	2,360	2,510	2,670	95	82	85	102	5	7	9	
El Salvador	1,850	2,300	2,490	2,560	89	99	103	98	37	46	81	
Grenada	2,240	2,280	2,830	2,930	121	120	106	102	77	115	120	
Guatemala	2,080	2,290	2,350	2,230	81	83	96	98	15	22	31	
Guyana	2,280	2,500	2,350	2,790	80	74	59	101	18	14	17	
Haiti	1,950	2,040	1,780	2,110	152	153	114	98	22	34	40	
Honduras	2,150	2,120	2,310	2,340	146	132	111	136	9	14	24	
Jamaica	2,470	2,610	2,500	2,710	101	91	93	95	54	48	62	
Mexico	2,650	3,120	3,100	3,170	82	92	91	102	16	17	24	
Nicaragua	2,330	2,270	2,220	2,290	144	128	83	108	22	23	20	
Panama	2,330	2,270	2,320	2,300	130	119	108	96	16	28	37	
Paraguay	2,580	2,580	2,400	2,530	75	80	97	100	2	2	3	
Peru	2,250	2,130	1,960	2,580	88	69	67	106	32	31	26	
Saint Kitts and Nevis	1,940	2,270	2,580	2,730	117	157	110	100	234	234	318	
Saint Lucia	2,030	2,360	2,740	2,930	138	114	155	95	19	28	49	
Saint Vincent and the Grenadines	2,250	2,420	2,300	2,660	111	117	160	104	62	89	68	
Suriname	2,240	2,400	2,530	2,730	91	146	137	95	18	18	28	
Trinidad and Tobago	2,510	2,960	2,630	2,820	161	113	93	117	322	423	346	
Uruguay	2,950	2,850	2,660	2,920	80	77	82	102	7	6	9	
Venezuela	2,340	2,760	2,460	2,340	95	94	90	92	31	30	28	
MIDDLE EAST AND NORTH AFRICA									**34**	**37**	**38**	
Algeria	1,820	2,640	2,920	3,070	122	86	96	111	87	79	86	
Bahrain	–	–	–	–	–	–	–	–	576	484	740	
Egypt	2,350	2,900	3,200	3,330	70	68	80	104	26	24	22	
Iran, Islamic Rep. of	2,100	2,730	2,980	3,120	60	67	83	108	15	18	16	
Iraq	–	–	–	–	–	–	–	–	28	29	52	
Israel	3,140	3,150	3,410	3,610	105	111	108	101	48	55	65	
Jordan	2,240	2,610	2,820	2,730	99	95	125	119	112	127	119	
Kuwait	2,590	2,980	2,340	3,110	58	65	28	106	605	512	384	
Lebanon	2,330	2,710	3,160	3,190	58	72	125	96	35	41	50	
Libyan Arab Jamahiriya	2,440	3,450	3,270	3,380	67	104	92	96	138	97	117	
Morocco	2,470	2,750	3,030	3,110	93	84	110	118	21	29	35	
Occupied Palestinian Territories	–	–	–	2,240	–	–	–	97	–	57	46	
Oman	–	–	–	–	54	79	82	83	133	141	161	
Qatar	–	–	–	–	129	67	93	103	304	260	487	
Saudi Arabia	1,900	2,900	2,770	2,800	78	57	137	106	72	127	124	
Syria	2,380	2,950	2,830	3,070	71	114	95	115	15	10	16	
Tunisia	2,340	2,820	3,150	3,280	75	82	104	105	29	44	50	
United Arab Emirates	2,990	3,300	2,930	3,250	50	27	36	57	262	195	262	
Yemen	1,780	1,970	2,040	2,010	99	117	103	96	93	97	107	
EASTERN AND SOUTHERN EUROPE AND CIS									**9**	**8**	**8**	
Albania	–	–	–	2,870	–	–	–	104	22	20	28	
Armenia	–	–	–	2,340	–	–	–	123	34	30	28	
Azerbaijan	–	–	–	2,730	–	–	–	115	24	21	20	
Belarus	–	–	–	2,880	–	–	–	107	15	13	13	

GDP per capita (US$)	Poverty rate (%)			Inequality of income				Proportion of consumption spent on food			Road density
				Income share of lowest 20%		Gini coeficient					
2008	1990–1994	1995–1999	2000–2006	1990–1999	2000–2005	Year of survey	Gini coeficient	1990–1994	1995–1999	2000–2004	1993–2004
–	–	–	–	–	–	–	–	–	–	–	–
10,049	–	–	–	–	–	–	–	–	–	–	–
8,559	–	–	42.2	3.7	4.1	1998	47.4	–	–	–	–
7,518	–	46.0	–	3.3	–	1998	43.7	–	–	–	–
6,052	–	50.6	37.2	3.3	2.7	2000	53.2	–	–	–	–
11,232	–	–	–	–	–	–	–	–	–	–	–
4,900	–	–	56.2	3.2	3.9	2000	59.9	–	37.1	–	55
4,093	43.2	35.0	–	4.5	–	1999	43.2	–	–	–	–
1,330	–	–	–	–	2.4	–	–	–	–	–	–
4,261	–	52.5	50.7	3.3	3.4	1999	55.0	–	–	–	–
7,876	–	27.5	18.7	5.4	5.3	2000	37.9	–	55.0	–	–
14,582	–	–	17.6	4.0	4.3	2000	54.6	33.0	35.7	34.0	–
2,705	50.3	47.9	–	5.3	5.6	2001	43.1	–	–	–	28
11,255	–	37.3	–	3.4	2.5	2000	56.4	–	–	–	–
4,767	20.5	–	–	2.3	2.4	2002	57.8	–	–	–	–
8,585	–	–	53.1	4.4	3.7	2000	49.8	–	–	–	43
14,385	–	–	–	–	–	–	–	–	–	–	–
10,896	–	–	–	5.2	–	–	–	–	–	–	–
10,464	–	–	–	–	–	–	–	–	–	–	–
8,326	–	–	–	–	–	–	–	–	–	–	–
19,686	21.0	–	–	5.9	–	1992	40.3	–	–	–	–
12,707	–	–	–	4.4	4.5	2000	44.6	–	–	–	–
12,933	–	–	–	3.0	3.3	1998	49.1	–	–	–	–
6,927	–	22.6	–	7.0	–	1995	35.3	–	53.0	–	–
33,988	–	–	–	–	–	–	–	–	–	–	–
5,904	–	22.9	16.7	8.8	8.9	1999	34.4	–	–	–	–
11,209	–	–	–	5.1	6.5	1998	43.0	–	–	–	–
–	–	–	–	–	–	–	–	–	–	–	–
28,245	–	–	–	–	5.7	1997	35.5	–	–	–	–
5,172	–	21.3	14.2	7.5	6.7	1997	36.4	–	–	–	–
40,943	–	–	–	–	–	–	–	–	–	–	–
12,063	–	–	–	–	–	–	–	–	34.0	–	–
14,594	–	–	–	–	–	–	–	–	–	–	–
4,432	13.1	19.0	–	6.5	–	1998	39.5	–	–	–	–
–	–	–	–	–	–	–	–	–	–	–	–
26,095	–	–	–	–	–	–	–	–	–	–	–
86,670	–	–	–	–	–	–	–	–	–	–	–
24,120	–	–	–	–	–	–	–	–	–	–	–
4,668	–	–	–	–	–	–	–	–	–	–	–
8,020	7.4	7.6	–	5.6	6.0	2000	39.8	42.0	–	–	–
39,077	–	–	–	–	–	–	–	–	–	–	–
2,404	–	41.8	–	7.4	7.2	1998	33.4	55.0	–	–	21
6,797	–	–	25.4	8.7	8.2	2002	28.2	–	–	–	31
5,437	–	55.1	50.9	7.6	8.5	1998	37.9	–	64.5	68.0	–
8,958	–	68.1	49.6	6.9	7.4	2001	36.5	–	–	54.7	67
12,344	–	–	18.5	8.4	8.8	2000	30.4	–	65.0	47.5	64

	Dietary energy consumption (kcal/person/day)				Food production per capita (1999–2001 = 100)				Food imports as a percentage of food production		
	1969–1971	1979–1981	1990–1992	2002–2004	1969–1971	1979–1981	1990–1992	2002–2004	1990–1994	1995–1999	2000–2005
Bosnia and Herzegovina	–	–	–	2,730	–	–	–	100	9	20	34
Bulgaria	–	–	–	2,910	–	–	–	103	4	5	7
Croatia	–	–	–	2,800	–	–	–	99	11	12	15
Cyprus	3,140	2,790	3,100	3,280	122	100	96	102	59	69	78
Czech Republic	–	–	–	3,330	–	–	–	97	–	13	16
Estonia	–	–	–	3,220	–	–	–	106	12	29	29
Georgia	–	–	–	2,630	–	–	–	104	27	37	34
Hungary	–	–	–	3,590	–	–	–	102	5	6	8
Kazakhstan	–	–	–	2,820	–	–	–	109	1	1	2
Kyrgyzstan	–	–	–	3,110	–	–	–	99	22	6	5
Latvia	–	–	–	3,030	–	–	–	112	4	14	19
Lithuania	–	–	–	3,410	–	–	–	115	6	9	13
Macedonia, FYR	–	–	–	2,900	–	–	–	94	16	19	19
Malta	3,160	3,280	3,240	3,530	74	81	87	96	164	147	146
Moldova, Rep of	–	–	–	2,720	–	–	–	112	6	2	4
Poland	–	–	–	3,420	–	–	–	105	6	9	9
Romania	–	–	–	3,620	–	–	–	113	8	2	6
Russian Federation	–	–	–	3,090	–	–	–	112	13	9	9
Serbia and Montenegro	–	–	–	2,720	–	–	–	106	1	3	4
Slovakia	–	–	–	2,780	–	–	–	102	10	10	16
Slovenia	–	–	–	2,950	–	–	–	103	55	50	52
Tajikistan	–	–	–	1,900	–	–	–	133	70	31	19
Turkey	3,010	3,230	3,490	3,320	94	101	104	99	4	6	5
Turkmenistan	–	–	–	2,820	–	–	–	118	35	10	1
Ukraine	–	–	–	3,080	–	–	–	110	3	1	3
Uzbekistan	–	–	–	2,290	–	–	–	106	27	12	3

Indicator definitions and sources

Dietary energy consumption: Amount of kilocalories energy consumed per person per day. Average for three-year period. Data from 2002 to 2004 are preliminary.
Source: FAOSTAT. Available at: http://faostat.fao.org/.

Food production per capita: Index of net food production per capita (1999–2001 = 100). Average for three-year period.
Source: FAOSTAT. Available at: http://faostat.fao.org/.

Food imports as a percentage of food production: Total amount of food imported as percentage of total food production (in tons). Food includes crops and livestock. Average for considered period.
Source: FAOSTAT. Available at: http://faostat.fao.org/.

GDP per capita: Gross domestic product (GDP) per capita measured at purchasing power parity (PPP) in current prices.
Source: IMF, 2008c. Available at:
www.imf.org/external/pubs/ft/weo/2008/02/weodata/weoselgr.aspx.

Poverty rate: Percentage of the population living below the national poverty line. Data shown are the latest available for the considered period.
Source: United Nations Statistic Division, Millennium Development Goal Database.
Available at: http://data.un.org/.

Income share of lowest 20%: Share of poorest quintile in national consumption. Data shown are the latest available for the considered period.
Source: United Nations Statistic Division, Millennium Development Goal Database.
Available at: http://data.un.org/.

Gini coefficient: The area between the hypothetical line of equality and the Lorenz curve, which plots cumulative percentages of income against cumulative percentages of the population. A coefficient of 0 implies perfect equality and of 100 perfect inequality.
Source: UNDP, 2004.

Proportion of consumption spent on food: Percentage of food consumption in total consumption. Data shown are the latest available for the considered period.
Source: FAOSTAT. Available at: http://faostat.fao.org/.

Road density: Percentage of rural population with access to an all-season road.
Source: World Bank, 2007c.

GDP per capita (US$)	Poverty rate (%)			Inequality of income				Proportion of consumption spent on food			Road density
				Income share of lowest 20%		Gini coeficient					
2008	1990–1994	1995–1999	2000–2006	1990–1999	2000–2005	Year of survey	Gini coeficient	1990–1994	1995–1999	2000–2004	1993–2004
7,618	–	–	19.5	–	7.0	2001	26.2	–	–	–	–
12,372	–	36.0	12.8	10.0	8.7	2001	31.9	–	56.3	50.9	–
16,474	–	–	–	9.3	8.8	2001	29.0	–	37.1	28.5	–
28,381	–	–	–	–	–	–	–	26.2	–	–	–
25,755	–	–	–	10.3	–	1996	25.4	–	30.0	27.4	–
20,754	–	8.9	–	6.8	6.8	2000	37.2	–	42.0	34.5	–
5,001	–	–	54.5	6.0	5.4	2001	36.9	–	68.0	64.0	–
19,830	14.5	17.3	–	9.4	8.6	2002	26.9	–	–	–	–
11,563	–	34.6	15.4	6.7	7.4	2003	32.3	–	59.8	50.3	77
2,174	–	–	43.1	7.5	8.9	2002	34.8	–	–	–	76
17,801	–	–	5.9	7.3	6.8	1998	33.6	–	43.8	39.4	–
18,855	–	–	–	8.2	6.8	2000	31.9	–	54.0	46.7	–
9,128	–	–	21.7	8.5	6.1	1998	28.2	–	47.0	50.0	–
23,908	–	–	–	–	–	–	–	37.3	–	–	–
3,154	–	–	48.5	6.0	7.8	2002	36.9	–	–	68.3	–
17,560	23.8	14.6	–	7.9	7.4	2002	34.1	52.5	41.0	32.1	–
12,698	21.5	25.4	–	8.7	8.2	2002	30.3	–	57.0	56.0	89
16,161	30.9	31.4	19.6	5.5	6.1	2002	31.0	–	–	–	81
10,911	–	–	–	–	–	–	–	–	–	55.0	–
22,242	–	–	–	8.8	–	1996	25.8	–	30.0	–	–
28,894	–	–	–	9.1	8.3	1998	28.4	–	26.5	25.8	–
1,984	–	74.9	–	8.1	7.8	2003	32.6	–	87.7	73.6	74
13,447	28.3	–	27.0	5.8	5.3	2000	40.0	38.5	–	35.2	–
5,765	–	–	–	6.1	–	1998	40.8	–	–	–	–
7,634	–	–	19.5	8.8	9.0	1999	29.0	–	68.1	61.7	–
2,606	–	–	27.5	3.9	7.2	2000	26.8	–	34.7	–	57

Table 3 – International assistance

	Average annual food aid deliveries			Official development assistance (ODA)				
				ODA as % of GDP			% of ODA for agriculture	
	1990–1994	1995–1999	2000–2007	1990–1994	1995–1999	2000–2006	1995–1999	2000–2006
SUB-SAHARAN AFRICA	**4,521,109**	**2,774,050**	**3,902,418**	**6.9**	**3.9**	**3.5**	**7.4**	**3.9**
Angola	178,079	200,372	155,583	5.2	6.0	2.5	3.4	2.0
Benin	16,848	17,891	16,063	13.3	10.1	8.3	11.4	4.1
Botswana	9,958	2,880	0	3.0	1.7	0.5	3.7	3.2
Burkina Faso	53,814	40,814	38,258	14.3	15.6	12.7	13.4	8.8
Burundi	19,859	24,299	61,614	25.3	12.7	33.4	0.9	2.1
Cameroon	5,024	9,915	11,001	4.6	3.9	2.3	3.3	2.6
Cape Verde	56,659	60,020	34,669	31.7	23.3	15.2	5.0	3.1
Central African Republic	4,344	3,553	8,667	14.1	12.4	6.8	11.9	2.9
Chad	27,725	24,381	43,397	16.4	14.1	8.2	11.2	5.6
Comoros	5,565	3,318	23	19.6	14.6	8.9	4.0	3.9
Congo, Republic of	10,765	13,037	87,661	7.4	6.5	1.4	3.5	0.5
Congo, Democratic Rep. of the	67,574	39,579	16,190	4.0	2.7	12.2	0.7	1.2
Côte d'Ivoire	51,022	30,774	22,680	8.5	5.7	1.4	9.6	2.6
Djibouti	13,600	13,279	13,030	24.8	17.4	12.0	0.6	1.3
Equatorial Guinea	4,140	1,422	450	37.7	8.6	0.8	1.8	2.6
Eritrea	98,307	68,670	204,757	20.7	20.1	28.1	9.8	4.8
Ethiopia	899,890	599,453	1,036,161	9.9	8.4	14.7	13.8	6.0
Gabon	0	17	141	2.2	1.4	0.3	0.9	1.4
Gambia	9,866	6,300	9,186	26.4	9.4	14.2	29.6	5.9
Ghana	118,461	60,265	68,844	8.5	8.7	10.8	4.6	5.3
Guinea	30,475	13,387	31,809	11.6	8.7	6.2	12.7	5.8
Guinea Bissau	8,770	7,543	11,595	50.3	38.9	28.2	2.8	2.1
Kenya	204,248	88,489	237,728	7.6	4.0	3.6	8.8	8.5
Lesotho	38,635	20,903	30,969	16.7	8.1	6.8	11.5	2.5
Liberia	146,320	126,518	66,994	–	–	27.1	1.8	2.7
Madagascar	43,372	30,766	49,488	10.3	10.9	10.6	10.4	4.6
Malawi	305,877	108,480	120,297	29.5	22.6	19.7	6.4	5.9
Mali	35,793	20,040	26,368	15.9	14.8	12.3	8.3	8.8
Mauritania	54,632	31,100	51,187	18.6	16.5	15.2	6.9	8.4
Mauritius	6,757	362	0	1.7	0.8	0.4	21.1	5.6
Mozambique	574,048	211,953	176,319	47.7	24.8	21.6	5.8	3.8
Namibia	13,341	3,082	9,916	5.0	5.2	3.2	4.9	3.8
Niger	50,284	42,123	61,340	16.5	14.1	12.9	8.2	9.4
Nigeria	119	221	6,076	1.1	0.5	0.5	3.7	1.4
Rwanda	96,820	356,228	72,644	24.8	27.0	20.0	1.5	8.0
Sao Tome and Principe	8,485	4,330	3,443	45.1	37.4	30.3	12.6	5.9
Senegal	52,887	17,356	27,454	10.8	9.9	7.8	12.2	5.9
Seychelles	234	0	0	5.4	2.7	1.8	1.4	8.1
Sierra Leone	36,229	57,624	46,928	17.0	16.2	30.6	3.7	1.5
Somalia	163,229	39,663	66,474	–	–	–	1.9	1.1
South Africa	7,013	5,412	12,228	0.2	0.3	0.3	1.8	1.7
Sudan	457,180	159,906	400,024	7.9	2.2	3.7	1.5	1.1
Swaziland	14,951	5,218	11,615	4.3	2.2	1.5	22.5	19.9
Tanzania, United Rep. of	40,948	66,020	109,547	19.9	10.8	10.6	7.0	4.1
Togo	13,072	5,585	2,745	10.5	7.9	3.6	10.8	2.2
Uganda	62,174	75,818	191,214	22.9	11.2	14.3	4.8	4.5
Zambia	183,423	33,644	88,202	19.7	22.2	11.4	6.4	2.9
Zimbabwe	220,293	22,037	161,442	8.0	4.5	9.3	11.8	3.0

	Average annual food aid deliveries			Official development assistance (ODA)				
				ODA as % of GDP			% of ODA for agriculture	
	1990–1994	1995–1999	2000–2007	1990–1994	1995–1999	2000–2006	1995–1999	2000–2006
ASIA AND OCEANIA	**2,550,363**	**3,135,374**	**2,627,376**	**1.0**	**0.6**	**0.4**	**8.5**	**5.4**
Afghanistan	75,797	138,972	262,924	–	–	38.7	1.3	4.0
Bangladesh	919,427	836,594	344,201	5.3	2.5	2.0	5.1	3.4
Bhutan	4,555	4,975	4,542	24.2	18.6	11.7	7.4	8.2
Brunei Darussalam	0	0	0	0.1	0.1	–	–	–
Cambodia	57,258	50,034	40,395	8.1	11.3	9.8	9.7	6.8
China	137,294	167,593	47,416	0.5	0.3	0.1	6.2	5.0
Cook Islands	0	0	0	–	–	–	4.3	3.6
Fiji	0	0	0	3.4	2.1	1.9	0.6	3.2
Hong Kong (SAR)	2,476	0	0	0.0	0.0	–	–	–
India	341,688	341,892	181,031	0.7	0.4	0.2	12.2	9.0
Indonesia	47,704	345,409	202,108	1.2	0.8	0.6	9.0	5.7
Kiribati	0	0	0	60.0	36.5	20.0	1.7	2.2
Korea, Dem. People's Rep. of	0	761,680	1,016,242	–	–	–	26.9	3.0
Korea, Republic of	0	0	0	0.0	0.0	–	0.7	–
Lao People's Democratic Rep.	5,949	27,039	18,009	14.7	18.9	12.9	6.3	9.0
Malaysia	1,987	0	0	0.4	0.0	0.1	2.8	0.8
Maldives	2,463	3,355	6,944	10.5	7.3	4.6	5.4	0.0
Marshall Islands	0	0	0	–	–	–	–	0.1
Micronesia	0	0	0	–	–	–	–	0.1
Mongolia	14,820	20,574	36,128	9.5	18.0	14.5	5.2	5.0
Myanmar	371	4,534	14,560	4.9	1.0	1.2	8.5	3.9
Nauru	0	0	0	–	–	–	–	0.0
Niue	0	0	0	–	–	–	–	5.6
Nepal	21,064	39,600	48,232	10.5	7.6	6.0	20.0	7.3
Pakistan	299,145	171,725	136,862	2.1	1.1	1.6	11.1	3.4
Palau	0	0	0	–	–	–	–	0.7
Papua New Guinea	177	2,489	0	9.1	7.6	6.4	3.6	2.5
Philippines	149,915	63,164	132,176	2.6	1.0	0.7	10.3	6.5
Samoa	0	0	0	34.2	15.1	13.2	4.2	3.5
Singapore	0	0	0	0.0	0.0	–	–	–
Solomon Islands	2	52	0	18.4	12.0	36.8	0.4	1.3
Sri Lanka	319,788	92,721	77,481	7.4	2.8	2.8	13.5	4.5
Thailand	74,774	2,838	588	0.6	0.6	0.0	10.8	3.1
Timor-Leste	0	1,824	8,907	–	56.6	57.4	4.3	3.1
Tonga	0	0	0	20.5	17.4	13.4	8.7	1.0
Tuvalu	0	0	0	–	–	–	0.1	0.1
Vanuatu	2	0	0	23.2	14.7	12.8	1.4	2.7
Viet Nam	73,707	58,310	48,631	3.6	4.0	4.1	8.2	7.0
LATIN AMERICA AND CARIBBEAN	**1,916,014**	**912,237**	**704,795**	**0.4**	**0.2**	**0.2**	**6.3**	**5.8**
Antigua and Barbuda	200	626	0	0.9	1.0	1.0	12.4	–
Argentina	0	0	6	0.1	0.0	0.1	5.6	6.3
Bahamas	0	0	0	0.1	0.1	–	–	–
Barbados	0	0	19	–0.1	0.2	0.3	–	23.4
Belize	1	0	74	5.2	3.4	1.6	31.7	37.4
Bolivia	235,720	126,355	86,823	8.9	8.0	7.4	5.8	7.4
Brazil	25,606	244	40	0.0	0.0	0.0	4.6	4.4
Chile	7,599	116	46	0.3	0.2	0.1	3.0	2.4
Colombia	12,662	9,109	16,005	0.2	0.2	0.6	14.2	6.3
Costa Rica	38,818	756	0	2.0	0.0	0.1	7.9	4.8

	Average annual food aid deliveries			Official development assistance (ODA)				
				ODA as % of GDP			% of ODA for agriculture	
	1990–1994	1995–1999	2000–2007	1990–1994	1995–1999	2000–2006	1995–1999	2000–2006
Cuba	8,572	24,941	10,604	–	–	–	2.8	6.8
Dominica	751	1,936	0	8.0	9.4	7.6	30.5	30.4
Dominican Republic	19,389	29,144	15,024	0.8	0.8	0.4	8.2	5.7
Ecuador	41,802	19,018	47,421	1.6	0.9	0.7	15.6	6.8
El Salvador	137,739	33,215	33,544	4.5	2.3	1.3	4.9	3.7
Grenada	937	907	0	5.6	3.0	4.1	3.7	5.6
Guatemala	173,925	69,751	104,133	2.2	1.5	1.1	4.0	3.6
Guyana	43,208	41,449	18,859	20.4	12.6	13.6	8.9	6.4
Haiti	100,262	153,004	124,941	19.6	12.5	7.8	7.0	6.9
Honduras	124,671	65,224	66,493	6.5	7.4	5.7	5.2	3.5
Jamaica	224,932	29,070	11,846	1.3	0.7	0.4	3.0	6.7
Mexico	117,702	9,944	504	0.1	0.1	0.0	8.6	1.8
Nicaragua	136,119	91,494	56,889	30.5	15.1	13.8	4.7	4.6
Panama	6,253	1,172	0	1.5	0.4	0.2	1.8	4.2
Paraguay	2,028	534	5	1.7	1.2	0.8	20.7	6.0
Peru	434,745	189,182	110,085	1.3	0.7	0.7	6.4	10.5
Saint Kitts and Nevis	671	756	0	4.3	2.2	2.0	1.5	–
Saint Lucia	0	1,809	0	4.8	4.9	1.6	28.6	28.4
Saint Vincent and the Grenadines	0	1,714	0	6.5	8.1	1.7	–	37.2
Suriname	17,593	10,768	0	15.7	8.1	2.2	4.3	12.1
Trinidad and Tobago	0	0	0	0.2	0.4	0.0	0.2	0.6
Uruguay	4,110	0	0	0.5	0.2	0.1	6.8	3.0
Venezuela	0	0	1,435	0.1	0.0	0.1	0.4	6.8
MIDDLE EAST AND NORTH AFRICA	**1,851,828**	**484,139**	**719,795**	**1.4**	**0.8**	**0.5**	**7.3**	**2.2**
Algeria	24,770	29,734	36,628	0.5	0.6	0.4	1.4	2.4
Bahrain	0	0	0	1.6	0.9	0.6	11.9	0.9
Egypt	911,980	112,648	20,605	5.8	2.3	1.1	7.5	5.6
Iran, Islamic Rep. of	58,026	11,711	8,124	0.2	0.2	0.1	0.5	0.7
Iraq	62,615	75,503	151,545	–	–	–	0.4	0.5
Israel	1,005	0	0	2.3	1.3	–	0.0	–
Jordan	256,180	109,050	158,340	11.8	5.9	6.1	5.0	1.6
Kuwait	0	0	0	0.0	0.0	–	–	–
Lebanon	25,433	4,543	39,313	3.6	1.5	1.7	1.5	2.6
Libyan Arab Jamahiriya	0	0	0	0.0	0.0	0.1	–	6.4
Morocco	208,552	5,750	38,957	3.0	1.4	1.3	10.0	1.6
Occupied Palestinian Territories	37,658	31,754	130,845	–	–	–	–	–
Oman	0	0	0	0.4	0.4	0.1	4.0	1.1
Qatar	0	0	0	0.0	0.0	–	–	–
Saudi Arabia	0	0	0	0.0	0.0	0.0	0.5	0.4
Syria	33,105	27,411	14,413	3.3	1.4	0.4	–	–
Tunisia	149,914	13,089	473	2.0	0.8	1.3	18.2	1.8
United Arab Emirates	0	0	0	0.0	0.0	–	–	–
Yemen	82,589	62,947	120,552	1.7	4.1	2.8	4.5	5.2

	Average annual food aid deliveries			Official development assistance (ODA)				
				ODA as % of GDP			% of ODA for agriculture	
	1990–1994	1995–1999	2000–2007	1990–1994	1995–1999	2000–2006	1995–1999	2000–2006
EASTERN AND SOUTHERN EUROPE AND CIS	**3,426,996**	**2,330,403**	**845,974**	**0.6**	**0.7**	**0.9**	**5.4**	**4.4**
Albania	329,288	19,466	17,581	21.3	9.2	5.7	4.5	3.2
Armenia	105,547	185,188	44,211	21.1	13.4	8.0	7.7	11.3
Azerbaijan	47,989	127,997	36,435	5.3	3.8	3.0	10.4	10.5
Belarus	126,379	27,491	0	–	–	0.2	–	0.9
Bosnia and Herzegovina	220	58,121	35,959	–	18.8	7.4	2.5	1.5
Bulgaria	96,606	6,092	5,622	0.0	0.0	0.0	–	–
Croatia	2,385	14,811	0	0.4	0.3	0.4	2.0	3.0
Cyprus	0	0	22	0.6	0.2	–	–	–
Czech Republic	0	0	0	0.0	0.0	0.0	–	–
Estonia	83,814	0	0	0.0	0.0	0.0	–	–
Georgia	262,052	253,016	68,380	21.5	8.5	6.5	3.5	5.1
Hungary	0	0	0	0.0	0.0	0.0	–	–
Kazakhstan	14,214	2,750	759	0.4	0.7	0.7	0.6	0.8
Kyrgyzstan	53,196	85,309	52,955	11.7	16.4	11.5	20.0	8.8
Latvia	124,900	0	0	0.0	0.0	0.0	–	–
Lithuania	177,909	21,269	0	0.0	0.0	0.0	–	–
Macedonia, FYR	9,204	19,657	9,621	0.0	0.0	0.0	–	–
Malta	0	0	0	–	0.8	0.3	0.0	–
Moldova, Rep of	48,522	77,384	23,014	–	5.0	7.2	8.5	7.3
Poland	366,792	1	0	0.0	0.0	0.0	–	–
Romania	259,832	13	744	0.0	0.0	0.0	–	–
Russian Federation	937,920	963,017	241,682	0.0	0.0	0.0	–	–
Serbia and Montenegro	214,998	264,413	97,548	–	–	6.2	–	–
Slovakia	0	0	0	0.0	0.0	0.0	–	–
Slovenia	594	0	0	0.1	0.2	0.3	0.2	8.1
Tajikistan	48,263	133,675	122,281	5.3	10.5	11.9	16.6	10.1
Turkey	5,467	333	0	0.4	0.1	0.1	0.6	1.2
Turkmenistan	20,652	20,214	2,968	0.7	0.7	0.4	–	1.4
Ukraine	89,803	49,905	26,831	–	–	0.5	–	1.2
Uzbekistan	452	284	59,361	1.1	0.9	1.5	3.3	3.8

Indicator definitions and sources

Average annual food aid deliveries: Average annual food aid deliveries to recipient countries for the considered period. Cereals in tons of grain equivalent and non-cereals in actual tons.
Source: WFP, 2008a. Available at: www.wfp.org/interfais/index2.htm.

ODA as a % of GDP: Official development assistance (ODA) disbursements (net of debt relief) as a percentage of GDP (both in current US$). Average for considered period.
Source: IMF, 2008d, and OECD.Stat website. Available at: www.oecd.org/statistics.

% of ODA for agriculture: ODA commitments to agriculture as a percentage of total ODA commitments (both in current US$). Average for considered period.
Source: OECD.Stat website. Available at: www.oecd.org/statistics.

Part V Annexes

Abbreviations and acronyms

Glossary

Bibliography

Methodology for maps

ADMARC	Malawian Agricultural Development and Marketing Corporation
AIDS	acquired immune deficiency syndrome
AISP	Agricultural Input Subsidy Programme
BPL	below poverty line
BULOG	Indonesian Logistics Bureau
CAADP	Comprehensive African Agricultural Development Programme
CARE	Cooperative for Assistance and Relief Everywhere
CE	commodity exchange
CEPAL	Comisión Económica para América Latina y el Caribe (United Nations Economic Commission for Latin America and the Caribbean)
CIS	Commonwealth of Independent States
CPI	consumer price index
CPRC	Chronic Poverty Research Centre
CSB	corn–soya blend
DFID	Department for International Development
DHS	Demographic and Health Survey
DRC	Democratic Republic of the Congo
ECX	Ethiopia Commodity Exchange
EFSR	Emergency Food Security Reserve
EIU	Economist Intelligence Unit
EU	European Union
EWS	early-warning system
FANTA	Food and Nutrition Technical Assistance
FAO	Food and Agriculture Organization of the United Nations
FAPRI	Food and Agricultural Policy Research Institute
FAS	free alongside ship
FEWS NET	Famine Early Warning System Network
FFPRI	food and fuel price risk index
FOB	free on board
GDP	gross domestic product
GVI	global vulnerability index
HDI	Human Development Index
HH	household
HIPC	heavily indebted poor country
HIV	human immunodeficiency virus
HPRI	high price risk index
HRS	Household Responsibility System
HYV	high-yielding variety
IDP	internally displaced person
IFAD	International Fund for Agricultural Development
IFPRI	International Food Policy Research Institute
IGC	International Grains Council
IMF	International Monetary Fund
LDC	least developed country
LIFDC	low-income food-deficit country
MDG	Millennium Development Goal
MRP	maximum retail price
MT	metric ton
NEPAD	New Partnership for Africa's Development
NGO	non-governmental organization
ODA	official development assistance
OECD	Organisation for Economic Co-operation and Development
P4P	Purchase for Progress
PADETS	Participatory Agricultural Development and Extension Training Service
PCA	principal components analysis
PPP	purchasing power parity
PSNP	Productive Safety Net Programme
RATIN	Regional Trade Information Network
SAFEX	South African Futures Exchange
SENAC	Strengthening Emergency Needs Assessment Capacity
SIMA	Agricultural Market Information System
SOAS	School of Oriental and African Studies
SPS	sanitary and phytosanitary
TSC	Technical Steering Committee
UNAIDS	Joint United Nations Programme on HIV/AIDS

UNCTAD	United Nations Conference on Trade and Development
UNDP	United Nations Development Programme
UNICEF	United Nations Children's Fund
USAID	US Agency for International Development

USDA	US Department of Agriculture
VAT	value added tax
WFP	World Food Programme
WHO	World Health Organization
WR	warehouse receipt
WTO	World Trade Organization

Arbitrage

Actions by traders to ensure that the price differences of a *commodity* among locations (spatial arbitrage) or across time (temporal arbitrage) will be smaller than or equal to the cost of moving or storing the commodity from the region or period with the lower price to the region or period with the higher price. Through arbitrage, traders make profits from the price differences across space or time.

Asset

In a livelihood context, assets are the resources a household owns, or over which it has legal or customary usufruct rights. They fall into five broad categories: natural, social, physical, human and financial assets. Using these resources, a household can acquire food directly through production, or indirectly through exchange and transfer.

Bennett's law

As household income increases, a smaller share of calories comes from starchy staples as the diet becomes more diversified. This change in eating patterns generally entails the purchase of higher-quality foods.

Cash crop

A crop that is grown for trading purposes, as opposed to subsistence food crops, which are mostly consumed by the farmer. In developing countries, cash crops are usually exported. They include tropical fruits, cocoa, coffee, cotton and relatively expensive vegetables.

Commodity

A tangible good that has value and can be exchanged.

Competition

The rivalry among sellers to gain market share and profits. Competition may stimulate innovation, encourage efficiency and drive down prices. In economics, a perfectly competitive market has: (1) many buyers and sellers; (2) homogeneous products; (3) freedom of entry to and exit from the market; and (4) perfect information among market participants.

Consumer price index (CPI)

An index that measures the cost of a basket of goods and services, with weights reflecting the relative importance of each in the budget of an average household.

Contract farming

Agreement between a farmer and a processor or trader to supply specified agricultural output at a future date, often at predetermined prices. The buyer often supports the farmer through, for example, inputs and technical assistance.

Economies of scale

Declining average cost per unit produced as the volume of production increases. One cause is that overheads and other fixed costs can be spread over more units of output.

Effective demand

Actual demand for particular goods or services that is supported by a capacity to purchase. This is distinguished from notional demand, which is the desire or need for goods and services, which may not be supported by purchasing power, so cannot be communicated to suppliers through the price mechanism.

Efficiency

A situation where nobody can be made better off through exchange without making somebody else worse off. Loosely, efficiency ensures a maximum output with a given set of inputs. It does not necessarily imply equity.

Elasticity

A measure of the responsiveness of one variable, such as demand or supply, to changes in another, such as price or income. For instance, the price elasticity of demand refers to the percentage change in demand that results from a percentage change in price. A good is price-elastic when a change of 1 percent in price results in a change larger than 1 percent in demand. The change is smaller than 1 percent for an inelastic good. Staple foods are typically inelastic.

Engel's law

The observation made by Ernst Engel that people tend to spend a smaller share of their budget on food as their income rises.

Entitlements
The set of alternative bundles of goods and services that a person can acquire by converting his/her endowments, such as land and labour, through production, trade or gifts.

Food access
A household's ability to acquire adequate amounts of food regularly through a combination of production, purchases, barter, borrowing, food assistance or gifts.

Food availability
The amount of food that is present in a country or area through all forms of domestic production, imports, food stocks and food aid.

Food–price dilemma
The dilemma between increasing domestic *food availability* and increasing *food access*. High food prices provide production incentives to suppliers, but may obstruct access, especially for poor consumers. If prices are too low, producers may not be able to cover their costs. This conflict is at the heart of food security policy.

Food security
A condition that exists when all people, at all times, are free from hunger. Food security involves four aspects: (1) availability; (2) access; (3) utilization; and (4) stability.

Food utilization
The selection and intake of food and the absorption of nutrients. Food utilization depends on adequate diet, clean water, sanitation and health care.

Futures
A contract to buy or sell a commodity at a certain price at a future date.

Hazard
The probability that a potentially damaging phenomenon occurs within a given period and area.

Hedging
Cover against the risk of a price change by taking an opposite position, often by using futures.

Hunger
A condition in which people lack both the macronutrients, energy and protein, and the micronutrients, vitamins and minerals for fully productive, active and healthy lives. Hunger can be a short- or long-term problem with many causes and a range of effects, from mild to severe.

Institutions
The formal and informal rules and norms that shape human interaction. Institutions range from cultural customs to formal laws and government organizations. Together, they define the "rules of the game" or the environment in which social and economic interactions occur.

Liberalization
Policies intended to promote the role of markets, including through deregulation, removal of price controls and lowering of trade barriers, often accompanied by limiting the role of government.

Livelihoods
The capabilities, *assets* and activities a household requires to secure basic needs, including food, shelter, health and education.

Macronutrients
Include carbohydrates, protein and fat. They form the bulk of the diet and provide all energy needs.

Malnutrition
A physical condition in which people experience either nutrition deficiencies (undernutrition) or an excess of certain nutrients (overnutrition).

Market
The organized exchange of goods or services between buyers and sellers. Markets can be viewed as social arrangements that coordinate demand and supply, set prices and allocate resources.

Market failure
A market fails when it does not allocate resources efficiently. There are four broad causes of market failure:
1 the abuse of market power, which can occur when a single buyer or seller exerts significant influence over prices;

2 the presence of externalities, when the costs or benefits of a particular good or service, or its production process, are not fully reflected in the price;

3 public goods, when consumption of a good is non-excludable (i.e. it is difficult to exclude someone from enjoying it) and non-rival (i.e. consumption by someone does not detract from consumption by others); and

4 imperfect information, when there is incomplete information or uncertainty.

Market integration

The degree to which price changes are transmitted from one market to another. One measure is the correlation among prices in different markets for the same good or service. A high correlation between prices implies a high degree of market integration. *Arbitrage* plays an important role in market integration. For example, in a drought, markets are integrated if higher prices in the drought-affected area trigger trade from a surplus area, thereby reducing price differences. Market integration is an aspect of market functioning, which refers to whether or not a market is able to allocate resources. A functioning market is not necessarily efficient.

Market structure

Market characteristics that influence the behaviour of economic agents. It includes the numbers of buyers and sellers, their distribution, the degree of product differentiation, and entry barriers for new firms.

Marketing (or value) chain

The activities that bring a product or service from conception to end-use in a particular industry, ranging from input supply to production, processing, wholesale, and finally retail. Each step along the value chain adds to the final product in a different way; the value of each step is reflected in the *marketing margin*.

Marketing margin

The difference between prices at different levels of the *marketing chain*, for example, between the price paid by a consumer and that received by a farmer. Margins can be calculated all along the *marketing chain*. Each margin reflects the value added at that level of the chain.

Micronutrients

Include all the vitamins and minerals that in small amounts are essential for life.

Monetization

The open-market sale of food aid.

Option

A contract that gives the right – but not the obligation – to buy (a call option) or sell (a put option) a particular asset at a given price within a certain period.

Productivity

The ratio of output to input. It can be applied to individual factors of production or collectively. For example, labour productivity is usually calculated by dividing total output by the number of workers or the number of hours worked. Land productivity is the ratio of output to the area of land cultivated.

Price

The amount of money required for the exchange of a good or service to take place. Prices are an important source of market information, providing the incentive for market actors' decisions. There are different types of prices:

- *Farm-gate price:* the price a farmer receives for a product at the boundary of the farm, not including transport costs or other marketing services.
- *Wholesale price:* the price of a good purchased from a wholesaler. Wholesalers buy large quantities of goods and resell them to retailers. The wholesale price is higher than the farm-gate price because of the marketing margin.
- *Retail price:* the price of a good purchased from a retailer by a consumer. The retail price is higher than the wholesale price because of the marketing margin.
- *Import parity price:* the price paid for an imported good at the border, not including transaction costs incurred within the importing country.
- *Export parity price:* the price received for an exported good at the border, including transaction costs incurred within the exporting country.

Purchasing power

The quantities of goods and services that can be bought with a given amount of money. It depends on income and prices.

Risk

The probability that a negative impact occurs as a result of the interaction between a *hazard* and vulnerable conditions (see *vulnerability*).

Structure-Conduct-Performance (SCP) Paradigm

A framework or approach to market analysis based on the premise that the structure of a market (see *market structure*) influences the behaviour/conduct of its participants, which in turn influences the functioning or performance of the market.

Terms of trade (ToT)

The quantity of a good that can be acquired by giving up something else. They give an indication of *purchasing power*. In foreign trade, the ToT are the ratio of export prices to import prices. The ToT for pastoralists could refer to the kilograms of cereals they could buy by selling one goat, for example.

Thin market

A market that does not have large volumes of trade. The implication is that changes in supply or demand may result in large swings in prices. Prices obtained from thin markets are less reliable or informative about market conditions.

Transaction costs

Costs incurred during the buying and selling process that are above and beyond the costs associated with production. They include the costs of transportation, storage, information gathering, trade finance and contract enforcement. Markets function better with lower transaction costs.

Undernutrition

Physical manifestation of hunger resulting from inadequate intake of macro- and micronutrients or disease, and characterized by wasting, stunting or other clinical signs.

Vertical integration

The degree to which one firm carries out all the production and transaction for a particular good or service – the extent to which the firm owns its upstream suppliers and its downstream buyers, for example, farming, processing, transporting, marketing and retailing.

Vulnerability

Conditions that increase a household's susceptibility to the effect of *hazards*. It is a function of a household's exposure to a hazard and its coping capacity to mitigate the effect of that hazard.

Abdulai, A., Barrett, C.B. & Hazell, P. 2004. *Food Aid for Market Development in Sub-Saharan Africa*. Draft. Washington, DC, IFPRI.

Abdulai, A., Barrett, C.B. & Hoddinott, J. 2005. Does food aid really have disincentive effects? New evidence from sub-Saharan Africa. *World Development*, 33(10): 1689–1704.

Agyeman-Duah, F. 2006. Is a commodity exchange the answer to underdevelopment in Africa? *International Affairs Journal* at UC Davis, online edition. Posted at: http://davisiaj.com/content/view/69/95/.

Ahmed, A.U., Hill, R.V., Smith, L.C., Wiesmann, D.M. & Frankenberger, T. with assistance from **Gulati, K., Quabili, W. & Yohannes, Y.** 2007. *The World's Most Deprived: Characteristics and Causes of Extreme Poverty and Hunger*. 2020 Discussion Paper No. 43. Washington, DC, IFPRI.

Aker, J.C. 2007. *The Structure, Conduct and Performance of the Cereals Market in Niger: Implications for Grain Market and Food Security Policies during Crises*. Unpublished mimeo, University of California-Berkeley, USA.
___ 2008. *Droughts, Grain Markets and Food Crisis in Niger*. Posted at SSRN: http://ssrn.com/abstract=1004426

Aksoy, M.A. & Beghin, J.C. 2005. *Global Agricultural Trade and Developing Countries*. Washington, DC, World Bank.

Alderman, H. 2002. *Price and Tax Subsidization of Consumer Goods Social Protection*. Discussion Paper No. 0224. Washington, DC, World Bank.

Alderman, H. & Haque, T. 2006. Countercyclical safety nets for the poor and vulnerable. *Food Policy*, 31: 372–383.

Alderman, H. & Hoddinott, J. 2007. *Growth Promoting Social Safety Nets*. IFPRI Policy Brief. Washington, DC, IFPRI. Posted at: www.ifpri.org/2020Chinaconference/pdf/beijingbrief_alderman.pdf.

Alderman, H., Hoddinott, J. & Kinsey, B. 2006. Long term consequences of early childhood malnutrition. *Oxford Economic Papers*, 58: 450–474.

Alderman, H., Hoogeveen, H. & Rossi, M. 2006. Reducing child malnutrition in Tanzania: Combined effects of income growth and program intervention. *Economics and Human Biology*, 4(1): 1–23.

Angel, A. & Subran, L. 2008. *Alzas de los precios, mercados e inseguridad alimentaria en Centroamérica: Preocupaciones, intereses y acciones*. El Salvador, WFP.

Asfaw, A. 2008. Does supermarket purchase affect dietary practices of households? Some empirical evidence form Guatemala. *Development Policy Review*, 26(2): 227–243.

Banerjee, A.V. & Duflo, E. 2007. The economic lives of the poor. *Journal of Economic Perspectives*, 21(1): 141–167.
___ 2008. What is the middle class about? The middle classes around the world. *Journal of Economic Perspectives*, 22(2): 3–28.

Baro, M. & Deubel, T. 2006. Persistent hunger: Perspectives on vulnerability, famine, and food security in sub-Saharan Africa. *Annual Review of Anthropology*, (35): 521–538.

Barrett, C.B. 2002. Food security and food assistance programs. *In* B.L. Gardner and G.C. Rausser, eds. *Handbook of Agricultural Economics*. Amsterdam, North Holland.
___ 2005a. *Displaced Distortions: Financial Market Failures and Seemingly Inefficient Resource Allocation*. Ithaca, NY, Cornell University.
___ 2005b. Spatial market integration. *In* L.E. Blume and S.N. Durlauf, eds. 2008, *The New Palgrave Dictionary of Economics*. London, Palgrave Macmillan.
___ 2006. *Food Aid's Intended and Unintended Consequences*. FAO ESA Working Paper No. 06-05. Rome, FAO.
___ 2008. Smallholder market participation: Concepts and evidence from eastern and southern Africa. *Food Policy*, 33(4): 299–317.

Barrett, C.B. & Dorosh, P. 1996. Farmers' welfare and changing food prices: Nonparametric evidence from rice in Madagascar. *American Journal of Agricultural Economics*, 78(3): 656–669.

Barrett, C.B. & Maxwell, D.G. 2005. *Food Aid after Fifty Years: Recasting its Role*. New York, Routledge.

Bates, B., Kundzewicz, Z.W., Wu, S. & Palutikof, J. 2008. *Climate Change and Water*. Technical Paper of the Intergovernmental Panel on Climate Change. Geneva. IPCC.

Baulch, B. 2001. Food marketing. *In* S. Devereux and S. Maxwell, eds. *Food Security in Sub-Saharan Africa*. London, ITDG Publishing.

Behrman, J.R., Alderman, H. & Hoddinott, J. 2004. Hunger and malnutrition, *In* J. Lomborg, ed. *Global Crises, Global Solutions.* Cambridge, UK, Cambridge University Press.

Berdal, M.R & Malone, D.M. 2000. *Greed and Grievance: Economic Agendas in Civil Wars.* Boulder, CO, Lynne Rienner Publishers.

Berlage, L., Verpoorten, M. & Verwimp, P. 2003. Rural households under extreme stress: Survival strategies of poor households in post-genocide Rwanda. A report for the Flemish Interuniversity Council and the Belgian Department of International Cooperation under the Policy Research Program.

Bernstein, P.L. 1996. *Against the Gods – The remarkable story of risk*. New York, John Wiley and Sons.

Berry, R.A. & Cline, W.R. 1979. *Agrarian Structure and Productivity in Developing Countries*. Baltimore, MA, Johns Hopkins University Press.

Bhagwati, J. & Srinivasan, T.N. 2002. Trade and poverty in the poor countries. *American Economic Review*, 92(2): 180–183.

Binswanger, H. 1981. Attitudes toward risk: Theoretical implications of an experiment in rural India. *Economic Journal*, 91(364): 867–890.

Birdsall, N., Ross, D. & Sabot, R. 1995. Inequality and growth reconsidered: Lessons from east Asia. *World Bank Economic Review*, 9(3): 477–508.

Birthal, P.S., Joshi, P.K. & Gulati, A. 2005. *Vertical Coordination in High-Value Food Commodities: Implications for Smallholders*. MTID Discussion Paper No. 85. Washington, DC, IFPRI.

Black R., Biao, X., Collyer, M., Enghersen, G., Heering, L. & Markova, E. 2007. Migration and development: Causes and consequences. *In* R. Penninix, M. Berger and K. Kraal, eds. *The Dynamics of International Migration and Settlement in Europe: A State of the Art*. Amsterdam, Amsterdam University Press.

Block, S.A. 2004. Maternal nutrition knowledge and the demand for micronutrient-rich foods: Evidence from Indonesia. *Journal of Development Studies*, 40(6): 82–105.

Block, S., Kiess, L., Webb, P., Kosen, S., Moench-Pfanner, R., Bloem, M.W. & Timmer, C.P. 2004. Macro shocks and micro outcomes: Child nutrition during Indonesia's crisis. *Economics & Human Biology*, 2(1): 22–44.

Bonnard, P. 2001. *Improving the Nutrition Impacts of Agricultural Interventions: Strategy and Policy Brief.* Washington, DC, Food and Nutrition Technical Assistance (FANTA) Project, Academy for Educational Development.

Brett, E.A. 2001. *States, Markets and Civil Society: Autonomy, Diversity and Interdependence in Inter-Organizational Relationships.* Documentos de discusion sobre el Tercer Sector 15. Zinacantepec, Mexico, El Colegio Mexiquense.

Brinkman, H.J. 1996. Adjustment in Africa without development? *In* G. Köhler, C. Gore, U. Reich and T. Ziesemer, eds. *Questioning Development: Essays on the Theory, Policies and Practice of Development Intervention.* Marburg, Germany, Metropolis-Verlag.
___ 1999. Financial reforms in Africa and the lessons from Asia. *In* B. Herman, ed. *Global Financial Turmoil and Reform: A United Nations Perspective*. Tokyo, United Nations University Press.

Brinkman, H.J. & Gentilini, U. 2008. *Learning from WFP's Experience with Vouchers: Insights from Pakistan.* Pakistan, WFP.

Britto, T. 2008. The emergence and popularity of conditional cash transfer programmes in Latin America. *In* A. Barrientos and D. Hulme, eds. *Social Protection for the Poor and Poorest: Concepts, Policies and Politics.* London, Palgrave.

Buchanan-Smith, M. 2002. *Role of Early Warning Systems in Decision Making Process.* London, Overseas Development Institute.

Buchanan-Smith, M. & Jaspars, S. 2006. *Conflict, Camps and Coercion: The Continuing Livelihoods Crisis in Darfur. Final Report.* Sudan, WFP.

Byerlee, D., Jayne T.S. & Myers R.J. 2006. Managing food price risks and instability in a liberalizing market environment: Overview and policy options. *Food Policy*, 31(4): 275–287.

Cadot, O., Dutoit, L. & Olarreaga, M. 2006. *How Costly is it for Poor Farmers to Lift Themselves out of Subsistence?* World Bank Policy Research Working Paper No. 3881. Washington, DC, World Bank.

Carr, E.R. 2008. Men's crops and women's crops: The importance of gender to the understanding of agricultural and development outcomes in Ghana's central region. *World Development*, 36(5): 900–915.

Carter, M.R. & Barrett, C.B. 2005. The economics of poverty traps and persistent poverty: An asset-based approach. *Journal of Development Studies*, 42(2): 178–199. Posted at: http://ssrn.com/abstract=716162.

Carter, M.R., Little, P.D. & Mogues, T. 2007. Poverty traps and natural disasters in Ethiopia and Honduras. *World Development*, 35(5): 835–856.

CEPAL & WFP. 2007. *El Costo del Hambre: Análisis del Impacto Social y Económico de la Desnutrición Infantil en América Latina.* Santiago.

Chambers, R. 1995. Poverty and livelihoods: Whose reality counts? *Environment and Urbanization*, 7(1): 173–204.

Changing Times. 1974. Why food costs more? ABI/INFORM Global.

Chant, S. 1997. *Gender Aspects of Urban Economic Growth and Development.* Helsinki, UNU-WIDER.

Chastre, C., Duffield, A., Kindness, H., LeJeune, S. & Taylor, A. 2007. *The Minimum Cost of a Healthy Diet: Findings from Piloting a New Methodology in Four Study Locations.* London, Save the Children.

Chaudhuri, S. & Ravallion, M. 2006. Partially awakened giants: Uneven growth in China and India. *In* L.A. Winters and S. Yusuf, eds. *Dancing with Giants: China, India, and the Global Economy.* Washington, DC, World Bank Publications.

Chilowa, W. 1998. The impact of agricultural liberalisation on food security in Malawi. *Food Policy*, 23(6): 553–569.

Chronic Poverty Research Centre. 2008. *Social Protection: Top Priority to End Chronic Poverty.* Policy Brief. Manchester, UK, CPRC.

Clay, E., Dhiri, S. & Benson, C. 1996. *Joint Evaluation of European Union Programme Food Aid: Synthesis Report.* London, Overseas Development Institute.

Collier, P. 2007. *The Bottom Billion.* New York, Oxford University Press.

Collier, P. & Hoeffler, A. 1998. On economic causes of civil war. *Oxford Economic Papers*, 50: 563–573.

Conway, G. 1997. *The Doubly Green Revolution: Food for All in the 21st Century.* Ithaca, NY, Cornell University Press.

Coulter, J. 1998. *Commodity Exchange and Warehouse Receipts: Can They Improve the Performance of African Grain Markets?* Paper prepared for the AFMESA/FAO workshop Grain Commodity Trading and Commodity Exchanges. Pretoria.

Coulter, J. & Onumah, G. 2002. The role of warehousehold receipt system in enhanced commodity marketing and rural livelihoods in Africa. *Food Policy*, 27: 319–337.

Coxhead, I. 2000. Consequences of a food security strategy for economic welfare, income distribution and land degradation: The Philippine case. *World Development*, 25(1): 111–128.

Crawford, E., Kelly, V., Jayne, T.S. & Howard, J. 2003. Input use and market development in sub-Saharan Africa: An overview. *Food Policy*, 28(4): 277–292.

Creti, P. & Jaspars, S. 2007. *Cash Transfers Programming in Emergencies.* Oxford, UK, Oxfam Publishing.

Cummings Jr., R., Rashid, S. & Gulati. A. 2006. Grain price stabilization experiences in Asia: What have we learned? *Food Policy*, 31(4): 302–312.

Dana, J., Gilbert, C.L. & Shim, E. 2006. Hedging grain price risk in the SADC: Case studies of Malawi and Zambia. *Food Policy*, 31(4): 357–371. Posted at: www.sciencedirect.com/science/article/B6VCB-4JRVDB9-6/2/4ec9080085d146254f3b1f930cefa186.

Danielou, M. & Ravry, C. 2005. *The Rise of Ghana's Pineapple Industry. From Successful Take-off to Sustainable Expansion.* Report No. 34997. Washington, DC, World Bank.

Davies, S. & Davey, J. 2008. A regional multiplier approach to estimating the impact of cash transfers on the market: The case of cash transfers in rural Malawi. *Development Policy Review*, 26(1): 91–111.

Davis, B., Winters, P., Gero, C., Covarrubias, K., Quinones, E., Zedda, A., Stamoulis, K., Bonomi, G. & DiGiuseppe, S. 2007. *Rural Income Generating Activities: A Cross-Country Comparison.* ESA Working Paper No.07-16. Rome, FAO.

Dawe, D. 2008. *Have Recent Increases in International Cereal Prices been Transmitted to Domestic Economies? The Experience in 7 Large Asian Countries.* ESA Working Paper No.08-03. Rome, FAO.

Deaton, A. 1991. *Household Saving in LDCs: Credit Markets, Insurance, and Welfare.* Development Studies Paper No. 153. Princeton, NJ. Posted at: http://ideas.repec.org/p/fth/priwds/153.html.

Deaton, A. & Subramanian, S. 1996. The demand for food and calories. *Journal of Political Economy*, 104(1): 133–162.

de Brauw, A. & Hoddinott, J. 2008. *Must Conditional Cash Transfer Programs be Conditioned to be Effective?* IFPRI Discussion Paper No. 00757. Washington, DC. Posted at: http://papers.ssrn.com/sol3/papers.cfm?abstract_id=1011901.

Deininger, K. & Jin, S. 2008. Land sales and rental markets in transition: Evidence from rural Vietnam. *Oxford Bulletin of Economics and Statistics*, 70(1): 67–101.

Deininger, K., Zegarra, E. & Lavadenz, I. 2003. Determinants and impacts of rural land market activity: Evidence from Nicaragua. *World Development*, 31(8): 1385–1404.

de Janvry, A., Fafchamps, M. & Sadoulet, E. 1991. Peasant household behaviour with missing markets: Some paradoxes explained. *Economic Journal*, 101: 1400–1417.

del Ninno, C., Dorosh, P.A. & Smith, L.C. 2003. Public policy, markets and household coping strategies in Bangladesh: Avoiding a food security crisis following the 1998 floods. *World Development*, 31(7): 1221–1238.

de Pee, S. 2005. We know much about what to do but little about how to do it: Experiences with a weekly multimicronutrient supplementation campaign. *Food Nutrition Bulletin*, 27(4): S111–S114.

de Pee, S., Talukder, A. & Bloem, M.W. 2008. Homestead food production for improving nutritional status and health. *In* R.D. Semba and M.W. Bloem, eds. *Nutrition and Health: Nutrition and Health in Developing Countries*. 2nd edition. Totowa, NJ, Humana Press.

Dercon, S. 2002. Income risk, coping strategies, and safety nets. *World Bank Research Observer*, 17(2): 141–166.
___ 2004. Analyse micro-économique de la pauvreté et des inégalités: l'arbitrage équité-efficacité revisité. *Afrique Contemporaine*, 211: 73–97.
___ 2005. *Insurance against Poverty*. New York, Oxford University Press.

Dercon, S., Bold, T. & Calvo C. 2004. *Insurance for the Poor?* Paper prepared for financial markets and poverty project for the IADB. Washington, DC, IADB.

Dercon, S., Hoddinott, J. & Woldehanna, T. 2005. Consumption and shocks in 15 Ethiopian villages, 1999–2004. *Journal of African Economies*, 14: 559–585.

Devereux, S. 1988. Entitlements, availability and famine: A revisionist view of Wollo, 1972–74. *Food Policy*, 13(3): 270–282.
___ 2001. Famine in Africa. *In* S. Devereux and S. Maxwell, eds. *Food Security in Sub-Saharan Africa*. London, ITDG Publishing.

___ 2007a. *Case Study on Ethiopia's Productive Safety Net Programme.* Posted at: http://siteresources.worldbank.org/SAFETYNETSANDTRANSFERS/Resources/281945-1131468287118/1876750-1182180231533/Wiseman_EthiopiaPSNP_5-07.pdf.
___ 2007b. *The New Famines: Why Famines Persist in an Era of Globalization.* New York, Routledge.

Devereux, S. & Sabates-Wheeler, R. 2004. *Transformative Social Protection.* IDS Working Paper No. 232. Brighton, UK, Institute of Development Studies.
___ 2007. Debating social protection. *IDS Bulletin*, 3(38).

Devereux, S., Sabates-Wheeler, R., Tefera, M. & Taye, H. 2006. *Ethiopia's Productive Safety Net Programme (PSNP): Trends in PSNP Transfers Within Targeted Households.* Report commissioned by DFID Ethiopia. Brighton, UK, Institute of Development Studies and Addis Abeba, Indak International.

DFID. 2000. *Sustainable Livelihoods Guidance Sheets.* Posted at: www.livelihoods.org.
___ 2005a. *Making Market Systems Work Better for the Poor (M4P): An Introduction to the Concept.* Discussion paper prepared for the ADB-DFID learning event, ADB Headquarters, Manila. London, Department for International Development (DFID).
___ 2005b. *Reducing Poverty by Tackling Social Exclusion.* DFID Policy Paper. Posted at: www.dfid.gov.uk/pubs/files/social-exclusion.pdf
___ 2007. *A Record Maize Harvest in Malawi.* Posted at: www.dfid.gov.uk/casestudies/files/Africa%5Cmalawi-harvest.asp

Dolan, C. & Humphrey, J. 2000. Governance and trade in fresh vegetables: The impact of UK supermarkets on the African horticulture industry. *Journal of Development Studies*, 37(2): 147–176.

Dollar, D. & Kraay, A. 2002. Growth is good for the poor. *Journal of Economic Growth*, 7(3): 195–225.
___ 2004. Trade, growth and poverty. *Economic Journal*, 114(493): 22–49.

Donovan, C., McGlinchy, M., Staatz, J. & Tschirley, D. 2006. *Emergency Needs Assessments and the Impact of Food Aid on Local Markets.* MSU International Development Working Paper No. 87. Posted at: www.aec.msu.edu/fs2/papers/idwp87.pdf.

Dorosh, P. 2001. Trade liberalization and national food security: Rice trade between Bangladesh and India. *World Development*, 29(4): 673–689.

Dorosh, P., Dradri, S. & Haggblade, S. 2007. *Alternative Approaches for Moderating Food Insecurity and Price Volatility in Zambia.* International Development Collaborative Policy Briefs No. ZM-FSRP-PB-24, Department of Agricultural Economics. Ann Arbor, MI, Michigan State University.

Dorosh, P.A. & Subran, L. 2007. *Food Markets and Food Price Inflation in Ethiopia.* Mimeo. Washington, DC, World Bank.

Dorward. A. & Kydd, J. 2004. The Malawi 2002 food crisis: The rural development challenge. *Journal of Modern African Studies*, 42(3): 343–361.

Dorward, A., Kydd, J., Morrison, J. & Urey, I. 2004. A policy agenda for pro-poor agricultural growth. *World Development*, 32(1): 73–89.

Dorward, A., Kydd, J. & Poulton, C. 1998. *Smallholder Cash Crop Production under Market Liberalisation: A New Institutional Economics Perspective.* Wallingford, UK, CAB International.

Dorward, A., Poole, N., Morrison, J., Kydd, J. & Urey, I. 2003. Markets, institutions and technology: Missing links in livelihoods analysis. *Development Policy Review*, 21(3): 319–332.

Dradri, S. 2007. *A Market Analysis of the Food Security Situation in Southern Africa in 2007/08.* Johannesburg, WFP.

Dubey, A. 2003. *Levels and Determinants of Hunger Poverty in Urban India during the 1990s.* World Bank Urban Research Symposium 2003. Posted at: www.worldbank.org/urban/symposium2003/docs/papers/dubey.pdf.

Easterly, W. & Levine, R. 1997. Africa's growth tragedy. *Quarterly Journal of Economics*, 112(4): 1203–1250.

The Economist. 2005. Niger's harvest last year was not so terrible. Why is the country now so hungry? *The Economist*, 1 September.
___ 2008. Food and the poor. The new face of hunger. *The Economist*, 17 April.

EIU. 2008. *Global Outlook*, July 2008. Economist Intelligence Unit (EIU).

Emran, M., Morshed, A. & Stiglitz, J. 2007. *Microfinance and Missing Markets.* New York. Posted at: http://papers.ssrn.com/sol3/papers.cfm?abstract_id=1001309.

Evenson, R.E. & Gollin, D. 2003. Assessing the impact of the green revolution: 1950–2000. *Science*, 300: 758–762.

Fafchamps, M. 2004. *Market Institutions in Sub-Saharan Africa: Theory and Evidence.* Cambridge, MA, MIT Press.

Fafchamps, M. & Hill, R.V. 2005. Selling at the farm-gate or travelling to market. *American Journal of Agricultural Economics,* 87(3): 717–734. Posted at: www.economics.ox.ac.uk/members/marcel.fafchamps/homepage/.

Fallon, P.R. & Lucas, R.E.B. 2002. The impact of financial crises on labor markets, household incomes, and poverty. *World Bank Research Observer*, 17(1): 21–45.

Faminow, M.D. 1995. Issues in valuing food aid: The cash or in-kind controversy. *Food Policy*, 20(1): 3–10.

Fang, C. & Yang, D. 2006. The changing nature of rural poverty and new policy orientations. *The Chinese Economy*, 39(4): 10–24.

FANTA. 2003. *Food Access Indicator Review.* Washington, DC, Food and Nutrition Technical Assistance (FANTA) Project, Academy for Educational Development.

FAO. 2002. *World Agriculture towards 2015/2030: Summary Report.* Rome. Posted at: www.fao.org/docrep/004/Y3557E/Y3557E00.HTM.
___ 2006a. *Faostat.* Posted at: www.fao.org/faostat/foodsecurity/Files/NumberUndernourishment_en.xls.
___ 2006b. *Rapid Growth of Selected Asian Economies: Lessons and Implications for Agriculture and Food Security.* Bangkok, FAO Regional Office for Asia and the Pacific.
___ 2006c. *State of Food and Agriculture.* Rome.
___ 2006d. *The State of Food Insecurity in the World: Eradicating World Hunger – Taking Stock Ten Years after the World Food Summit.* Rome.
___ 2008a. *Food Outlook.* November. Rome.
___ 2008b. *Soaring Food Prices: Facts, Perspectives, Impacts and Actions Required.* High-Level Conference on World Food Security: The Challenges of Climate Change and Bioenergy. HLC/08/INF/1. Rome.
___ 2008c. *The State of Food Insecurity in the World.* Rome.

FAO & WFP. 2004. *Crop and Food Supply Assessment Mission to Niger.* Niger.
___ 2008a. *Crop and Food Supply Assessment Mission to Southern Sudan. Special Report.* Rome.
___ 2008b. *Crop and Food Supply Assessment Mission to Zimbabwe. Special Report.* Rome.

FAOSTAT. http://faostat.fao.org/site/567/DesktopDefault.aspx?PageID=567.

FAPRI. 2008. *2008 World Agricultural Outlook.*, Ames, IA.

Farina, E.M.M.Q. & Reardon, T. 2000. Agrifood grades and standards in the extended Mercosur: Their role in the changing agrifood system. *American Journal of Agricultural Economics*, 82(5): 1170–1176.

FEWS NET. 2005. *Niger: An Evidence Base for Understanding the Current Crisis*. Washington, DC.
___ 2007. *Northern Wheat Trader Survey and Afghan Food Security: A Special Report prepared by the Famine Early Warning System Network (FEWS NET)*. Washington, DC.

Folbre, N. 1986. Cleaning house: New perspectives on households and economic development. *Journal of Development Economics*, 22: 5–40.

Forsen, Y. & Subran, L. 2008. *Wheat Price Increase and Urban Programming in Afghanistan. Assessment Mission Report*. Rome, WFP.

Freebairn, D.K. 1995. Did the green revolution concentrate incomes? A quantitative study of research reports. *World Development*, 23(2): 265–279.

Gabre-Madhin, E.Z. 2005. *Getting Markets Right*. Paper presented to the workshop Managing Food Price Instability in Low-Income Countries. Washington, DC.

Gabre-Madhin, E.Z. & Haggblade, S. 2004. Successes in African agriculture: Results of an expert survey. *World Development*, 32(5): 745–766.

Garton, G. & Rouwenhorst, K.G. 2004. *Facts and Fantasies about Commodity Futures*. NBER Working Paper No.10595. Cambridge, MA, National Bureau of Economic Research.

Gentilini, U. 2007. *Cash and Food Transfers: A Primer*. Rome, WFP.
___ 2009. Social protection in the "real" world: Issues, models, and challenge. *Development Policy Review*, 27(2): 147–166.

Gentilini, U. & Carucci, V. 2008. *Increasing the Economic Opportunities for the Vulnerable*. Paper presented at the AU-NEPAD Food Security Workshop. Johannesburg, South Africa.

Gibbon, P. 2003. Value chain governance, public regulation and entry barriers in the global fresh fruit and vegetable chain into the EU. *Development Policy Review*, 21(5–6): 615–625.

Gibson, A., Scott, H. & Ferrand D. 2004. *Making Markets Work for the Poor: An Objective and an Approach for Governments and Development Agencies*. South Africa. Posted at: www.dfid.gov.uk/news/files/trade_news/adb-workshop-makingmarkets.pdf.

Govereh, J., Haggblade, S., Nielson, H. & Tschirley, D. 2008. *Report 1: Maize Market Sheds in Eastern and Southern Africa*. Report prepared by Michigan State University for the World Bank under contract No. 7144132, Strengthening Food Security in Sub-Saharan Africa through Trade Liberalization and Regional Integration. Washington, DC, World Bank.

Guabao, W. 2006. *Access to Credit, Poverty and Inequality: Some Findings from China Using Grouped Rural Household Data*. China. Posted at: www.networkideas.org/feathm/Oct2006/PDF/Wu_Guobao.pdf.

Gulati, A., Minot, N., Delgado, C. & Bora, S. 2005. *Growth in High-Value Agriculture in Asia and the Emergence of Vertical Links with Farmers*. Paper presented at the workshop Linking Small-scale Producers to Markets: Old and New Challenges. Washington, DC.

Haddad, L. 2000. A conceptual framework for assessing agriculture–nutrition linkages. *Food and Nutrition Bulletin*, 21(4): 367–373.

Haddad, L., Hoddinott, J. & Alderman, H. 1997. *Intrahousehold Resource Allocation in Developing Countries: Models, Methods and Policy*. Baltimore, MA, Johns Hopkins University Press.

Haggblade, S., Hazell, P. & Reardon, T. 2007. *The Rural Nonfarm Economy: Pathway Out of Poverty or Pathway in?* Paper presented at the International Research Workshop Future of Small Farms, June 2007. Washington, DC.

Hagos, F. & Holden. S. 2006. Tenure security, resource poverty, public programs, and household plot-level conservation investments in the highlands of northern Ethiopia. *Agricultural Economics*, (34): 183–196.

Hamid, A.R., Salih, A.A.A., Bradley, S., Couteaudier, T., El Haj, M.J., Hussein, M.O. & Steffen, P. 2005. *Markets, Livelihoods and Food Aid in Darfur: A Rapid Assessment and Programming Recommendations*. Report commissioned by USAID and European Commission. Sudan.

Harvey, P. 2005. *Cash and Vouchers in Emergencies*. London, Overseas Development Institute.
___ 2007. *Cash-Based Responses in Emergencies*. HPG Report No. 24. London, Overseas Development Institute.

Harvey, P. & Adams, L. 2007. *Learning from Cash Responses to the Tsunami*. London. Posted at: www.odi.org.uk/hpg/papers/cashissue1.pdf.

Harvey, P. & Savage, K. 2006. *No Small Change: Oxfam GB Malawi and Zambia Emergency Cash Transfers Projects: A Synthesis of Key Learning.* London, Overseas Development Institute.

Hayami, Y. & Ruttan, V.W. 1985. *Agricultural Development: An International Perspective.* Baltimore, MA, Johns Hopkins University Press.

Hazell, B.R. 2003. Green revolution: Curse or blessing? *In* J. Mokyr, ed. *The Oxford Encyclopedia of Economic History.* Oxford, Oxford University Press.

Henson, J.S. 2006. *The Role of Public and Private Standards in Regulating International Food Markets.* Paper presented at the IATRC Symposium, Bonn, Germany.

Hess, U., Robertson, T. & Wiseman, W. 2006. *Ethiopia: Integrated Risk Financing to Protect Livelihoods and Foster Development.* Rome, WFP, Washington, DC, World Bank and Addis Abeba, DFID Ethiopia. Posted at: www.wfp.org/policies/introduction/background/index.asp?section=6&sub_section=1#.

Hoddinott, J. 2008. *Social Safety Nets and Productivity Enhancing Investments in Agriculture.* Washington, DC, IFPRI.

Hoddinott, J., Maluccio, J.A., Behrman, J.R., Flores, R. & Martorell, R. 2008. Effect of a nutrition intervention during early childhood on economic productivity in Guatemalan adults. *The Lancet*, 371(2): 411–416.

Hoddinott, J. & Yohannes, Y. 2002. *Dietary Diversity as a Household Food Security Indicator.* Washington, DC, Food and Nutrition Technical Assistance Project (FANTA).

Hoffman, I. & Bernhard, B. 2007. Meat marketing in Burkina Faso after the devaluation of the FCFA: Insights into the functioning of informal markets. *Food Policy*, 32(2): 229–245.

Horton, S. & Mazumdar, D. 1999. *Vulnerable Groups and Labor: The Aftermath of the Asian Financial Crisis.* Paper presented at the World Bank–International Labour Organization Seminar on Economic Crisis, Employment, and Labor Markets in East and Southeast Asia. Geneva, ILO.

Humphrey, J., McCulloch, N. & Ota, M. 2004. The impact of European market changes on employment in the Kenyan horticulture sector. *Journal of International Development*, 16(1): 63–80.

Husain, A. & Subran, L. 2008. *A Food and Fuel Price Risk Index.* Internal working paper. Rome, WFP.

IFAD. 2003a. *Agricultural Marketing Companies as Sources of Smallholder Credit in Eastern and Southern Africa. Experiences, Insights and Potential Donor Role.* Rome.
___ 2003b. *Promoting Market Access for the Rural Poor in Order to Achieve the Millennium Development Goals.* Roundtable Discussion Paper for the Twenty-Fifth Anniversary Session of IFAD's Governing Council. Rome.

IFPRI. 2002a. *Ghana: The Accra Urban Food and Nutrition Study.* Washington, DC.
___ 2002b. *Living in the City: Challenges and Options for the Urban Poor.* Washington, DC.
___ 2008. Personal communication from Mark Rosegrant, updating von Braun, 2007.

IGC. 2007a. *Grain Market Report. GMR No. 370. 23 August 2007.* London.
___ 2007b. *Grain Market Report. GMR No. 371. 27 September 2007.* London.
___ 2007c. *Grain Market Report. GMR No. 372. 25 October 2007.* London.
___ 2007d. *Grain Market Report. GMR No. 373. 22 November 2007.* London.
___ 2008a. *Grain Market Report. GMR No. 374. 24 January 2008.* London.
___ 2008b. *Grain Market Report. GMR No. 384. 30 October 2008.* London.

IMF. 2008a *The Balance of Payments Impact of the Food and Fuel Price Shocks on Low-Income African Countries: A Country-by-Country Assessment.* Washington, DC, IMF African Department.
___ 2008b. *Food and Fuel Prices: Recent Developments, Macroeconomic Impact and Policy Responses: An Update.* Washington, DC.
___ 2008c. *World Economic Outlook. Financial Stress, Downturns, and Recoveries,* Washington, DC.
___ 2008d. *World Economic Outlook. Housing and the Business Cycle,* Washington, DC. Posted at: www.imf.org/external/pubs/ft/weo/2008/01/index.htm.
___ *Data and Statistics.* Posted at: www.imf.org/external/np/res/commod/index.asp.

Jaffee, S. & Henson, S. 2005. Agro-food Exports from Developing Countries: The Challenges Posed by Standards. *In* M.A. Aksoy and J.C. Beghin, eds. *Global Agricultural Trade and Developing Countries.* Washington, DC, World Bank Publications.

Jaspars, S. 2006. *From Food Crisis to Fair Trade: Livelihoods Analysis, Protection and Support in Emergencies.* ENN Special Supplement Series No. 3. Washington, DC, Emergency Nutrition Network.

Jayne, T.S. 1994. Do high food prices constrain cash crop production? Evidence from Zimbabwe. *Economic Development and Cultural Change*, 42(2): 387–402.

Jayne, T.S. & Jones, S. 1997. Food marketing and pricing policy in eastern and southern Africa: A survey. *World Development*, 25(9): 1505–1527.

Jayne, T.S., Yamano, T., Weber, M., Tschirley, D., Benfica, R., Neven, D., Chapoto, A. & Zulu, B. 2001. *Smallholder Income and Land Distribution in Africa: Implications for Poverty Reduction Strategies*. International Development Paper No. 24. Lansing, MI, Michigan State University, Department of Agricultural Economics, Department of Economics.

Jayne, T.S., Zulu, B. & Nijhoff, J.J. 2006. Stabilizing food markets in eastern and southern Africa. *Food Policy*, 31: 328–341.

Johnston, B.F. & Kilby, P. 1975. *Agriculture and Structural Transformation: Economic Strategies in Late-Developing Countries*. New York, Oxford University Press.

Joshi, P.K., Gulati, A. & Cummings, R. 2007. *Agricultural Diversification in South Asia: Beyond Food Security*. Washington, DC, IFPRI. Posted at: www.ifpri.org/pubs/otherpubs/agdiversesach02.pdf.

Keen, D. 1994. *The Benefits of Famine: A Political Economy of Famine and Relief in Southwestern Sudan, 1983–89*. Princeton, NJ, Princeton University Press.

Kelly, V., Adesina, A.A. & Gordon, A. 2003. Expanding access to agricultural inputs in Africa: A review of recent market development experience. *Food Policy*, 28(4): 379–404.

Kennedy, J., Ashmore, J., Babister, E. & Kelman, I. 2008. The meaning of build back better: Evidence from post-tsunami Aceh and Sri Lanka. *Journal of Contingencies and Crisis Management*, 16(1): 24–36.

Key, N. & Runsten, D. 1999. Contract farming, smallholders, and rural development in Latin America: The organization of agroprocessing firms and the scale of outgrower production. *World Development*, 27(2): 381–401.

Keynes, J.M. 1926. *The End of Laissez-Faire*. Amherst, NY, Prometheus Books.

Khan, M.S. & Khandker, A. 2006. Let them eat poison. *Slate Magazine*, September 2006. Posted at: www.newagebd.com/slate/2006/sep/01.html.

Kherallah, M. 2000. *Access of Smallholder Farmers to the Fruits and Vegetables Market in Kenya*. Washington, DC, IFPRI.

Kherallah, M., Delgado, C., Gabre-Mahdin, E., Minot, N. & Johnson, M. 2002. *Reforming Agricultural Markets in Africa*. IFPRI Food Policy Statement No. 38. Washington, DC, IFPRI.

Kindleberger, C.P. 2000. *Manias, Panic and Crashes: A History of Financial Crises*. New York, John Wiley & Sons Inc.

Klitgaard, R. 1991. *Adjusting to Reality: Beyond "State versus Market"*. San Francisco, CA, USA, ICS Press.

Kurosaki, T. 2006. Consumption vulnerability to risk in rural Pakistan. *Journal of Development Studies*, 42(1): 70–89. Posted at: http://ideas.repec.org/a/taf/jdevst/v42y2006i1p70-89.html.

Kurosaki, T. & Fafchamps, M. 2002. Insurance market efficiency and crop choices in Pakistan. *Journal of Development Economics*, 67: 419–453.

Kydd, J. & Dorward, A. 2004. Implications of market and coordination failures for rural development in least developed countries. *Journal of International Development*, 16: 951–970.

Lacey, M. 2006. Food aid program takes out insurance on Ethiopia weather. *New York Times*, 8 March. Posted at: www.nytimes.com/2006/03/08/international/Africa/08ethiopia.html.

Legge, A., Orchard, J., Graffham, A., Greenhalgh, P. & Kleih, U. 2006. *The Production of Fresh Produce in Africa for Export to the United Kingdom: Mapping Different Value Chains*. Report. Chatham, UK, Natural Resource Institute.

Lemos, S. 2006. *Minimum Wage Effects in a Developing Country*. Discussion Papers in Economics No. 06/1. Leicester, UK, Department of Economics, University of Leicester.

Lentz, E., Barrett, C.B. & Hoddinott, J. 2005. *Food Aid and Dependency: Implications for Emergency Food Security Assessments*. Study prepared for WFP (SENAC). Rome, WFP.

Levine, S. & Chastre, C. 2004. *Missing the Point. An Analysis of Food Security Interventions in the Great Lakes*. An HPN Network Paper. London, Overseas Development Institute.

Levinsohn, J. & McMillan, M. 2005. *Does Food Aid Harm the Poor? Household Evidence from Ethiopia*. NBER Working Papers No.11048. Cambridge, MA, National Bureau of Economic Research. Posted at: http://ideas.repec.org/p/nbr/nberwo/11048.html.

Lipton, M. 2001. Challenges to meet: Food and nutrition security in the new millennium. *Proceeding of the Nutrition Society*, 60: 203–214.

___ 2007. Plant breeding and poverty: Can transgenic seeds replicate the "green revolution" as a source of grains for the poor? *Journal of Development Studies*, 43(1): 31–62.

Lipton, M. & Longhurst, R. 1989. New seeds and poor people. *Agricultural Systems*, 33(4): 378–380.

Little, P. 2008. Food aid dependency in rural Ethiopia: Myth or reality? *World Development*, 36(5): 860–874.

Lohmar, M. 2003. Market reforms and policy initiatives: Rapid growth and food security in China. *In* USDA, *Food Security Assessment*. USDA, Economic Research Service.

___ 2006. Feeling for stones but not crossing the river: China's rural land tenure after twenty years of reform. *The Chinese Economy*, 39(4): 85–102.

Lundberg, M. 2005. Agricultural market reforms. *In* A. Coudouel and S. Paternostro, eds. *Analyzing the Distributional Impact of Reforms: A Practitioner's Guide to Trade, Monetary and Exchange Rate Policy, Utility Provision, Agricultural Markets, Land Policy and Education*. Washington, DC, World Bank Publications.

Maertens, M. & Swinnen, J.F.M. 2006. *Trade Standards and Poverty: Empirical Evidence from Senegal*. LICOS Discussion Paper 177/2006. Leuven, Belgium, LICOS Centre for Institutions and Economic Performance. Posted at: www.econ.kuleuven.be/LICOS/DP/dp.htm.

Malthus, T.R. 1982 (first edition 1798). An Essay on the Principle of Population. Penguin Books Ltd.

Maluccio, J. 2005. *Coping with the "Coffee Crisis" in Central America: The Role of the Nicaraguan Red de Protección Social*. Washington, DC, IFPRI. Posted at: www.ifpri.org/divs/fcnd/dp/papers/fcndp188.pdf.

Martin-Prével, Y., Delpeuch, F., Traissac, P., Massamba, J.P., Adoua-Oyila, G., Coudert K. & Trèche. S. 2000. Deterioration in the nutritional status of young children and their mothers in Brazzaville, Congo, following the 1994 devaluation of the CFA franc. *Bulletin of the World Health Organization*, 78(1): 108–118.

Masine, L. 2008. Malawi: Fertiliser success stuns Western donors. *African Business*, May.

Maunder, N. 2006. *The Impact of Food Aid on Grain Markets in Southern Africa: Implications for Tackling Chronic Vulnerability*. Regional Hunger and Vulnerability Programme. Posted at: www.wahenga.net/uploads/documents/reports/Food_aid_Report.pdf.

Maxwell, D., Ahiadeke, C., Levin, C., Armar-Klemesu, M., Zakariah, S. & Lamptey, G.M. 1999. Alternative food-security indicators: Revisiting the frequency and severity of "coping strategies". *Food Policy*, 24(4): 411–429.

Maxwell, D. & Caldwell, R. 2008. *The Coping Strategies Index: Field Methods Manual*. 2nd edition. Atlanta, GA, CARE, WFP, TANGO and Tufts University.

Maxwell, D. & Wiebe, K. 1999. Land tenure and food security: Exploring dynamic linkages. *Development and Change*, 30: 825–849.

McMillan, J. 2002. *Reinventing the Bazaar: A Natural History of Markets*. New York, W.W. Norton & Company.

Meadows, D.H., Meadows, D.L., Randers, J. & Behrens, W.W. 1972. *The Limits to Growth*. New York. Universe Books.

Meier, G.M. 1984. *Leading Issues in Economic Development*. New York, Oxford University Press.

Mendoza, R.U. & Thelen, N. 2008. Innovations to make markets more inclusive for the poor. *Development Policy Review*, 26(4): 427–458.

Micronutrient Initiative and UNICEF, 2004. *Vitamin and Mineral Deficiency: A Global Progress Report*. Ottawa.

Minot, N. 2007. *Contract Farming in Developing Countries: Patterns, Impact, and Policy Implications*. Case Study No. 6-3 of the Program: Food Policy for Developing Countries: The Role of Government in the Global Food System. Ithaca, NY. Posted at: http://cip.cornell.edu/DPubS?service=UI&version=1.0&verb=Display&handle=dns.gfs&collection=Cornell.

Minot, N. & Ngigi, M. 2003. *Are Horticultural Exports a Replicable Success Story? Evidence from Kenya and Cote D'Ivoire*. EPTD/MTID discussion paper. Washington, DC, IFPRI.

Minten, B. & Kyle, S. 1999. The effect of distance and road quality on food collection, marketing margins, and traders' wages: Evidence from former Zaire. *Journal of Development Economics*, 60(2): 467–495.

Minten, B., Randrianarison, L., & Swinnen, J.F.M. 2006. *Global Retail Chains and Poor Farmers: Evidence from Madagascar*. LICOS Discussion Paper No.16406. Leuven, Belgium, LICOS Centre for Institutions and Economic Performance.

Mittal, A. & Mousseau, F. 2006. *Sahel: A Prisoner of Starvation? A Case Study of the 2005 Food Crisis in Niger.* Oakland, CA, The Oakland Institute.

Moron, C. 2006. Food-based nutrition interventions at community level. *British Journal of Nutrition*, 96, Suppl.1, S20–S22.

Muller, C. 2002. Prices and living standards: Evidence ftom Rwanda. *Journal of Development Economics*, 68(1): 187–203.

Murray, M. & Mwengwe, E. 2004. *Food Security and Markets in Zambia.* London, International Humanitarian Practice Network.

Myers, R.J. 2006. On the costs of food price fluctuations in low-income countries. *Food Policy*, 31(4): 288–301.

Myhrvold-Hanssen T.L. 2003. *Democracy, News Media, and Famine Prevention: Amartya Sen and The Bihar Famine of 1966–67.* Oxford, UK, Oxford University Press.

Narayan, D., Patel, R., Schafft, K., Reademacher, A. & Koch-Shulte, S. 2000. *Voices of the Poor: Can Anyone Hear Us?* Washington, DC. Posted at: http://web.worldbank.org/WBSITE/EXTERNAL/TOPICS/EXTPOVERTY/0,,contentMDK:20619302~isCURL:Y~menuPK:336998~pagePK:148956~piPK:216618~theSitePK:336992,00.html.

Newbery, D. & Stiglitz, J. 1981. *The Theory of Commodity Price Stabilization.* Oxford, UK, Oxford University Press.

North, D.C. 1990. *Institutions, Institutional Change and Economic Performance.* Cambridge, UK, Cambridge University Press.
___ 1991. Institutions. *Journal of Economic Perspectives*, 5(1): 97–112.
___ 1995. The new institutional economics and third world development. *In* J. Harris, J. Hunter and C.M. Lewis, eds. *The New Institutional Economics and Third World Development.* London, Routledge.

Nurkse, R. 1953. *Problems of Capital Formation in Underdeveloped Countries.* Oxford, UK, Oxford University Press.

OECD. 2008. *The Relative Impact on World Commodity Prices of Temporal and Longer Term Structural Changes in Agricultural Markets*, Document: TAD/CA/APM/CFS/MD(2008)6. Paris, OECD.

OECD & FAO. 2008. *Agricultural Outlook 2008–2017.* Paris, OECD.

Ó Gráda, C. 2007. Making famine history. *Journal of Economic Literature*, 45(1): 5–38.

Omamo, S.W., Diao, X., Wood, S., Chamberlin, J., You, L., Benin, S., Wood-Sichra, U. & Tatwangire, A. 2006. *Strategic Priorities for Agricultural Development in Eastern and Central Africa.* IFPRI Research Report No.150. Washington, DC, IFPRI.

Oxfam. 2002. *HIV/AIDS and Food Insecurity in Southern Africa.* Oxford, UK, Oxfam.

Perry, G., Arias, O., Lopez, J., Maloney, W. & Serven, L., eds. 2006. *Poverty Reduction and Growth: Virtuous and Vicious Circles.* Washington, DC, World Bank.

Pinstrup-Andersen, P. 1988. Food subsidies: Consumer welfare and producer incentives. *In* W.J. Mellor and R. Ahmed, eds. 1998. *Agricultural Price Policy for Developing Countries.* Baltimore, MA, John Hopkins University Press.

Polaski, S. 2006. *Winners and Losers: Impact of the Doha Round on Developing Countries.* Washington, DC, Carnegie Endowment for International Peace.

Poulton, C., Kydd, J. & Dorward, A. 2006a. Overcoming market constraints on pro-poor agricultural growth in sub-Saharan Africa. *Development Policy Review*, 24(3): 243–277.

Poulton, C., Kydd, J., Wiggins, S. & Dorward, A. 2006b. State intervention for food price stabilisation in Africa: Can it work? *Food Policy*, 31: 342–356.

Rangaswami, A. 1985. Failure of exchange entitlements: Theory of famine, a response. *Economic and Political Weekly*, 20(41): 747–751.

Rao, N. 2005. Land rights, gender equality and household food security: Exploring the conceptual links in the case of India. *Food Policy*, 31: 180–193.

Rao, S.K. 1989. Agriculture and economic development. *In* J. Eatwell, M. Milgate and P. Newman, eds. *The New Palgrave: Economic Development.* New York, W.W. Norton & Company.

Ravallion, M. 1987. *Markets and Famines.* Oxford, UK, Clarendon Press.
___ 1997. Famines and economics. *Journal of Economic Literature*, 35(3): 1205–1242.
___ 2003. *Targeted Transfers in Poor Countries: Revisiting the Tradeoffs and Policy Options.* World Bank Policy Research Working Paper No. 3048. Washington, DC, World Bank. Posted at: SSRN: http://ssrn.com/abstract=412803.

___ 2006. Looking beyond averages in the trade and poverty debate, *World Development*, 34(8): 1374–1392.

___ 2007. Inequality is bad for the poor. *In* J. Micklewright and S. Jenkins, eds. *Inequality and Poverty Re-examined*. Oxford, UK, Oxford University Press.

___ 2008. *Are there Lessons for Africa from China's Success against Poverty?* Policy Research Working Paper No. 4463. Washington, DC, World Bank. Posted at: http://papers.ssrn.com/sol3/papers.cfm?abstract_id=1080478.

Ravallion, M., Chen, S. & Sangraula, P. 2007. *New Evidence on the Urbanization of Global Poverty.* Policy Research Working Paper No. 4199. Washington, DC, World Bank.

Ray, R. 2007. Changes in food consumption and the implications for food security and undernourishment: India in the 1990s. *Development and Change,* 38(2): 321–343.

Reardon, T. 1997. Using evidence of household income diversification to inform study of the rural nonfarm labor market in Africa. *World Development*, 25(5): 735–747.

Reardon, T., Barrett, C., Berdegué, J. & Swinnen, J. forthcoming. Agrifood industry transformation and small farmers in developing countries. *World Development*. Forthcoming.

Reardon, T. & Berdegué, J. 2002. The rapid rise of supermarkets in Latin America: Challenges and opportunities for development. *Development Policy Review*, 20(4): 371–388.

Reardon, T., Cordon, J.M., Bush, L., Bingen, J. & Harris, C. 1999. Global change in agrifood grades and standards: Agribusiness strategic responses in developing countries. *International Food and Agribusiness Management Review*, 2(3): 421–435.

Reardon, T. & Swinnen, J.F.M. 2004. Agri-food sector liberalization and the rise of supermarkets in former state-controlled economies: Comparison with other developing countries. *Development Policy Review*, 22(4): 317–334.

Reardon, T., Taylor, J.E., Stamoulis, K., Lanjouw, P. & Balisacam, A. 2000. Effects of non-farm employment on rural income inequality in developing countries: An investment perspective. *Journal of Agricultural Economics*, 51(2): 266–288.

Reardon, T., Timmer, C.P., Barrett, C. & Berdegué, J. 2003. The rise of supermarkets in Africa, Asia and Latin America. *American Journal of Agricultural Economics*, 85(5): 1140–1146.

Reed, B.A. & Habicht, J.P. 1998. Sales of food aid as sign of distress, no excess. *The Lancet*, 351(10): 128–131.

Renkow, M., Hallstrom, D.G. & Karanja, D.D. 2004. Rural infrastructure, transactions costs and market participation in Kenya. *Journal of Development Economics*, 73(3): 349–367.

Rockefeller Foundation. 2006. *Africa's Turn: A New Green Revolution for the 21st Century.* New York, Rockefeller Foundation.

Rodríguez, F. & Rodrik, D. 1999. *Trade Policy and Economic Growth: A Skeptic's Guide to the Cross-National Evidence.* NBER Working Paper No. 7081. Cambridge, MA, National Bureau of Economic Research.

Rodrik, D. 2006. Goodbye Washington consensus, Hello Washington confusion? A review of the World Bank's economic growth in the 1990s: Learning from a decade of reform. *Journal of Economic Literature*, 44(4): 973–987.

Sahn D.E. & Stifel, D.C. 2003. Urban–rural inequality in living standards in Africa. *Journal of African Economies*, 12(4): 564–597.

Sanders, D.R. & Irwin, S. 2008. Futures imperfect. *The New York Times*, 20 July. Posted at: www.nytimes.com/2008/07/20/opinion/20irwinsanders.html?ref=opinion.

Sanders, D.R., Irwin, S. & Merrin, R.P. 2008. *The Adequacy of Speculation in Agricultural Futures Markets: Too Much of a Good Thing?* Marketing and Outlook Research Report 2008-02. Urbana, IL, Department of Agricultural and Consumer Economics, University of Illinois at Urbana-Champaign.

Sanogo, I. 2009. Global food price crisis and household hunger: A review of recent food security assessments findings. *Humanitarian Practice Network Papers*, forthcoming.

Schmidhuber, J. 2006. *Impact of an Increased Biomass Use on Agricultural Markets, Prices and Food Security: A Longer-Term Perspective*. Paper prepared for the International symposium of Notre Europe. 27–29 November 2006. Paris.

Schubert, B. & Slater, R. 2006. Social cash transfers in low income African countries: Conditional or unconditional? *Development Policy Review*, 24(5).

The SEEP Network. 2007. *Market Development in Crisis-Affected Environments: Emerging Lessons for Achieving Pro-poor Economic Reconstruction*. Washington, DC. Posted at: www.seepnetwork.org/content/article/detail/5659.

Sen, A. 1981. *Poverty and Famines. An Essay on Entitlement and Deprivation.* Oxford, UK, Oxford University Press.

___ 1989. Food and freedom. *World Development*, 17(6): 769–781.

___ 1993. Hunger and Public Action. *In* A. Sen and J. Drèze, eds. 1999. *The Amartya Sen and Jean Drèze Omnibus*. New Delhi, Oxford University Press.

___ 2000. *Development as Freedom.* New York, Anchor Books.

Shiller, R.J. 2000. *Irrational Exuberance.* Princeton, NJ, Princeton University Press.

Slater, R. & Dana, J. 2006. Tackling vulnerability to hunger in Malawi through market-based options contracts: Implications for humanitarian agencies. *Humanitarian Exchange*, 33: 13–17.

Smith L.C. & Haddad, L. 2000. *Overcoming Child Malnutrition in Developing Countries: Past Achievements and Future Choices.* IFPRI 2020 Briefs No. 64. Washington, DC, IFPRI.

SOAS. 2008. *Evaluation of the 2006/7 Agricultural Input Subsidy Programme, Malawi, Final Report.* London, School of Oriental and African Studies.

Sogge, D. 1994. Angola: Surviving against rollback and petrodollars. *In* J. Macrae and A. Zwi, eds. *War and Hunger: Rethinking International Response in Complex Emergencies.* London, Zed Books.

The Sphere Project. 2004. *Humanitarian Charter and Minimum Standards in Disaster Response.* Oxford, UK, Oxfam Publishing.

Srinivasan, P.V. 2003. *Food Security and Agriculture.* Paper prepared for the Roles of Agriculture International Conference. 20–22 October 2003. Rome, FAO.

Stephens, E. & Barrett, C.B. 2008. *Incomplete Credit Markets and Commodity Marketing Behavior.* SAGA Working Paper. Ithaca, NY, Strategies and Analysis for Growth and Access.

Stiglitz, J.E. 1989. Sharecropping. *In* J. Eatwell, M. Milgate and P. Newman, eds. *The New Palgrave: Economic Development.* New York, W.W. Norton & Company.

Stites, E., Young, H., Titus, S. & Walker, P. 2005. *Non Food Responses to Food Insecurity in Emergencies.* SENAC Project, Rome, WFP Emergency Needs Assessment Branch.

Swift, J. & Hamilton, K. 2001. Household food and livelihood security. *In* S. Devereux and S. Maxwell, eds. *Food Security in Sub-Saharan Africa.* London, ITDG Publishing.

Swinnen, J.F.M. & Maertens, M. 2007. Globalization, privatization, and vertical coordination in food value chains in developing and transition countries. *Agricultural Economics*, 37(2): 89–102.

Swinnen, J.F.M. Maertens, M., Verpoorten, M. & Vandeplas, A. 2007. *Access to Markets: Constraints, Developments and Implications for Food Security.* Background paper for the WHS. Rome, WFP.

Takane, T. 2004. Smallholders and nontraditional exports under economic liberalization: The case of pineapples in Ghana. *African Monographs Study*, 25(1): 29–43.

Time. 1974. The world food crisis. *Time*, 11 November. Posted at www.time.com/time/magazine/article/0,9171,911503-4,00.html.

Timmer, C.P. 1986. *Getting Prices Right: The Scope and Limits of Agricultural Policy.* Ithaca, NY, Cornell University Press.

___ 1989. Food price policy: The rationale for government intervention. *Food Policy*, 14(1): 17–27.

___ 2000. The macro dimensions of food security: Economic growth, equitable distribution, and food price stability. *Food Policy*, 25: 283–295.

___ 2002. *Food Security and Rice Price Policy in Indonesia: Reviewing the Debate.* Working Paper No. 12, June 2002. Jakarta, Indonesian Food Policy Program.

___ 2008. Rural changes stimulate rising giants. *Science*, 321(5889). Posted at: www.sciencemag.org/cgi/content/summary/321/5889/642.

Timmer, C.P., Falcon, W.D. & Pearson, S.R. 1983. *Food Policy Analysis.* Baltimore, MA, World Bank/Johns Hopkins University Press.

Torlesse H., Kiess L. & Bloem, M.W. 2003. Association of household rice expenditure with child nutritional status indicates a role for macroeconomic food policy in combating malnutrition. *Journal of Nutrition*, 133: 1320–1325.

Traill, B.W. 2006. The rapid rise of supermarkets? *Development Policy Review*, 24(2): 163–174.

UNAIDS/UNICEF/USAID. 2004. *Children on the Brink: A Joint Report of New Orphan Estimates and a Framework for Action.* New York. Posted at: http://library.cph.chula.ac.th/Ebooks/HIV-AIDS/Children%20on%20the%20Brink%202004.pdf.

UNCTAD. 2005. *Economic Development in Africa: Rethinking the Role of Foreign Direct Investment.* New York and Geneva.
___ 2008. *Development and Globalization: Facts and Figures.* New York and Geneva.

Underwood, B. 2000. Overcoming micronutrient deficiencies in developing countries: Is there a role for agriculture? *Food and Nutrition Bulletin*, 21(4): 356–360.

UNDP. 2004. *Human Development Report 2004.* New York.

UNICEF. 1990. *Strategy for Improved Nutrition of Children and Women in Developing Countries.* UNICEF Policy Review. New York.
___ 2003. *Iodine Deficiency still Leaves Millions of Children at Risk of Mental Retardation.* Press Release.
___ 2007. *A World Fit for Children Statistical Review.* New York.
___ 2008. *The State of the World's Children 2008, Child Survival.* New York.

United Nations. 1999. *World Economic and Social Survey 1999.* New York.
___ 2000. *World Economic and Social Survey.* New York.
___ 2008a. *Comprehensive Framework for Action.* New York, United Nations High-level Task Force on the Global Food Security Crisis.
___ 2008b. *Millennium Development Goals Report 2008*, New York.
___ 2008c. *World Economic Situation and Prospects 2008.* New York.

United Nations Millennium Project Task Force on Hunger. 2005. *Halving Hunger: It Can Be Done.* New York. Posted at: www.unmillenniumproject.org/documents/HTF-SumVers_FINAL.pdf.

Unnevehr, L.J. 2000. Food safety issues and fresh food product exports from LDCs. *Agricultural Economics*, 23(3): 231–240.

USAID. 2005. *Malawi – Food Insecurity November 14.* Washington, DC.
___ 2006a. *Notes from the Field: Weather Insurance Mitigates Risk.* Washington, DC.
___ 2006b. *Southern Africa – Food Insecurity. Situation Report No. 1, November 14.* Washington, DC.

USDA. 2008a. *Global Food Security Assessment (GFA)* Posted at: www.ers.usda.gov/Briefing/GlobalFoodSecurity/.
___ 2008b. *USDA Agricultural Projections to 2017.* Interagency Agricultural Projections Committee. Washington, DC.

Victora, C.G., Adair, L., Fall, C., Hallal, P.C., Martorell, R., Richter, L. & Singh Sachdev, H. 2008. Maternal and child undernutrition: Consequences for adult health and human capital. *The Lancet*, 371: 340–357.

Vincent, K., Tanner, T.M. & Devereux, S. 2008. *Climate Change, Food Security and Disaster Risk Management.* Input paper to the Expert Meeting on Climate Change and Disaster Risk Management, FAO, Rome, and Institute of Development Studies, Brighton, UK.

Vollrath, D. 2007. Land distribution and international agricultural productivity. *American Journal of Agricultural Economics*, 89(1): 202–216.

von Braun, J. 2007. *The World Food Situation: New Driving Forces and Required Actions.* Food Policy Report No. 18. Washington, DC, IFPRI.

von Braun, J., Robles, M. & Torero, M. 2008. *When Speculation Matters.* Mimeo. Washington, DC, IFPRI.

von Braun, J. & Torero, M. 2008. *Physical and Virtual Global Food Reserves to Protect the Poor and Prevent Market Failure.* IFPRI Policy Brief No. 4. Washington, DC, IFPRI. Posted at: www.ifpri.org/pubs/bp/bp004.pdf.

Vranken, L. & Swinnen, J. 2006. Land rental markets in transition: Theory and evidence from Hungary. *World Development*, 34(3): 481–500.

Watkins, K., von Braun, J., Díaz-Bonilla, E. & Gulati, A. 2003. *Trade Policies and Food Security.* Washington, DC, IFPRI.

Weatherspoon, D.D. & Reardon, T. 2003. The rise of supermarkets in Africa: Implications for agrifood systems and the rural poor. *Development Policy Review*, 21(3): 333–356.

Webb, P. 1998. Isolating hunger: Reaching people in need beyond the mainstream. *In* WFP. *Time for Change: Food Aid and Development.* Rome, WFP.

Webb P., Coates, J., Frongillo, E.A., Lorge Rogers, B., Swindaale, A. & Bilinsky, P. 2006. Measuring household food insecurity: Why it's so important and yet so difficult to do. *Journal of Nutrition*, 136(5): 1404S–1408S.

Webb, P. & Thorne-Lyman, A. 2006. *Entitlement Failure from Food Quality Perspective.* Research Paper No. 20076/140. Helsinki, UNU World Institute for Development Economics Research.

Welch, R.M. & Graham, R.D. 2000. A new paradigm for world agriculture: Productive, sustainable, nutritious, healthful food systems. *Food and Nutrition Bulletin*, 21(4): 361–366.

WFP. 2004. *WFP and Food Based Safety Nets: Concepts, Experiences and Future Programming Opportunities.* Policy Issues, Agenda Item No. 4. WFP/EB.3/2004/4-A. Rome.

___ 2005a. *Angola: Comprehensive Food Security and Vulnerability Analysis.* Rome, SENAC Project, WFP Emergency Needs Assessment Branch.

___ 2005b. *Definition of Emergencies.* Policy Issues, Agenda Item No. 4, WFP/EB.1/2005/4-A/Rev.1. Rome.

___ 2005c. *Emergency Needs Assessment, Pakistan Earthquake. October 2005.* Pakistan.

___ 2005d. *Mali: Comprehensive Food Security and Vulnerability Analysis.* Rome, SENAC Project, WFP Emergency Needs Assessment Branch.

___ 2005e. *Niger: Analyse de la Sécurité Alimentaire et de la Vulnérabilité (CFSVA).* Rome.

___ 2005f. *Niger: Profile of Cereal Markets.* Rome.

___ 2005g. *Post Earthquake Relief and Recovery Operation – South Asia.* Agenda Item No. 8. Rome.

___ 2005h. *Republic of Uganda: Comprehensive Food Security and Vulnerability Analysis.* Rome, SENAC Project, WFP Emergency Needs Assessment Branch.

___ 2006a. *Comprehensive Food Security and Vulnerability Analysis, Liberia.* Rome.

___ 2006b. *Greater Monrovia: Comprehensive Food Security and Nutrition Survey.* Monrovia.

___ 2006c. *Rwanda: Comprehensive Food Security and Vulnerability Analysis.* Rome, SENAC Project, WFP Emergency Needs Assessment Branch.

___ 2006d. *Technical Meeting Report: Cash in Emergencies and Transition.* Addis Abeba.

___ 2007a. *Cameroun: Analyse Globale de la Sécurité Alimentaire et de la Vulnérabilité (CFSVA).* Rome, SENAC Project, WFP, Emergency Needs Assessment Branch.

___ 2007b. *Lao PDR: Comprehensive Food Security and Vulnerability Analysis.* Rome, SENAC Project, WFP Emergency Needs Assessment Branch.

___ 2007c. *Malawi: Assessment of Appropriateness and Feasibility of Cash Response Options. Special Initiative for Cash and Vouchers Programming.* Rome.

___ 2007d. *Markets in Darfur, Sudan.* Mimeo. Rome.

___ 2007e. *Sudan: Comprehensive Food Security and Vulnerability Analysis.* Rome, SENAC Project, WFP Emergency Needs Assessment Branch.

___ 2007f. *Where We Work: Malawi.* Rome.

___ 2008a. 2007 Food Aid Flows. INTERFAIS. *The Food Aid Monitor,* June 2008. Rome.

___ 2008b. *Recent Food Price Developments in Most Vulnerable Countries.* Issue No. 2. Rome.

___ 2008c. Rising Commodity Prices. *Market Watch 3,* February 2008. Posted at: www.reliefweb.int/rw/ RWB.NSF/db900SID/MUMA-7BS98J?OpenDocument.

___ 2009. *Comprehensive Food Security and Vulnerability Analysis Handbook.* Rome.

WFP, FAO & MADR. 2007. *Guinee-Bissau: Commerce du cajou et du riz: Implications pour la sécurité alimentaire. Emergency Needs Assessment.* Rome.

WFP & NEPAD. 2004. *NEPAD Study to Explore Further Options for Food-Security Reserve Systems in Africa.* Posted at: www.reliefweb.int/rw/rwb.nsf/db900SID/ JWIN-67PKCX?OpenDocument.

WFP & UNICEF. 2008. *Rising Food Prices: Interventions Required to Prevent Deterioration of Health and Nutritional Status.* Issues Brief. Rome and New York.

Whiteside, M., Chuzo, P., Maro, M., Saiti, D. & Schouten, M.J. 2003. *Enhancing the Role of Informal Maize Imports in Malawi Food Security.* Consultancy Report for DFID. London, DFID.

Williamson, J. 2003a. *From Reform Agenda to Damaged Brand Name: A Short History of the Washington Consensus and Suggestions for What to Do Next.* Washington, DC, IMF Finance and Development.

___ 2003b. The Washington consensus and beyond. *Economic and Political Weekly,* 38(15): 1475–1481.

World Bank. 1999. *Global Economic Prospects and the Developing Countries 2000.* Washington, DC.

___ 2001. *Social Protection Sector Strategy: From Safety Net to Springboard.* World Bank Report No. 21643. Washington, DC. Posted at: www-wds.worldbank.org/ external/default/WDSContentServer/WDSP/IB/2001/01/26/ 000094946_01011705303891/Rendered/PDF/ multi_page.pdf.

___ 2005. *Managing Food Price Risks and Instability in an Environment of Market Liberalization.* Washington, DC.

___ 2006. *Repositioning Nutrition as Central to Development: A Strategy for Large-Scale Action.* Washington, DC.

___ 2007a. *From Agriculture to Nutrition: Pathways, Synergies, and Outcomes.* Washington, DC.

___ 2007b. *Malawi, Fertilizer Subsidies and the World Bank.* Washington, DC.

___ 2007c. *World Development Report 2008: Agriculture for Development.* Washington, DC.

___ 2008a. *Double Jeopardy: Responding to High Food and Fuel Prices.* Washington, DC.

___ 2008b. *Food Price Crisis Imperils 100 Million in Poor Countries, Zoellick Says.* Posted at: http://web.worldbank.org/WBSITE/EXTERNAL/NEWS/ 0,,contentMDK:21729143~pagePK:64257043~piPK: 437376~theSitePK:4607,00.html.

___ 2008c. *Global Economic Prospects 2008.* Washington, DC.

___ 2008d. *Niger: Food Security and Safety Nets.* Washington, DC.

___ 2008e. *Rising Food Prices: Policy Options and World Bank Response.* Note prepared by PREM, ARD and DEC for a Development Committee meeting. Washington, DC.

___ 2009. *Global Economic Prospects 2009.* Washington, DC.

World Bank & IFPRI. 2005. *Agriculture and Achieving the Millennium Development Goals.* Agriculture and Rural Development Department Report No. 32729-GLB. Washington, DC.

Young, J.E. 2008. *Speculation and World Food Markets.* Washington, DC, IFPRI.

Zeller, M., Schrieder, J., von Braun, J. & Heidhues, F. 1997. *Rural Finance for Food Security for the Poor: Implications for Research and Policy.* Washington, DC. Posted at: www.ifpri.org/PUBS/FPR/SYNOPSES/FPRSYN4.htm.

Zlotkin, S.H. 2007. *Sprinkles: An Innovative, Cost-Effective Approach to Provide Micronutrients to Children.* Technical paper for the WHS. Rome, WFP.

Zlotkin, S.H., Schauer, C., Christofides, A., Sharieff, W. & Tondeur, M.C. 2005. Micronutrient sprinkles to control childhood anemia. *PLoS Medicine, 2*(1). Posted at: http://medicine.plosjournals.org/perlserv/?request=get-document&doi=10.1371/journal.pmed.0020001&ct=1.

Zlotkin, S.H. & Tondeur, M. 2006. Successful approaches: Sprinkles. *In* K. Kraemer and M.B. Zimmermann, eds. *Nutritional Anemia.* Basel, Sight and Life Press.

Zulu, B., Jayne, T.S. & Beaver, M. 2007. *Smallholder Household Maize Production and Marketing Behaviour in Zambia and its Implications for Policy.* Paper No. ZM-FSRP-WP-22 in the International Development Collaborative Working Papers Series. Ann Arbor, MI, Department of Agricultural Economics, Michigan State University.

Country boundaries

All map boundaries used in this publication are based on FAO GAUL – Global Administrative Unit Layer http://www.fao.org/geonetwork/srv/en/ metadata.show?id=12691

Map projection

World maps A and B in this publication are in Flat Polar Quartic projection, datum WGS84.

The maps in this publication may be downloaded from VAM-SIE http://vam.wfp.org/vamsie.

Map construction

Map A – Underweight children
Data are from Table 1 of the Resource Compendium (underweight for 2003–2005).

Map Figures 1.2a and 1.2b – Underweight and transportation costs in sub-Saharan Africa
The figures show the relation between transport costs, averaged over districts, and the prevalence of underweight among children under 5. The maps are constructed as follows. The Demographic and Health Surveys (DHS, see www.measuredhs.com for details) register, among many other items, the weights of children, and report the percentage of sampled children that are underweight. Usually, these data are available at the province or district level and differentiate between urban and rural areas. Data on transport costs for primary, secondary and tertiary roads are based on information from WFP country offices. The maps use the average transport costs by district, rather than depicting the transport costs by road type. To highlight the relation between poor nutrition status and remoteness of areas as reflected in high transport costs, areas with average transport costs of less than US$1.5 per MTkm are designated as low-cost areas, and other areas as high-cost areas. For each of these two categories, data on underweight children are projected to arrive at the two maps included in Figure 1.2. The maps were compiled by the Centre for World Food Studies of Free University, Amsterdam.

Map B – Food and fuel price risk
See the box on the food and fuel price risk index on page 100, and Husain and Subran, 2008.

Map B – Vulnerability to increases in food commodity and fuel prices

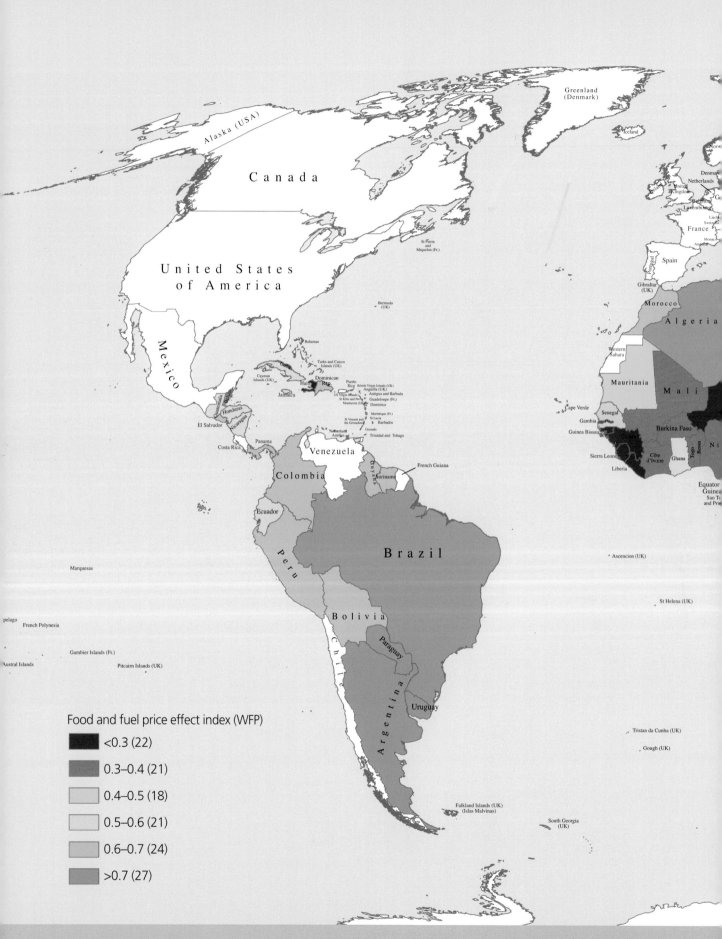

Food and fuel price effect index (WFP)

- ■ <0.3 (22)
- ■ 0.3–0.4 (21)
- ☐ 0.4–0.5 (18)
- ☐ 0.5–0.6 (21)
- ☐ 0.6–0.7 (24)
- ■ >0.7 (27)

The boundaries and names shown and the designations used on this map do not imply any official endorsement or acceptance by the United Nations.

Map produced by WFP Food Security Analysis Service September 2008.